1972

TWENTIETH CENTURY VIEWS

The aim of this series is to present the best in contemporary critical opinion on major authors, providing a twentieth century perspective on their changing status in an era of profound revaluation.

Maynard Mack, *Series Editor*
Yale University

E. E. CUMMINGS

A COLLECTION OF CRITICAL ESSAYS

Edited by

Norman Friedman

Prentice-Hall, Inc. A SPECTRUM BOOK *Englewood Cliffs, N.J.*

Grateful thanks are due to Mrs. Martha Nemeth and Mrs. Mimi Penchansky of the Queens College Library for their help in duplicating and locating materials needed for the preparation of this book.

In Memory of My Mother
Eva Nathanson Friedman
1905–1968

 ISBN: C 0-13-195552-7; P 0-13-195545-4. *Library of Congress Catalog Card Number 74-163857.* Printed in the United States of America.

10 9 8 7 6 5 4 3 2 1

PRENTICE-HALL INTERNATIONAL, INC. (*London*)
PRENTICE-HALL OF AUSTRALIA, PTY. LTD. (*Sydney*)
PRENTICE-HALL OF CANADA, LTD. (*Toronto*)
PRENTICE-HALL OF INDIA PRIVATE LIMITED (*New Delhi*)
PRENTICE-HALL OF JAPAN, INC. (*Tokyo*)

Contents

Introduction

by Norman Friedman

I

Cummings' supporters have always outnumbered his detractors—and among the former he has had his share of very good critics indeed, critics who have been appreciative and discerning rather than merely adulatory, critics such as (and I name only the most conspicuous) Marianne Moore, Robert Graves, Ezra Pound, Allen Tate, and William Carlos Williams. And among those who, while they may not be counted with his supporters, nevertheless have seen fit to take him seriously are found Edmund Wilson, Kenneth Burke, Louis MacNeice, Robert Penn Warren, and John Crowe Ransom.

Yet, in spite of such criticism and a continuing and flourishing popularity in many circles, there exists about his reputation an aura of inadequacy, a sense of some important establishment to which he has failed to gain admission, an air of unseriousness about his stature, as if he were somehow good but not quite good enough. Not that I think this anomalous position bothered Cummings or that we need to find some means of sanctioning his career for some sort of academy—did he not relish his position as an individualist, a nonconformist, one who would go his own way no matter what?

It is about ourselves that I am concerned and the deprivation we inflict upon our lives by mistaken exclusions. I am concerned about our understanding of our poetic heritage, about the powers and limitations of our critical fashions, and about the reading lists, anthologies, and matters of instruction in our schools, colleges, and universities. I want to ask what it is that has caused us to attribute to Cummings that slight flavor of illegitimacy, and I want to suggest how it may be remedied. For I think we are ready now for a fairer assessment of the case; perhaps this volume will be a step in that direction.

II

In the 1920s Cummings was known as a conspicuous member of the avant-garde, an arch-experimentalist, a modernist, and a bohemian.

The New Criticism, which was just beginning to germinate in the writings of T. E. Hulme, Ezra Pound, T. S. Eliot, and I. A. Richards, had not yet noticed any serious discrepancy between its own principles and the writings of Cummings. The real hostility he aroused was among the antimodernists—Max Eastman and Stanton A. Coblentz, for example, and, in later decades, critics such as John Sparrow and Ivor Winters—men who were attacking Pound and Eliot as well. There is no real problem here, for, while it cannot be said that the critics, favorable or otherwise, really understood what Cummings was about, neither can it be said that he himself had altogether found his way. It was suspected—and it was probably partly the case at the time—that he was a poet of sensations rather than of thoughts, and this notion has continued to haunt his reputation ever since, despite the obvious truth that he did in fact develop a vision of life as he matured. Indeed, it is one of the great flaws of Cummings criticism that it has pretty consistently failed to develop as he developed, that it has remained fixated upon early attitudes to his early work.

In the 1930s firmer lines began to be drawn. It was becoming clear by then that Cummings was antirational, anticollectivist, and antipolitical, both in theme and technique, and that he was therefore a threat to another kind of antimodernist—the leftist critic. To be sure, many regarded these qualities favorably, seeing in a poet who stood for the living human being and his personal responses to life a social as well as an artistic value. Yet even the emerging New Criticism, spearheaded in this case by the austere R. P. Blackmur, although pleased with Cummings' concern for experimentation and his dislike of mass culture, was made uneasy by his romantic vagueness and his ostensibly simplistic answers to the times. The affirmation of love, spring, and the individual did not seem a sufficiently serious reaction to the tragedy of twentieth-century history, which was then reaching its climax in a depression and in preparations for a second world war.

In the 1940s critics such as Paul Rosenfeld, William Carlos Williams, Theodore Spencer, and Lloyd Frankenberg realized that there was more to Cummings than this, that underlying his interest in love, spring, and the individual was a vision that served to give depth and meaning to both his anarchic techniques and his anarchistic beliefs. In describing this vision, however, they were still more or less limited to such concepts as freshness, originality, accuracy, directness, precision, and immediacy, and they therefore produced no full and consistent analysis of the character of his thought. Hostile critics such as F. O. Matthiessen and Robert Martin Adams could, therefore, still dismiss him as an adolescent sentimentalist and sensationalist despite the fact that he had vividly recorded at firsthand two of the most significant events of our century—the beginnings of concentration-camp existence in World War I and the subsequent rise of the Soviet state.

The demand on Cummings to develop—to be more "mature," more sophisticated, more aware of how good and evil are intermingled, and more appreciative of the meaning of history and society—increased during the 1950s. Though it was still not realized that an appreciation of his qualities required terms and concepts that had not been evolved, several critics—George Haines IV, Robert E. Maurer, John Logan, Barbara Watson, and Ralph J. Mills, Jr.—were already pushing beyond the customary notions of freshness and precision, moving deeper toward concepts of transcendence, mysticism, and timelessness, and S. V. Baum and Rudolph Von Abele were conducting detailed analyses of techniques and themes. Unfortunately, the New Criticism's methods of close analysis, which had by now become fairly standard in college and university courses in literature and criticism, did not often suit Cummings' poems very well; the kinds of irony, paradox, ambivalence, ambiguity, and symbolism looked for by that method were frequently not to be found.

Nevertheless, as the 50s gave way to the 60s and 70s, a sharper awareness of the nature of his vision gradually emerged. It became clear, for one thing, that we were significantly hampered by the limits of contemporary criticism, since he wrote to a large degree outside of these limits. Eliot and Stevens and Auden, for example, were easier to deal with critically, for they wrote within them. Even when we know we *like* Cummings, we lack the appropriate language for explaining why. Theoretically, our problem is to expand our ideas of what constitutes valid poetry; practically, it is to find out what other kinds of poet we think are worthwhile—apart from and in addition to those who have the "unified sensibility" that the New Critics have taught us to appreciate. We must, in other words, widen our historical and critical frames of reference.

III

Take the matter of love, for instance. Although Cummings is no mere "romantic" love poet and has written some of the most effective poems about sex in the language, the fact remains that he does not always depict the worm within the rose, the skull beneath the skin. His characteristic love poems are based on a single wholeness of feeling—praise, reverence, joy, passion, devotion—rather than upon the mixed feelings favored by the New Criticism. He is perfectly aware that his lady is mortal, that she sweats, and that she performs the natural functions, but he prefers to go beyond that awareness toward moments of affirmation. If we compare his "somewhere i have never travelled,gladly beyond" (263: LVII*) to Auden's "Lay your sleeping head, my love," we find that Cummings' emotion is not "qualified" —but that does not mean that it is sentimental. His singleness comes not from exclusion, but rather from transcendence, which is a different thing altogether.

When it comes to the means by which such an emotion is embodied —structure, technique, style—Cummings is indeed an innovator and, as such, is in line with the predispositions of contemporary critics. Although he is more traditional than he often seems at first glance, he was never content to rest easily within inherited conventions. Here again, instead of favoring the more usual devices of the modernists —juxtaposition, self-mockery, reflexive meanings, complex symbols, learned allusions—Cummings went on to develop many of his own. Thus he juxtaposes words and parts of words instead of images, anecdotes, and incidents, and his chief structural invention is typographical —or perhaps linguistic—rather than compositional. He distorts grammar and syntax by changing word order and parts of speech instead of exploiting the many levels of meaning in the connotations of words.

He aims at simultaneity and instantaneousness, then, rather than at irony and ambiguity; at reawakening encapsulated meanings rather than at multiplying them. He often writes lyrics that are truly lyrical —poems that are, in the best sense, like songs—for he aims at joyfulness rather than at meditativeness, and the result is more musical and melodious, while at the same time authentic, than any love poetry since the sixteenth and seventeenth centuries.

On the other side, of course, there is hate. It would be hard to find satires as barbed and brilliant as his after the eighteenth century, for there is exuberance and joy too in Cummings' hate, and with a few exceptions his satires are spirited, witty, and large-hearted. A good lover will be a good hater, and a transcendentalist will regard the descendental with full-bodied dismay. In comparison, Pound is mean and Auden is clever. As for the rest, satire is no more a typical modernist genre than is the love lyric, which also requires more single-mindedness than the New Criticism allows. If the contemporary critic agrees with Cummings' attacks on a mechanized civilization, he does not agree with the basis of that attack nor with the implied or expressed solution, for it is not so much the individual he would rescue as society.

The characteristic modernist genre is, in fact, either the meditative lyric or the meditative archetypal-mythic "epic" (or some combination of the two), and Cummings has written neither. He is not, however,

* A key to the references is given at the end of the Introduction, p. 14.

a simple one- or two-note man. In addition to the love lyric and the satire he works typically with the descriptive and reflective nature poem—which, significantly, deals as often with urban as with rural landscapes—and with poems about, and in praise of, people.

It is a matter of expectations, then, and the criticism of the first half of this century formed a set of expectations that Cummings often did not meet, expectations about feeling, about techniques, and about genres. So too it was with the expectation about artistic growth and development. Yeats set the pattern, making himself over three times during a long and fruitful career. Pound put behind him the lyrics of his earlier period to go on to *The Cantos*—as Hart Crane and William Carlos Williams went on to their "epics." Eliot progressed from "Prufrock" to *The Waste Land,* through *Ash Wednesday* to the *Four Quartets* and on to the later plays. Auden went from Marx to Freud to Christianity. Cummings simply became more Cummings, and so the impression has gained currency that he has not changed, not matured. There are different kinds of growth, however, and one can develop and deepen along a single course as well as reverse oneself or take up a new tack; one way is not necessarily more mature than the other. Stevens, although more sophisticated and ambivalent than Cummings, developed pretty much along the lines he had laid down early in his career. So did Frost, Marianne Moore, and D. H. Lawrence.

The fact is that Cummings changed quite markedly all through his life. His love poetry, for example, became less erotic and more transcendental. His typography exploded—and then imploded. His linguistic distortions became more meaningful and luminous. Most important of all, his vision of life deepened and crytallized to a degree not yet sufficiently appreciated by the critics, for the current expectations about vision are the most excluding of all.

IV

The world in which the New Criticism conceives of itself and its favored authors as living is the world that has been created by History up to now. It is a world that has become more and more fragmented since the seventeenth century—or the Middle Ages, or perhaps even Eden—and which artists and cultivated men must try to put back together before it is too late. It is a world that has to be controlled by means of discriminations, definitions, categories, conventions—a world, as Cummings calls it, of clocks and calendars. It is an archetypally religious—sometimes Christian—world of Sin, the Fall, and the hope of Redemption. Improvement will come about not by denying the principle of discrimination, but rather by finding the right set of discriminations. An art that reflects this world must reflect its fragmentation as well as its hope of unification. Because its reality is many-sided, the poem must be complex. Because he is fallen, the poet must be aware of his own contradictoriness. Thus the poem must be paradoxical, ambivalent, suggestive, polysemous, symbolic. It must reconcile opposites; it must earn its affirmations.

Surely this version of the world is so familiar to us that we are perpetually in danger of taking it as the only possible one. But there is another version of the world—equally archetypal, equally religious—that says that the hope of Redemption is Now, that nature and human life have but to be seen freshly in order to be experienced freshly. History is the result of mental rigidity, a nightmare from which we can awaken. The way to improvement is not by finding the right set of discriminations, but rather by denying the principle of discrimination itself. Such a world will not lack values; rather they will emerge and fade, grow and die, in a natural way. Thus a revolution in consciousness can bring about a revolution of the world.

Lest this sound, on the one hand, not very different from the New Criticism's concept of "unified sensibility" or, on the other, altogether too like the transcendental pap sold to the young today by certain cheapjack prophets, let us pursue it further. Though both world views see unity as their objective, each thinks of it in a different way. For the New Criticism, it is to be achieved tenuously and after much tension and conflict—in effect, unity is to be gained by piecing together what is given and binding it with an act of the imagination. For the true transcendentalist, however, unity is there to be experienced once the windows of perception have been cleansed. For the former, fragmentation is a given of History and unity has to be created; for the latter, unity is the given and fragmentation has been created. The favored poetry of the New Criticism does not reject the stale, depersonalized, and artificial categories of society so much as it works *with* them. Its joy is tinged with sadness, its sense of life with death, and its imagination is anchored in the ordinary world of habit and routine. Programmatically, it assures us, nothing can be pure. The poetry of transcendence, on the other hand, tries to recapture or reawaken the sense of life we had *before* we became bound to conventional categories; it seeks a purer vision, one that will be outside those categories and consequently free of the usual polarities. To reject History is not to reject Time but only its official version; to reject Society is not necessarily to reject Community but only its stereotype.

Thus the ultimate awareness we must try to grasp, according to this second world view, is not so much an integration of polarities—thought and feeling, for example—as a rising *above* them. It is the result of an attempt not to control and understand the world, but rather to receive and experience it. It says that timelessness is attained when past and future become less important than absorption in the present moment—where a sense of the eternal Now can permeate consciousness. It says we do not achieve selfhood by rejecting what we hate and becoming the opposite, but rather by going into ourselves and discovering what is authentically there. It says that although we may work for goals, we should not make our sense of ourselves depend upon winning them. It is an achievement beyond the will to achieve, a transcendence of categories, a strength strong enough to surrender and forgive—surrender our need to control, forgive the world for not living up to our expectations. Taoist wisdom, with which Cummings was familiar, puts it this way:

> The man in whom Tao
> Acts without impediment
> . . . is not always looking
> For right and wrong
> Always deciding "Yes" or "No."[1]

And so does Cummings, at the conclusion of his Introduction to *Collected Poems* (1938):

> Never the murdered finalities of wherewhen and yesno,impotent nongames of wrongright and rightwrong;never to gain or pause,never the soft adventure of undoom,greedy anguishes and cringing ecstasies of inexistence;never to rest and never to have:only to grow.

This attitude underlies Cummings' work from the beginning. It shows up specifically in his first volumes of the early 20s in such poems as "o sweet spontaneous" (39–40: II), and in 1926 in such well-known pieces as "voices to voices, lip to lip" (189–90: XXXIII) and "since feeling is first" (208–9: VII). It grows deeper and steadier throughout his career, appearing as a contrast to the ordinary world in his satires; as a basis for love poems; as emerging from some intense moment of responsiveness to a vivid experience of the natural world; as a way of praising individuals and lovers; and as a way of talking about harmony with and surrender to natural process over and above the usual polarities. Compare, for example, "one's not half two. It's two are halves of one" (398: XVI); the familiar "what if a much of a which of a wind" (401: XX); and "dive for dreams" (*95 poems*, #60), which concludes:

> never mind a world
> with its villains or heroes

[1] Thomas Merton, *The Way of Chuang Tzu* (New York: New Directions, 1965), p. 91. Cf. also William McNaughton, *The Taoist Vision* (Ann Arbor: University of Michigan Press, 1971).

(for god likes girls
and tomorrow and the earth)

Let us take a single poem and look at it more closely in order to give weight to my central point and to illustrate its usefulness:

being to timelessness as it's to time,
love did no more begin than love will end:
where nothing is to breathe to stroll to swim
love is the air the ocean and the land

(do lovers suffer?all divinities
proudly descending put on deathful flesh:
are lovers glad?only their smallest joy's
a universe emerging from a wish)

love is the voice under all silences,
the hope which has no opposite in fear;
the strength so strong mere force is feebleness:
the truth more first than sun more last than star

—do lovers love?why then to heaven with hell.
Whatever sages say and fools,all's well *95 poems, #94*

This is one of the many poems in which Cummings praises love and lovers, and as such it is in the great tradition of the love lyric from Catullus to the courtly troubadors and from the Elizabethans to the Romantics—as we see, the poem is a sonnet—in treating erotic love in an exalted way. So much is clear from a first and second reading, and so much has been fully acknowledged by the critics. After seeing these things we can say either that the poem is fine, if a bit archaic, or that it is, for these times, downright silly and sentimental. But then, if we continue to allow the poem to speak to us, we begin to notice that the diction, syntax, rhythm, ideas, imagery, structure, and so on, reflect Cummings' special consciousness and style. The opening word, for example, by virtue of its place in the line, does double duty as a verb and as a noun—meaning "since love is" and also implying "state of existence." Further, the first line as a whole is based on Cummings' characteristic use of what Lloyd Frankenberg calls "the algebra of the heart"—since x is to y as x is to z. As we shall see, the meaning of "nothing" in the third line is both ordinary and Cummingsesque, and the concept of lovers as divinities is both conventional and special. The poem exemplifies neither mere traditional hyperbole nor modernist ambivalence. It is, rather, a way of seeing love in terms of the alternative world view.

Since love stands in the same relation to timelessness as it does to time—that is, has no reference either to time or to its opposite and thereby stands outside of the whole polarity—it does not exist in the world of History. In that other world where "nothing" exists—that is, that world above the world of ordinary perceptions and habits—love is the "something," the substance—put, it may be noticed, in terms of Nature, for the natural world is the ground of that reality grasped by the vision of transcendence.

So far, then, love has been taken out of the usual categories and placed in the categoryless world—or rather, it has been identified with its "material." The second stanza begins by putting this "definition" in an explicitly religious context; lovers are seen as sacrificial gods who put on mortality for the sake of redeeming mankind. The point is that those who possess such an awareness must perforce enact their destiny in the ordinary world, and this is a form of suffering (cf. Cummings' "Foreword to Krazy"). On the other hand, the joy of lovers creates worlds out of wishes—which might seem sentimental if it were not for the counterposing context of their pain. Their wishes create worlds not because love is simply a fantasy of fulfilment, but rather because the inner reality reflects the outer.

After love has been placed in the categoryless world and then defined in relation to the ordinary world, its categorylessness must be exemplified in terms of this ordinary world, for it is difficult to understand things in any other terms. This Cummings does by playing on the usual polarities of sound and silence, hope and fear, strength and weakness, day and night, and cancelling them out. He takes extremes and puts love beyond them: it is the sound within silence, the hope not opposed by fear, the strength beyond force, a truth that extends from before daybreak until after nightfall (echoing and developing "love did no more begin than love will end").

Finally, when lovers love, hell becomes a part of heaven—thereby abolishing *that* fatal polarity—and whatever either sages or fools say, all is well. It does not matter whether wise men or stupid men say anything, for love is beyond wisdom and stupidity and has nothing to do with how we may intellectualize or verbalize about it. Thus are opposites transcended.

The reason, therefore, that Cummings does not display the self-mockery, ambivalence, struggle before affirmation, and other characteristics prized by the New Criticism is that his vision is directed toward a state of unified awareness beyond, outside of, and apart from such conflicts. This is not to say that it is easy, for it is a rare and difficult thing and not to be confused with promiscuous self-abandonment. Giving up the principle of categories, surrendering to a reality experienced directly, daring to act out one's deepest and innermost being: these attainments are not to be confused with what many do today who think of themselves as spontaneous and original when they are only skimming the top off themselves and evading rather than facing the actual job of self-realization and self-transcendence.

V

Thus it is possible to define a kind of poetry that is valid although it falls outside the critically fashionable definitions—a kind of poetry that Cummings wrote for forty years. Poems written in this mode do not need to find the villain within, for theirs is a world beyond villains and heroes.

Or it should be. And here we confront a dilemma, for the world of Cummings' poems does have, as we have seen, its villains and heroes, and they crop up not only in the satires but also in the love lyrics. If a good lover is also a good hater, his hate will be tempered by forgiveness. It is easy to explain the *presence* of villains in the satires; it is less easy to account for the quality and intensity of some of Cummings' *feelings* about them—scorn, for example, or contempt, or condescension—as if Cummings were indeed blaming the world for not living up to his expectations.

In Cummings' own terms, while it might be appropriate to reject the non- and antitranscendental, it is not appropriate to despise it.[2] A man who has gone beyond ambivalence is obliged by his own attainment to feel sympathy for those who have not yet made it. A man who is at peace with himself may not suffer fools gladly, and he may energetically work toward correcting the abuses of society, but he should not betray that self-congratulatory reaction, concealing a lack of self-confidence, that is sometimes found in Cummings. For his own teachings amount to a rejection not only of stereotypes and categories but also of spite. When Krazy is hit by a brick, a heart flowers in the "balloon" above her head; when Cummings was hit by a brick, too often he replied with savage invective. In consequence, he sometimes projects a feeling of us–against–them that offends many and that denies his own view of life. Even in a love lyric he will sometimes pause to negate something or somebody, thereby betraying, through over-insistence, a certain defensiveness:

> and here is a secret they never will share
> for whom create is less than have . . .
> that we are in love,that we are in love:
> with us they've nothing times nothing to do . . .

[2] Cf. Robert G. Tucker, "Cummings the Chivalrous," in *The Twenties,* R. E. Langford and W. E. Taylor, eds. (DeLand, Fla.: Everett Edwards Press, 1966), pp. 25–27.

this world(as timorous itsters all
to call their cowardice quite agree)
shall never discover our touch and feel. . . . (464–5: 66)

Is his love the more valuable in proportion to the few who can share it?

The New Criticism seems to me wrong in saying that poetry needs polarization, but I would agree that if you *do* polarize, you should not violate your audience's sense of reality by sharply dividing the world into villains and heroes. You cannot apply the mood of certainty, which is appropriate to the transcendent world, to the social criticism of this world, where it is not appropriate. The appropriate mood of the transcender, when he turns from the ecstacy of his vision to contemplate the ordinary world—as Cummings himself has shown us—is surrender, love, and forgiveness. As he wrote in the legend attached to Mrs. Cummings' photograph of Marianne Moore in *Adventures in Value* ([1962] IV 3):

in a cruel world—to show mercy. . .
in a hateful world—to forgive

Or, to quote again from Chuang Tzu:

[The Taoist man]
Does not bother with his own interests
And does not despise others who do. . . .
He goes his way
Without relying on others
And does not pride himself
On walking alone.
While he does not follow the crowd
He won't complain of those who do. . . .

The Way of Chuang Tzu, p. 91

Either this, or you must be ambivalent—you must see that what you hate in others is also in yourself. If you do not transcend the categories, then you must play the category game wisely and humanely. Complacency, spite, and defensiveness are a false combination as well as an unattractive one. Thus, though I cannot agree with the monism of current criticism, I do agree that a lack of charity is troubling. Cummings was not always strong enough himself to surrender, love, and forgive, and one needs an especial strength to surrender, love, and forgive oneself. Patricia Tal-Mason Cline's excellent essay, included here, traces Cummings' spiritual struggle with himself; she is soon to bring out a book on this topic that should prove illuminating indeed.

Cummings was shy, sensitive, and self-protective in the extreme: it must have been very difficult for him to strive toward the givingness and openness he sang of so often and so well—as indeed it is difficult for any of us. It is a sign of the magnitude of his achievement that he got as far as he did; even the question I have been discussing, if I am right, is best viewed as evidence of the intensity of the struggle as well as of the preciousness of the attainment. None of his contemporaries is without his own blind spot. Pound, Eliot, Frost, Stevens, even Yeats, are all short-sighted and cranky in certain ways.

What then has Cummings left us? On the simplest and most basic level, he has significantly expanded the language, not so that we may imitate his tricks and devices, but rather that we may develop a greater sense of its possibilities for ourselves. Few poets have done more with words than he: his sense of and delight in style were extraordinarily vivid, musical, and almost tactile. Further, he carried on and developed, as we have seen, the tradition of the lyric, of lyric style and structure, to an extent which has not been surpassed in our time even by Yeats. In his satires, whatever their occasional failings, he was among the first to point out and diagnose the most dangerous features of our society—features which, alas, seem to have gotten worse as he wrote, and which have been provoking more and more desperate reactions among us. Finally, when he reaches those moments of pure transcendence—as he does often—he gives us something more important than any merely clairvoyant social criticism. He gives us a vision of what it means to achieve, beyond achievement, our full and fully human potential:

> (now the ears of my ears awake and
> now the eyes of my eyes are opened) (464: 65)

VI

The essays that follow have been chosen primarily for the information they give about and the insight they offer into the actual nature of Cummings' accomplishment. I have avoided the presentation of controversy for controversy's sake, and I have preferred depth and breadth of analytical penetration to cleverness, appreciation, tribute, testimonial, or memoir. I have also avoided, with one or two exceptions, essays that are already in Baum's collection or otherwise available in book form, and essays that are mainly explicative of a single poem or two or a part of a poem—although, as will be seen, analyses of single longer works are included.

The essays selected fall into three groups: the first four deal with Cummings' view of life; the next five with his language, style, and techniques; the final five with his four longer works. Haines and Watson provide the main pioneering studies of the 1950s, presenting Cummings' vision at a depth and in a detail that had hardly been approximated before that time. Haines' examination of his attitude toward and use of abstraction and Watson's interpretation of his responses to security and freedom are landmarks in Cummings criticism—informed, sophisticated, and intelligent. My own essay represents a concerted attempt, in the 1960s, to fit all the pieces together into an articulate and intelligible pattern. Mrs. Cline's, as I have already suggested, is unique in its attempt to trace out Cummings' spiritual struggle to reach his difficult vision of transcendence.

Blackmur's original attack on Cummings' language in 1931 is too well known to be reprinted here, but since it has deflected the course of Cummings criticism for forty years, I have taken this opportunity to reprint three reactions to it. The first was written in 1932 by Tate, who, although he shares many of Blackmur's critical assumptions, nevertheless is more favorably disposed toward Cummings as a poet. The second is by Blackmur himself in 1941, in his hitherto neglected review of *50 POEMS,* in which he in effect makes something of a retraction. The third is a 1955 essay by Maurer, one of the best of Cummings' younger critics. From the 1940s comes William Carlos Williams' delighted and perceptive exclamation over Cummings' use of language; and from the 1950s Baum's painstaking analysis of Cummings' techniques, the first of its kind in thoroughgoing detail and critical intelligence.

Studies of *The Enormous Room* seem to have been proliferating lately, but Smith's of 1965 impresses me as particularly valuable because it is more about the book itself than about its backgrounds and conditions. Maurer's 1956 essay on *Him* is the first full analysis of that play and still remains one of the most helpful. Rosenfeld's 1946 study of *Eimi,* although somewhat eccentric, is astonishingly brilliant and endlessly suggestive, as is so much written by this many-faceted critic. Finally, the 1954 reviews of *i:Six Nonlectures* by Kazin and Graves round out this consideration of Cummings' longer works by revealing what two distinguished writers have to say about a major poet at the climactic point in his career.

This is a rich harvest because there was much to choose from. My regret is that I had, of necessity, to omit a good number of excellent essays. But if this collection as it stands stimulates its readers to turn more to their Cummings, and perhaps to think and write and talk about him in a more understanding way, then it will have served its purpose.

The essays are reprinted largely as they were published (with the exception of the essays by Professors Watson and Cline, who have authorized certain stylistic changes); only mechanical errors have been corrected, and any missing references for the quotations have been supplied. All citations of poems, unless otherwise noted, are to page and poem numbers in *Poems 1923–1954*; references to *The Enormous Room* are to the Modern Library edition, unless otherwise noted; references to *A Miscellany Revised* are to Firmage's collection; references to *Eimi* are to the Grove Press edition (although I believe the plates and pagination are the same for all editions). The Selected Bibliography at the end of this volume should be consulted to clarify any of these matters. All footnotes are the authors', except where specifically indicated.

I wish to acknowledge here, finally, the use I made of Barry Marks' Chronology in his *E. E. Cummings,* of Charles Norman's *The Magic-Maker,* and of the list of Events and Characters in F. W. Dupee and George Stade's *Selected Letters of E. E. Cummings* in compiling the Chronology of Important Dates at the end of this book.

: : 2 : 1

The World and E. E. Cummings

by George Haines IV

We live today in the twilight of a great creative era in the arts and sciences, and nowhere is this revealed more clearly than in literature and its criticism. No longer do we argue over the right of this or that writer to preeminence; we are concerned rather to discover the philosophical, psychological, or sociological significance of accepted works. This is a useful occupation. Such matters are relevant to the ultimate social effects of creative procedures and constitute the proper business of the critic as expositor, academician, journalist. The artist inevitably protests the futility of these studies; he prefers that we simply praise him. And quite understandably. Until we have granted his importance, such work is meaningless for it can be—and often is—done as well for the tenth as for the first or second rate. But the time has come. We know now who the best men are.

We have been long arriving at that certainty concerning E. E. Cummings. By comparison with his only slightly older contemporaries, he has been neglected. And even today, hearing him praised, I wonder if we know what we are about. How, the poet must occasionally ask, do they think I differ from Mr. Vinal? That this poet, whose faith in the sheer vitality of the living impulse seems often but a secular evocation of a pantheist or transcendental faith, who delights in American distortions of the English language and in our pleasure in oblique and random epithets, whose technique is that of a Yankee whittler in words, that he should be neglected suggests we are not yet free of all cultural provincialism. He is one of us. Not least because his spiritual dilemma is the spiritual dilemma of America. And this being, as Gertrude Stein told us, America's century, his and our dilemma is the Western world's.

Our period has been dubbed many names, but D. H. Lawrence

": : 2 : 1 The World and E. E. Cummings," by George Haines IV. From *The Sewanee Review,* 59 (1951), 206–27.

early said "abstraction" and Lawrence was right. He knew quite well what it was he hated. For him, however, it was still just possible—though he had continually to chase about the world—to hate a little less this than to love that other, in Cummings' language, that "actual universe or alive of which our merely real world or thinking existence is at best a bad, at worst a murderous, mistranslation" (*Eimi,* pp. 104–5). Just possible, for *der Tag* of abstraction, the day when men would become numbers rather than individuals, when life would be interpreted in rationalized generalities rather than the sharp experiencing of being, when

whichs
turn
in
to whos
. . .
people
be
come
un (333: 1)

had in his time just begun. With the American poet, the balance hangs more perilously even. Each of his volumes can be divided into two: one part violent loathing, one part gentlest love. It is abstraction he loathes—and in that loathing his expression is often most concrete; his love finds as often only abstraction by means of which to express itself: *One Times One.*

Obviously, there is a difficulty here, a difficulty that is resolved, I believe, only by distinguishing between abstractions. I shall begin with the first kind of abstraction, the kind against which many of our artists have rebelled; through an analysis of Cummings' procedures, we shall arrive at a notion of a second kind.

The abstraction of the modern world which arouses our protests is a reflection of the mechanical sciences of the Nineteenth Century and of the social applications of the machine pattern. That pattern presupposes a fixed purpose with respect to which all elements of a society find their function. Hence we live in a relatively regimented society, where the virtues of conformity to an austerely ascetic, bureaucratic ideal prevail. Whether in the professions, in administration, or on the assembly line, the life of a man is expected to be devoted to his special function in relation to the group's purpose. Only that particular aspect of the whole man is engaged or valued. This is "dead land"; this is the land of "hollow men." It is a world of mechanized thought, feeling, and action. Few artists have denounced this world more scathingly than has Cummings. But it is insufficient to denounce.

If this is unreal, what is real? If this is "cactus land," where is the land of milk and honey?

In seeking the truly real, Cummings, again like many of his contemporaries, turned to the primitive, to the folk. But unlike our collectors of folk-lore, he did not neglect what is perhaps most widely characteristic of expression at the folk level, whether among country peasants or city proletariat, an emphasis upon the sexual in bawdy terms. In the cheap dance hall, at the burlesque show, at the circus, he found an earthy reality uninfluenced, uninhibited, by the prevailing conventions, the antithesis to the scientific and industrial asceticism. So he wrote bawdy lyrics and *no thanks* to a host of conventional publishers.

For a considerable time, it seemed that the celebration of a simple sensualism was adequate for him. Despite a clear recognition of something more in many poems, a recognition of "what we/everywhere do not touch)deep/things" (211–12: XI); despite an awareness of the "supremely welcome mystery,the mystery of growing:the mystery which happens only and whenever we are faithful to ourselves" (p. 331), this something more seemed to be little else than a veneer of sentimentality. His celebrations of "all shining things" (35: V), of flowers, April, spring, were phrased in terms of "frail," "crisp," "delicate," "fragile," terms only occasionally suggesting anything more than a tired, tag-end romanticism. It was still the celebration of a simple "I feel" before the descent into "the sawdust of forgetfulness," before going "wonderfully down into the Big Dirt . . . bumped with the last darkness" (*The Enormous Room,* p. 293).

Yet a phase of his reaction against the standardized, abstract world was a reaction against the standardized vocabulary of romantic lyricism, the vocabulary of "these gently O sweetly/melancholy trillers amid the thrillers" (167–8: II). Throughout the early poems one feels the writer is struggling to find an idiom of expression adequate to such purpose as he has. But neither purpose nor idiom was adequately enough realized to be of service to the other.

His struggle to form an idiom was complicated by a desire to satisfy an eye-aesthetic as well as an ear-aesthetic. He has said he lives "In China. . . . Where a painter is a poet" (*A Miscellany Revised,* pp. 316–17), and in his writing he has attempted to create ideographs; in other words, he has sought to convey his "meaning" simultaneously through the words and by the arrangement of the words and letters on the page. To object to the attempt is ridiculous. And if in many instances the distortions of the words fail to create a poem, the failure does not automatically disqualify the technique. Like any other technical procedure, this one is justified if and when it accomplishes what cannot be as well achieved by other means. And just as Joyce discovered he could reveal new dimensions of meaning by combining words, so Cummings discovered he could reveal new dimensions of meaning by separating a word into several parts, thus making the single word serve more than a single meaning. The craftsmanship involved is often nothing less than extraordinary, as I shall presently demonstrate. Meanwhile, if we had no other work but *Eimi,* this would alone be adequate to justify his technical mannerisms.

Eimi is a landmark in Cummings' development both in the quality of his thinking and in his mastery of words. The difficulty one felt regarding his early work was a certain sophomoric impatience; he was facing the problems at too simple a level. Individual aspects of our society were attacked as if each existed in isolation from every other, as if each alone were a cause for exasperation. Nor was his love any more whole, but made up of discrete mosaics of agreeable moments. His poetry was pleasant, amusing; but too often it seemed that when he sought to reveal his more profound intuitions, his words lacked the authority of even a private metaphysic. What happened to change this was, I surmise, the experience which produced *Eimi.*

From the first word: "SHUT" to the final: "OPENS," *Eimi* is a vivid account of his travels in the U.S.S.R., of his life among the dead or the damned. As a travel book, it ranks with a very select number of those produced in our time. But more importantly for its author, it was an experience of one kind of logical extreme to which our world of abstraction leads, or as I should phrase it, the kind of logical extreme to which the abstraction of the Nineteenth Century tends. Here was the actuality of what in Western Europe and the United States was as yet only a nightmare of foreboding; here was realized as daily routine what had seemed elsewhere to some degree hardly more than an accident of war. The U.S.S.R. was the Enormous Room on so monstrously enlarged a scale that escape from it was unthinkable. No longer was it a room: it was a world.

All the technical devices he had experimented with found their just and happy employment in the composition of this work. The device of the incomplete line (where the completing word is either obvious, and hence unnecessary, or is supplied in a later context) which forces the reader to carry the meaning of the incomplete line into the context of the following or later line; the device of parenthesis to force the realization of the contemporaneity of two events; the device of employing prefixes and suffixes in unconventional ways, especially the prefix "un" and the suffix "less" to distinguish between the living dead and the sensitively alive creatures; these devices and others constitute a simple means for conveying what otherwise might have become hopelessly involved or incommunicable. Since this is a mass world where few rise to the dignity of being persons, the "nonmen" and "nonwomen" exist for us only by the phenomenal accidents of place, occupation, or appearance; integers are known by no names, but only by descriptive epithets: "blond," "M.D.," "Shine," "mentor," "New Englandish," etc.

The theme of the book is the unreality of any mechanized life, of life under a "shrill collective myth," and the artist's testimony against it. As in the *Inferno* of Dante, which Cummings took as his model, the visitors descend gradually to the lowest levels, so in *Eimi* the final degradation of human beings in the U.S.S.R. is revealed toward the end:

> ?O
> Dante,O comrade poet;aid me now,
> beyond that wire(moveunmoving)seem not beings but items,unearthly integers,shapeless corruptions,baleful unobjects;not creatures not things but grotesquely how hideous entities(or such foul monstrosities as might arrive only with the disintegration of a universe;only behind life's final sunset,awfully vomited out of depthless nightmare. . .)
> &,as we approached,awfully(there dreadfully & fearfully here)appear omens,signs,tokens,disastrous hints;resemblances and presently the very (but everywhere immeasurably deformed)lineaments of mankind:now I am beholding,faintly and sick at heart,some unimaginable parody of human flesh-and-blood;am viewing a demented most preposterous distortion—now itself cruelly this catastrophe reveals:now my eyes celebrate the transposing of man and of woman(and of their natures flesh spirit or proportions)into such fathomless vocabularies of unrecognition as must dwell beyond any dream of every darkness.[1]

Though this is a description of a mud bath, it is also a kind of summation of the effects of living in the Soviet Union.

I cannot undertake to do justice to this book here, but another quotation is required. In the confused mass of humanity, two or three "shining forms" stand apart from others. In one episode, Cummings meets a man "Not quite Latin Quarterishly apparelled (suddenly am sick for unimaginable Paris!)," a man of the old regime, a fellow-traveller. In the following, it is this man speaking in the first paragraph; the "(K)" stands for Kem-min-kz as the author was known to the "comrades":

> . . . This is my street—how much?(to a forlorn slenderful unyouth clumsily whose both wings hug white frail trafficshaken flowerings. And stooping,LQ inhales)"incroyable. Ca sent la vie." (He chose,dropped slowly coinless coins into the un's outstuck handless hand)smell. (And we pass on). Isn't it Spring? Is there anything more beautiful—even a woman—than a flower? And women are so rarely beautiful;that's why we

[1] *Eimi*: New York, 1933, p. 329.

worship them if they are. Whereas flowers almost never succeed in being ugly,therefore we are inclined scarcely to notice them.

(K)there is an I Feel;an actual universe or alive of which our merely real world or thinking existence is at best a bad,at worst a murderous, mistranslation;flowers give me this actual universe.

Give(he said)yes(he stopped. Eyes:looking dreamily toward me with something beneath shyness;through me with dreamingly something beyond agony or all pain). Thank you;poets don't speak often.[2]

Reading *Eimi,* I am reminded of the paintings of Giorgio de Chirico. At one period of his career this artist was fond of depicting figures molded in tights with egg-shaped, expressionless heads, inhabiting a geometric world. These strange figures were denizens of an abstract world, a world of "nonbeing," and themselves suggested automatons. In another mood, Chirico painted "Les Plaisirs du Poète," a vision of a child or poet who wanders lonely, and almost overwhelmed, among handsome deserted buildings above which wistful flags fly bravely against miraculously beautiful skies. In *Eimi* the juxtaposition of these two worlds creates a dramatically intense reality.

For Cummings, the experience of Russia matured his vision of the world and matured his idiom. The brilliantly selective glare of the world of the U.S.S.R. cast into clear perspective the essentials of his loves and hates. *no thanks* immediately revealed the fact; *50 POEMS* confirmed it. Long before those critics who complained that the author of the latter volume was a child who had not grown up, Cummings had achieved such a sense of the realities of the contemporary world as they would acquire only after the Potsdam Conference.

Reviewing the morality play, *Santa Claus,* Lloyd Frankenberg cogently observed that Cummings had "set an abstraction to catch an abstraction." It is the essence of his technique. The poet, whose function is to make affirmations, to celebrate life, must fulfill that function by using an idiom of his own time and place. In a world of abstraction, the individual instance to gain universal significance must become itself an abstraction. Only so will it, in religious terminology, speak to or minister to our condition.

I have said the Cummings' maturity was immediately reflected in *no thanks.* His words acquired the authority of a poet whose particular poem arises from a whole metaphysic. Consider the sonnets: "does yesterday's perfection seem not quite" (296: 31); "how dark and single,where he ends,the earth" (299: 35); "conceive a man,should he have anything" (300: 37) with its foreshadowing of one of his great poems in the lines: "(his autumn's winter being summer's spring;" "love's function is to fabricate unknownness" (321: 61), foreshadowing

[2] *Eimi,* pp. 104–5.

the metaphysic of his love poems in *One Times One*; "reason let others give and realness bring" (325: 69). Or consider the lyrics: "love is a place" (318: 58), "death(having lost)put on his universe" (324: 66); or the perhaps rehearsal for another of his undoubted masterpieces, "this mind made war" (315: 56). Or the magnificent "Jehovah buried, Satan dead" (314: 54); or "worshipping Same" (314: 55); or the "kumrads die because they're told" (296: 30) with the pitying insight of its conclusion: "(because they are afraid to love," a bit of wisdom we have scarcely begun to understand. A dozen poems that one would have thought sufficient to make the name of any poet.

I have used the word "authority" to suggest my feeling of the accomplishment of these poems. But it is a vague word. What precisely in terms of craft has Cummings done? that is the question to be answered. For this purpose, I shall take 34 from *50 POEMS*, since a kind of parallel to it can be found in his earlier work. In *Collected Poems*, 218 (253: XLIII) is on his mother. First published in *ViVa* (1931), it reads in part:

> if there are any heavens my mother will(all by herself)have
> one. It will not be a pansy heaven nor
> a fragile heaven of lilies-of-the-valley but
> it will be a heaven of blackred roses
>
> my father will be(deep like a rose
> tall like a rose)
>
> standing near my
>
> (swaying over her
> silent)
> .[3]

Compare this with the following excerpts:

> my father moved through dooms of love
> through sames of am through haves of give,
> singing each morning out of each night
> my father moved through depths of height
>
> * * *
>
> and should some why completely weep
> my father's fingers brought her sleep:
>
> * * *
>
> scorning the pomp of must and shall
> my father moved through dooms of feel;

[3] *Collected Poems,* N.Y., 1938.

his anger was as right as rain
his pity was as green as grain

* * *

septembering arms of year extend
less humbly wealth to foe and friend
than he to foolish and to wise
offered immeasurable is[4] (373)

* * *

The assured movement of the second contrasts with the vague and tentative phrasing of the first. Perhaps "green as grain" is relatively commonplace compared to roses "deep" or "tall"? At least, it reflects the certainty of a man who can say what he means and who means what he says. And "right as rain" has itself a rightness that makes any flowers used to describe a heaven seem platitudinous. The great difference in the use of words, however, is the increased abstractness of the idiom. The effects of the first depend largely upon our sense of the concrete associations of the words. Pansies, lilies-of-the-valley, roses have a meaning for us in the concrete world, specific, almost individual meanings. "dooms of love," "sames of am," "haves of give" have literally no concrete, specific references. We are not called upon to imagine any doom situation or love event; rather, we are expected to recognize that love may be a kind of fate, a grievous fate, that love may be of a kind that suffers a thousand deaths, that the poet's father lived in that kind of love's realm; so "sames of am," we realize, means constant, continuous living, means living in the actual world of "I Feel." The reference is to the qualities of certain concepts.

The substantival use of verbs, adverbs, adjectives is perhaps most fortunate in the line "and should some why completely weep." Did the poet wish to conjure up for us human sufferers asking the eternally unanswerable questions? Lo! it is accomplished and yet made individual in that miraculous "why." So in the last stanza quoted the general meaning, harvest, is given a qualitative individuality by personification in "septembering arms of year extend," while retaining the general reference. This is the great magic of Cummings' matured idiom; it preserves the quality of individuality in the phraseology of the universal and the abstract.

But this is only one aspect of a change in idiom which appears first with any regularity in *no thanks.* Equally marked is the increasing use of unexpected comparisons: "far less lonely than a fire is cool";

[4] *50 POEMS,* N.Y., 1940, Number 34.

his addiction to sharp antitheses which are perceived to be interrelated: "and dark beginnings are his luminous ends" (300: 37). Related to these is his delight in lines beginning and ending with the same phrases or word. All of these, we observe, are means of integrating dissimilarities; the incongruities or antitheses of the phenomenal world are reconciled in the world of abstraction.

All of these technical means are employed to create the sorcery of "anyone lived in a pretty how town" (370–1: 29). Again abstract words are used to denote simultaneously a particular and a general meaning. "anyone" means what it says but means, also, its opposite: a particular one. The last line of the third stanza reads:

> that noone loved him more by more

and the word "noone" has at once its conventional meaning, but also refers to the "she" of the next stanza:

> when by now and tree by leaf
> she laughed his joy she cried his grief
> bird by snow and stir by still
> anyone's any was all to her

The same double reference marks the climax of the poem in the line:

> (and noone stooped to kiss his face)

The remarkable compression of meanings achieved in such dialectical phrases as "when by now," "tree by leaf," "bird by snow," and so on, can only be appreciated by careful analysis. But the fact that many of these represent the poet's technical interest in repetition in beginning and ending of phrases, repetition often suggested by rhymes, alliterations, is clear. This seemingly technical interest is triumphantly vindicated in the exact synthetic repetitions of "all by all and deep by deep/and more by more . . .", phrases so simple, yet so moving because of their affirming power, a power partly, at least, created by the repetition itself, though conveyed in terms of meaning in the two lines following:

> noone and anyone earth by april
> wish by spirit and if by yes

These are certainly technical triumphs, yet they do not justify his experiments in what may be called the fragmentation of words. To indicate the completeness of his achievement in picturing meaning, it is necessary to have a complete poem before us. For this, number 48 of *50 POEMS* will serve, though others are equally available:

mortals)

climbi
ng i
nto eachness begi
n
dizzily
swingthings
of speeds of
trapeze gush somersaults
open ing
hes shes
&meet&
swoop
fully is are ex
quisite theys of re
turn
a
n
d
fall which now drop who all dreamlike

(im (385)

Many of the effects of this poem are necessarily lost in any oral reading: it is a poetry for the eye as well as for the ear. At a time when nearly all poetry is read silently, this should be regarded as an extension rather than a restriction of the possibilities of poetry. It is, also, another example of establishing relations between diverse "meanings" by abstraction. And before beginning my analysis, I wish to note that my remarks, if sometimes obvious, are not intended to be considered as inclusive of all or exclusive of other meanings. They are intended primarily to counteract the notion that in such poems Cummings is deliberately making poetry a game of puzzles. His purpose in these as in his other poems is to realize completely his meaning.

The poem begins by stating its subject, "mortals)" the simplest state of being; and at this point the parenthesis may be interpreted as marking off the word as title, a reversal, as it were, of the practice of Marianne Moore, whose titles are detached components of her first lines. These mortals are seen "climbing into eachness" and at once from the mixture of terms describing internal and external events we learn that the poem is to be read on two levels of meaning: the level of a description of things seen, and the level of psychic or spiritual meaning. In the first half (through "trapeze gush somersaults") we witness on the descriptive level mortals mounting to their individual trapezes and turning a few preparatory whirls.

Simultaneously, however, this is literally placed on the page in the printing of the lines. It would be superfluous to indicate the movement created by the broken lines (though the trapezelike form of the phrases "climbi" through "dizzily" may not be obvious). In addition, the separation of "climbi," of "i," and "begi" from their concluding letters: "ng," "nto," and "n" emphasizes what Marianne Moore has called the "I of each," the individuality of the performers, while the separation also provides the pleasure of a number of eye-rhymes in both the "i" and "n," the latter lined up to form the bar of the trapeze, and provides the model for the later pattern of "a/n/d." The beginning and end of line repetition or rhyme in "of speeds of" not only pictures the back and forth motion of the trapeze, but again prepares for a similar pattern later in "&meet&." But both of these picture a further meaning. Recalling the line already cited from an earlier poem, "and dark beginnings are his luminous ends," we may remember T. S. Eliot's "In my beginning is my end," varied by Eliot to show its circularity in "In my end is my beginning." The circularity implied by these to exist in human experience is in Cummings' poem visually set forth on the page. We shall see its significance underlined in an extension of the device.

The "act" is now about to begin and the slight separation made in the word "open ing" mirrors on the page at once the openness, the spatial arrangement of the trapezes, the static moment preceding the actual beginning of the act, and the beginning of the figure performance by the group, the latter indicated by the immediately following "hes shes."

But to this point the poem may also be interpreted as a description of the growth of mortals through childhood ("climbing into eachness," "swingthings," "gush") through flowering youth "open ing") to maturity as "hes shes."

"&meet&" conveys the precise sense of graceful, swift encounters of the acrobats, the swinging together of "hes shes" whether in acrobatic performances or elsewhere. "swoop" hardly calls for comment. But the "fully" both continues the sense of movement (as it may complete the word "swoop"), and prepares another statement, the one of which it is a linear part. In this line the meaning of the second level clearly dominates. "fully is are ex" may be translated as: the individual "i's" and the "hes shes" (by the "is" and "are") are now "ex," that is to say, have entered into the realm of the unknown (always symbolized by "x" of which "ex" is the spelling), or have entered into the transcendental realm of the imagination; they are now seen as objectified or realized dream as the word "theys" in the next line delicately hints. Of course "they" are "exquisite" in the precision and control of their motion, while the "re/turn" is pictured, and the drop of the line continues the motion to the next movement of the figures. The fall at the conclusion is visually set forth in the now deserted bar of the trapeze, "a/n/d," and the following long line hangs like a rope from one end of the bar. What was suggested by the line "fully is are ex" is now made more explicit in "who all dreamlike." The final line, so typical of this poet, justifies his contention that precision creates motion. To read that last line, to give completeness to it and to the parenthesis, one must literally on the page return to the first line of the poem. Here is the visual experience, the form objectifying the reality of: "In my beginning is my end" and the truth of "the dark beginnings are his luminous ends."

To recapitulate: the mortals, after achieving individuality and maturity, have through their encounters achieved a kind of immortality. The circle has always been a favorite symbol not only of eternal motion, but of any kind of wholeness, whether of completeness of achievement in life or of immortality. The argument is reproduced and reinforced by the very medium of its expression. This is a triumph of the poet as painter.

We may now indicate something of that metaphysic earlier postulated as lying behind this poetry. For in these thirty-five or six words is adumbrated a metaphysic respecting human life. Whether or not metaphysic is the precise word is doubtful since my reference is not to anything very systematic, but I do not know of a better one for a kind of unity of thought and feeling which finds expression in a variety of ways yet remains always one thing. And this one thing in Cummings is ultimately the transcendence of individuality through love. Increasingly manifested in the poetry of *no thanks* and *50 POEMS, One Times One* is, as the title indicates, its fullest exposition.

Once again all the peculiarities of his idiom find their just use. What could better suggest the togetherness of love in the conclusion of the lyric: "yes is a pleasant country" (412: XXXVIII) than the contraction in the final line "(and April's where we're)" since the conventional "we are" is two! Who would accuse the poet of constructing puzzles in XLI (414) when he inserts "(two be/tween sto/nes)" *between* the two syllables of "squir . . . ming"? Or when he separates the "t" from the "hou" in order to reproduce in the last word the poem's first word, "how"? Finally, if "old mr ly" (404: XXVII) seems only a technical extravaganza, the importance of Cummings' technique has escaped the reader.

Since the theme of the volume is the going beyond individuality through love into an immortality of togetherness, those poems which are not love poems are inevitably concerned with the failure of those who do not transcend their limited individual visions, "not excluding mr u" (394: XI), nor the expositor of "ygUDuh" (393: VII), nor the wayward soldier of "plato told" (396: XIII); or else it is the failure of those who, as scholars, seek reality in the lonely sterility of books (422–3: LIV).

Again some of the profound expressions of his theme are found in the sonnets, a form virtually recreated by him and in which he has no contemporary equals.

> one's not half two.   It's two are halves of one:
> which halves reintegrating,shall occur
> no death and any quantity;but than
> all numerable mosts the actual more

with its conclusion:

> we(by a gift called dying born)must grow
>
> deep in dark least ourselves remembering
> love only rides his year.
>   All lose,whole find
>
> (398: XVI)

The relation of this poem's theme to that of "mortals)" must be clear. Here is no possibility of confusing love with sensual pleasure alone; here is the more one could hardly glimpse in his early work. And the concluding lines contain the essence of that quotation from Saint John, "Except a grain of wheat fall into the earth and die, it abideth by itself alone, but if it die, it beareth much fruit," the truth of which, as Harry Levin noted in *James Joyce,* has been discovered by so many writers of the last half century. Individuality is not enough. Cummings has found it out.

For the deeply committed individualist the discovery of this truth is peculiarly hard since it requires a voluntary renunciation of some degree of individual liberty. Yet the way of love has always been the way of cooperation and the sharing of experiences for the realization of a community with one's fellows through the transcendence of self. This is the romantic individualist's profoundest insight.

This insight should not, however, be confused with a belief in any kind of political socialism. Cummings is an anti-political poet. Only occasionally when some form of power moves him to deep anger do his political verses rise to the level of poetry. Otherwise, he is not concerned with power in any of its forms: political, economic, or social.

In the "Forword" to *Krazy Kat* (N.Y., 1946: *A Miscellany Revised,* pp. 323–28) he pictured the individual as ever at war with society, any and every society. Individual fulfillment can be achieved only in society's despite.

This anarchical attitude is often dismissed as a mere reflection of the Greenwich Village of the Twenties. Such dismissal ignores the *raison d'être* both of the attitude and that society. Greenwich Village was a relatively unimportant instance of a European-wide rebellion against the evolution of a scientific, utilitarian, bureaucratic society. Similarly, the anarchical attitude, frequently viewed as a precursor to authoritarian regimes, might better be understood as the only possible resource of the individual driven to extremes by either fully achieved or rapidly evolving authoritarian orders.

From Cummings' perspective the "socially-minded" are the servants, deceivers and deceived alike, of the mechanics and collectivities of worldly power. The world of the factory, of mass production and mass consumption, of mass pleasure and mass murder, is their preoccupation. This is the nightmare world of unreality. Against such power the individual can only protest by living in the real world of I Feel. Reality and life everlasting blossom out of innocence:

> but the proud power of himself death immense
> is not so as a little innocence (456)

or out of the creative imagination:

> and goeffrey and all)come up from the never of when
> come into the now of forever come riding alive
>
> down while crylessly drifting through vast most
> nothing's own nothing children go of dust[5] (463)

and, of course, out of love.

We can now explore further the implications of Cummings' metaphysic. Modern expressionist art, whether poetry or painting, manifests an idealist metaphysic. The expressionist approach to the phenomenal world is characterized by an effort to penetrate to the true reality lying behind, beyond, or within that world. The natural world is an expression of the noumenal. The expressionist seeks to penetrate to the essential forces which elude the concepts of phenomenal analysis. This of necessity involves penetration to an unspeakable level since language symbols, through social usage, inevitably congeal into phenomenally definable and restricted concepts. The burden of the expressionist is to adapt a symbol system, already fitted to conceptual usage for dealing with the phenomenal realm, to the needs of a formal expres-

[5] From Nos. 51 and 63, *XAIPE seventy-one poems* by e e cummings: N.Y., 1950.

sion adequate for revealing insights relative to the realm of the noumenal.

This is the secret of Cummings' technical devices and of his metaphysic: only as the contradictions or antitheses of the phenomenal world are recognized as having their resolution in the noumenal, in the realm of the spirit, does one understand the actual or alive universe. The parentheses and other devices do not merely impart a feeling of immediacy of experience but also bring the antitheses into juxtaposition as elements of a verbal and ideographic pattern and so reveal the phenomenally antithetical as harmonious in the world of the actual.[6]

Cummings is an expressionist and, like most modern expressionists, is an anti-intellectual. This anti-intellectualism is a carry-over from the nineteenth-century romanticism which was a reaction against the rationalism of a naïvely realistic and utilitarian science, its implications and applications. But the recourse to the self and its sensations is but the reverse side of the same coin. Precisely such abstractions and separations as the sharp distinction between the individual and the group, the perceptual and conceptual, fact and fiction, led to the barbarous mysticism of the Third Reich and the dialectical materialism of the U.S.S.R. Our own society shares, of course, in both tendencies without having yet run completely to either extreme. The dilemma of the modern West is how to reconcile individual and collective values, perceptual and conceptual values. And if spiritual transcendence has any meaning whatever, probably only by such transcendence can these antitheses be resolved.

An indication of Cummings' advance beyond the older romanticism appears in his distinction between feelings: true feeling and unfeeling. But is there not thinking and unthinking also? Are not most of our "scientists" and "thinkers" as unthinking as most of our "artists" are unfeeling? There is feeling creative and feeling destructive, and there is thinking creative and thinking destructive. In *Santa Claus* the mob is as unthinking as it is unfeeling. And at his best, when most truly a poet, Cummings recognizes this. The poet who wrote the following lines:

> so many selves(so many fiends and gods
> each greedier than every)is a man

[6] I have heard Cummings' work described as analogous to Cubism because of his fragmentation technique. This seems to me to misunderstand either Cummings or Cubism. Only if one confuses Cubism and Expressionism is this possible. The metaphysics of Cubism is that of a critical *realism;* in this connection, the essays of Clement Greenberg on Cubism in the *Partisan Review* are informative. Many Expressionists have utilized Cubist techniques for their own purpose; the analogy of techniques, if not pursued far enough, can be misleading.

(so easily one in another hides;
yet man can,being all,escape from none)

so huge a tumult is the simplest wish:
so pitiless a massacre the hope
most innocent(so deep's the mind of flesh
and so awake what waking calls asleep)[7] (435)

that poet cannot but be profoundly aware of the brotherhood of thinking and feeling in the world of the transcendent spirit. When Cummings' work is least satisfactory, when it is trivial and vulgar as it sometimes is even in his latest volume, it is because the metaphysical transcendence of sensation and idea has not been attained, but the poet himself has been guilty of unfeeling and unthinking. His technical idiosyncrasies are then mere verbal fireworks and his love and anger belong to the all too human world of unreality. He has, in brief, fallen into the world of intellectual abstractions dangerously reified and so mistaken for the real.

Our salvation does not lie in denouncing all intellectual abstractions in favor of individual sensations, but rather in mounting to a higher level of symbolic abstraction, a level at which we can retain or recover the individual quality and vision in the universal as Cummings achieves this in the idiom and metaphysic of his best work. We must recognize that today we have only a choice between the reified abstractions of the Eighteenth and Nineteenth Centuries and the symbolic abstractions of the Twentieth. Whether in the sciences, in the plastic arts, or in literature, the symbolic abstractions of our day are efforts, however tentative or misconceived, to bring an harmonious order out of the chaos of our inheritance.

In his "Notes Toward a Supreme Fiction," Wallace Stevens wrote: "It must be abstract. . . ." So indeed it must, for on the level of the concrete no resolutions are possible. Man and woman, men and women, must never remain separate and distinguishable creatures in the concrete world. The best that can be attained on that level is the incomplete resolution of addition: one plus one equals two, which assures us that the resolution is ultimately false. Only in the abstract world of the imagination, the world of love and logic, does the equation one times one equals one hold possible implications of truth.

[7] *Ibid.*, No. 11.

The Dangers of Security: E. E. Cummings' Revolt against the Future

by Barbara Watson

The recent *Poems 1923–1954* of E. E. Cummings shows more clearly than ever that, without announcing his intentions, Cummings has written a body of verse strongly and consistently in rebellion against the future, not the removed future of any utopian ideal, but the future now arriving, out of which, like mountaineers cutting their steps out of the very glacier that resists them, we are already cutting our days.

In the Cummings Issue of *The Harvard Wake* in 1946, there was a statement by Allen Tate which I take to be a reference to the same fact in other terms. In speaking of a man who has often been considered a minor and a wayward poet, he cites a juncture of qualities that is again and again called into the argument when literary greatness is being discussed: ". . . in looking back over the war years I see only one American poet who kept his humanity and his poetry, and that man is Estlin Cummings. . . . Among the men of our age some kept their humanity, some their poetry; but none, I think, both."

Among the partial and guarded appreciations of technique, temperament and spontaneity which make up most of the criticism in this special issue, such a tribute might seem incongruous, except that, looking simply for the qualities of his humanity and his poetry, I cannot find evidence that either element has had to be sacrificed with the passing of time and the onslaught of events.

If this poet's unstated scheme has held together better than those of his contemporaries through the earthquakes of the past twenty years, without losing its relevance, he must have related to his world in some way better adapted to the artist's special part in it than the ways of others, most of whom addressed themselves more deliberately to its problems.

"The Dangers of Security: E. E. Cummings' Revolt Against the Future," by Barbara Watson. From *The Kenyon Review,* 18, no. 4 (1956), 519–37.

Throughout his work, Cummings has fought the intellectualizing, devitalizing and neutering of emotion, which were paving the way for mass societies based on a standard unit, which is the sum-of-the-group divided by the total number. This second operation is the one minimized by the optimists of group procedure. In human affairs this arithmetic yields, rather than a quantitative, a qualitative change.

I

If the protest found in most *avant garde* writing of the Twenties seemed to be based on certain general principles (of individualism, a new honesty, and the primacy of the aesthetic sense), and if nevertheless there was a difference in the viability of the approach (though not necessarily of the products), that difference may indicate how crucial is the concrete embodiment of ideas and the techniques by which it is achieved, not merely for their effective expression, a truism of aesthetics, but in the active formation of their meaning. If this be circular, so is life, and one can only seek more useful entrances and exits.

The first obvious fact about Cummings as a literary innovator is that, without fully sharing his contemporaries' orientation to life, he did share with them the advantages of a liberation of means. The post-war artists accepted this liberation without necessarily realizing that it was itself a part of the past to which, in its own language, they were saying good-bye. They spoke as though the Victorian and Georgian ways had been the last efforts of a moribund society to hamper the free development of each human being. I would argue that, in fact, they were the posthumous children of that era.

World War I, which rebellious men claimed as their cradle, was not the beginning of the upheaval, although it was the bloodiest and most destructive stage. The causes of the war, whether analyzed according to Marxist, patriotic, or more inclusive theories, had already been the causes of a revolution in the arts, long before cracks appeared in the surface world where champagne suppers, cartel economics, emperor cousins, cooks in kitchens, capital gains, "good" families, and security, appeared still to the sheltered children of these "good" families, as part of a pre-ordained scheme of the universe. To most of them, respectably reared in middle-class comfort, the pre-war years permitted an enviable childhood in which things *seemed* settled, and the confidence of their elders that strength and goodness were one, and wars and upheavals safely caged in the past or in the continents belonging to the past, gave them steady ground to tread on while they went about the business of being children.

Yet in this comfortable setting, Malcolm Cowley, self-appointed spokesman for his generation, tells us: "At seventeen . . . we had come to question almost everything we were taught at home and in school." That would have been in 1915, before the war could mean anything personally to a high school boy in Pittsburgh, and it casts doubt on his reiterated statements that the war cut these young men off from their boyhood and led to a completely new point of view. Perhaps it seemed to do so, especially for the men of his age, because it entered their lives at the moment when they would in any case have had to learn a new role and, in playing it, to pass the point beyond which, in war or peace, no return to boyhood is possible for any man.

I am not denying the effect of that sudden gruesome thunder, especially on middle-class Americans, brought up to recognize neither blood nor death. When they arrived in France and saw with their own eyes the horrors possible in their own world, the meaning must have been real to them even though it had as yet no name. It meant that the strikes, the beatings, the corruptions, the inhumanities, which they had been taught to view as flaws being slowly purified out of the social order, were in fact symptoms of incurable disease.

But they were very young, male, bachelors, foreigners. In this war of decimation and pauperization from which no European country ever quite recovered, the Americans were as adventurers; and the sense of power, luck and pride which the young carry away after a bout with danger and hardship, made up much of the momentum which carried the Lost Generation through the Twenties in creative exuberance.

Their response to the war and to France was probably heightened by the fact that the young intellectuals went to war conscious of their own ripeness for rebellion. These clever adolescents had by no means invented themselves. Already at hand was the whole machinery of modernism, so complete that, even for their exceptionally inventive work, they would never really have to retool. The new painting and the new music were no longer new. And every old literary convention had been mined, if not already blown sky-high.

Even the jazz age, which seems to be so tidily explained as a reaction to the war experience (the release by transportation and danger, the recoil from fear, death and discomfort), began before the war. Samuel Eliot Morison says, in *Three Centuries of Harvard,* that during those pre-war years when Cummings was a student there: "there were other things in the air . . . than reform and literary expression. The dance mania hit the college hard. . . . Never was college so exciting, or drunks so drunken, or the generous feelings of ardent youth so exalted. . . ."

Then they had come through the war, with suffering that was real and disillusionment that was real, but neither of the most damaging kind, and none of it unselfconscious. Cowley has pointed out that what these writers called "disillusionment" was really a rebellion which "implies faith in one's ability to do things better than those in power," a quite different feeling from the disillusionment of the Fifties. Full of what now seems like optimism, and a characteristic product of the time called "pep," they came home to protest against a world of hypocrisy and brutality. They set themselves up as a new kind of coroner's jury, to declare the past dead and thus to kill it.

And the contrast that Cowley sets up between the older humanism at Harvard and the new aesthetics who seemed to be re-creating the Oxford of the Nineties, dims before our eyes when it is seen in the glaring light of the success civilization that stood opposed to both. Poise, proportionateness, decorum, the Inner Check: reversed, they became ecstasy, immoderation, revolt from middle-class standards, self-expression. But it was not in this war that the blood of the poets was to be shed. The success civilization did not merely *reverse* the ideals of an older order, as in a sense Cummings did. Instead it opened a new dimension, and the war of ideals was, like the wars of religion, never settled, only superseded.

II

When Campion wrote "Rose-Cheeked Laura," no one had heard of parity prices, precision instruments, AT&T or poison gas, or seen biophysics labs, junkyards, or Radcliffe students with "uneyes safely ensconced in thick glass." (236–7: XVIII) No dunghill, no slatternly servant girl carrying out slops, no unwashed mistress with chilblains, is so intractable to a lyricist as these products of steel and abstraction. Those who least wish to write about them can least ignore their presence. This new pole—abstract, inhuman and unmanageable—opposed dunghill and rose garden alike, and it made new forms in literature inevitable.

Eliot, Pound, Auden, even when the aerodromes are offstage, show us, mainly by the attitude of watchful reserve and control in their lyrical work, that they are of a high order of the mind-dominated man of the 20th Century, whose control is exercised at the source, before he begins to be bouleversé by the sticky little leaves of spring. This is not to say that these poets are devoid of lyricism, sensibility or emotion, or are incapable of writing poetry which stirs us to a response sometimes less guarded than itself. But their approach to life seems to be primarily practical and intellectual, controlled and controlling, willing and building.

Cummings could be neither Campion nor Auden. Perhaps some of those "supposedly indigenous throstles" whom Cummings assassinates in "POEM, OR BEAUTY HURTS MR. VINAL" (167–68) could sit down at the typewriter wearing doublet and hose. But imitation of the past has never produced any art better than an amusing or decorative *divertissement.* Why is it not possible, at least in theory, to produce excellence by the conventions of the past? Perhaps it is that the writer is then paying tribute to literature, not to life, admitting an inability to be moved to creation without the aid of a printed go-between, and that initial dependence mars the performance in some mysterious but deadly fashion. Cummings knew that these same lyric emotions, having come to him unsolicited on Eighth Street, neither need nor could be cast from an antique mold.

If lyric impulses are found alive in the modern world, though naked, toothless and illegitimate, it must be possible to render them by a new validity in modern forms. But the modern forms being developed by others were scarcely more useful to Cummings. And the only way I know to explain this special quality and special need in Cummings, would be to explain how any human being becomes himself, for reasons so many, so modulated, so hidden, so intercomplicating that no answer is possible.

There are some partial answers in the gratitudes of the *i:Six Nonlectures* delivered by Cummings at Harvard. From them we learn that the child born with who knows what endowment of intelligence, receptivity and strength, was at least partly shaped into a self in a home where gentleness, intelligence, character and love flowed naturally, a community in which intellect and tradition were valued, a town which could still offer a mysterious gentle sanctuary of flowers growing under trees, and privacy; a way of life in which there was the time and the heart for all the unproductive pleasures that surround poetry.

The man who responded in a certain way to a world war, to a vast slap-happy, fast and callow, citified, mechanized nation, was the kind of man who could grow harmoniously from these origins and remain, even in Greenwich Village, so loyal to them that he seems at times almost provincial, though with a peculiar New England provincialism which sticks so closely to classical and religious teaching that it ends by making boundaries meaningless.

Cummings solved his probably unformulated problems with a virtuosity which becomes, when its effects are finest, too subtle to analyse. But that does not prevent our talking about the more obvious things.

In the first place, if the lyric is not to seem false and cloying to the modern reader, it must include also the negatives of lyricism, if only to prevent an emotional vacuum into which the neutralities of life would rush.

This same method also fights the peculiarly modern prudery that rejects joy in a dirty dress. If spring is exquisite, Cummings tells us, spring is messy, too. If love is the highest, the most beautiful, the most this, the most that, it is also messy, and those who will have it only in a tidy form will have to do without it altogether, like Miss Gay, "to whom nobody seems to have mentioned ye olde Freudian wish" (236–7: XVIII); but

> spring slattern of seasons you
> have dirty legs and a muddy
> petticoat, drowsy is your
> mouth your eyes are sticky
> with dreams and you have
> a sloppy body
> from being brought to bed of crocuses (51: IX)

In the second place, if you are speaking, as William Carlos Williams suggested in the *Harvard Wake* issue, "a christian language—addressing the private conscience of each of us in turn,"[1] you do not try to be "readable," because then you can say only those things which are already so well known they will be dead upon arrival. If you want to say something new or forgotten, you must demand attention. If what you are saying is as strange to the temper of the time as the sermons of E. E. Cummings, it may demand, even more intensely than most poetry, details of attention and imagination which leave, for the second, third or twentieth reading, distinctive shapes which retain their sharpness of meaning.

The most trivial means may serve to etch these shapes: the misplaced capitals which make mOOns; the separated words which chime through the time-bound poem as reminders of the simultaneity of complex elements in emotional experience; the strung-together words which tauten rhythms and give pace to relationships; supra-grammatical constructions to render more precise meanings, like:

> down above all with love
> and everything perverse
> or which makes some feel more better
> when all ought to feel less worse (335: 4)

Then there is punctuation halting the facile movements of habit, or fastening things together like little hooks and eyes. More important are the images, often startling in their justness, and the rhythms which move, in the poems most expressive of himself, with the measured flow of less nervous times.

These are by no means all. But one complete poem may show better the link between the problem—intense emotion of lyrical apprehen-

[1] [From "Lower Case Cummings," reprinted herein, pp. 100–3. —Editor's note.]

sion—and the solution, the concrete placing of abstractions in metaphors designed to capture things scarcely known, inside a shape which can be held:

sometimes
            in)Spring a someone will lie(glued
among familiar things newly which are
transferred with dusk)wondering why this star
does not fall into his mind
                        feeling
throughout ignorant disappearing me
hurling vastness of love(sometimes in Spring
somewhere between what is and what may be
unknown most secret i will breathe such crude
perfection as divides by timelessness
that heartbeat)
            mightily forgetting all
which will forget him(emptying our soul
of emptiness)priming at every pore
a deathless life with magic until peace
outthunders silence.
                And(night climbs the air (307: 45)

Kenneth Burke says, "An art may be of value purely through preventing a society from becoming too hopelessly, too assertively, itself." These techniques enable Cummings to say in our language the things this language was built to exclude, and in doing so to liberate possibilities which may not have existed before.

III

The most distinctive thing about this inventive modernist is his rejection, not of the past that is present, but of the future that is present. He writes, even in his earliest books, as though he had already witnessed collectivism, concentration camps, security programs, sedition laws, the "return" to "God," the increasing massiveness of mass media, and all the other paraphernalia of conformity.

Prophecy is not an altogether mysterious business, and there is no mystique implied in this instance of it. Neither is there an analytical clarity like that which enabled Tocqueville, at longer range, to find out similar dangers. A mind like Tocqueville's can fly by instrument, but for the poet presence is everything. And around Cummings in the Twenties, and even earlier, flourished the plants from whose power the jungle was building itself. They flourished equally around all his contemporaries, but the effect was not the same. The two things that made Cummings into a prophet *malgré lui* were his high sensitivity to every denial of the right of homo sapiens to be himself, and his lack of any program or any longing for a program to improve society.

Those who seized life with their minds saw faults and proposed remedies. In both aspects of their rebellion they were trammelled within the assumptions of the society itself. For Cummings, who did not try to theorize about, but only to respond to, problems of injustice, war, imprisonment, the barriers of expectation and probability did not exist.

Being to an unusual degree a poet, he was, as Gertrude Stein would say, in love with nouns, with things being, not as the novelists are, with verbs, with the way things happen, which makes it easier for the novelist to manipulate events, and therefore more difficult for him to render them justice. The poet is so carried away by the prolific surprise and excitement of life as it falls, that all his inventiveness is consumed in the task of doing justice to that experience. Cummings is a poet who opens himself to experiences humbly (though in other respects humility is not his pride) and without condescension:

> and when i timidly hinted "novocaine?"
> the eyes outstart, curl, bloat, are newly baked
>
> and swaggering cookies of indignant light (165–6: II)

Those who tried to give themselves some sense of control over the universe by understanding it schematically, set up expectations which led to programs of their own, in protest against a main stream which seemed to be carrying them to destruction. But the salvation by violence, by proletarian revolution, by the mysticism of sex, by the meliorism of schools and legislatures, by the elegant old ways or the respectable old religions, took them back, "by a commodious vicus of recirculation" into the impelling drag of the major current. Whereas Cummings evades:

> i mean that the blond absence of any program
> except last and always and first to live
> makes unimportant what you and i believe
> not for philosophy does this rose give a damn . . .
>
> While you and i have lips and voices which
> are for kissing and to sing with
> who cares if some oneeyed son of a bitch
> invents an instrument to measure Spring with?
>
> (189–90: XXXIII)

Last and always and first to live. To live by feeling. By feeling love and pleasure and the human quality of life, the human quality which is safeguarded by valuing the one-man being himself, by tolerating endlessly his dirt, deformity, obtuseness, sinfulness, crudity, sensuality, above all his law-breaking, demurring only at those who want to standardize others:

> . . . whether it's president of the you were say
> or a jennelman name misder finger isn't
> important whether it's millions of other punks
> or just a handful absolutely doesn't
> matter. . . . (394: IX)

This is the thread of principle that runs through all the poet's dislikes, which otherwise seem inconsistent, or even contradictatory. For example:

a politician: "is an arse upon/which everyone has sat except a man" (394: X)

a flic: "there are 50(fifty)flics for every/one(1)communist and/ . . . the communists have(very)fine eyes" (196–7:IX)

a Communist: "every kumrad is a bit/of quite unmitigated hate" (296: 30)

a salesman: "is an it that stinks to please" (394: IX)

a clergyman: "we are told/by is it Bishop Taylor who needs hanging/that marriage is a sure cure for masturbation" (125: XVI)

an intellectual: "proud of his scientific attitude" (359:13)

Miss Gay: "to whom nobody seems to have mentioned ye olde Freudian wish; . . . you try if we are a gentleman not to think of (sh)" (236–7: XVIII)

a Freudian: "who . . . studied with Freud a year or two/and when Freud got through/with Do—/nothing Do/—nothing could do/nothing . . ." (171:VI)

a polite poet: ". . . Art is O World O Life/a formula. . . ." (167–8: II)

a patriot: "of Sumner Volstead Christ and Co./. . . antibolshevistic gents" (191–2: I)

the Cambridge ladies: "who live in furnished souls" (58: I)

a streetwalker: "if she were alive, death was amusing" (83–4: XIII)

In this personal world which rejects shall and must, only the "i" is sacred. Robbed of the formal suit in which it had become indistinguishable from the crowd, the little naked swaggering "i" asserts its reference to one real and single being. Its size renders it unofficial, brings us to realize how brave it is. If against the antibolshevistic gents you do not join the bolshevistic gents, and vice versa, and the same for the Freudians, and so on, then you are indeed alone and small, and you must either be silent or be brave.

A writer cannot be silent, and Cummings is unmistakeably brave. He does not mind seeming to be wrong, and he does not care who likes it. To take the extreme case, his use of the taboo word "nigger," which is his unspoken assertion of the rights of love, and his quite different use of the equally taboo word "kike," justify doubts about a man whose prejudices are otherwise functional, but I do not think they justify Karl Shapiro's conclusion that "he ended by becoming a snob" (*Harvard Wake,* 5 [1946], 45). There must be some more accurate term for what I take to be an intellectual failing. His nastiest poem on the subject seems to indicate that a certain kind of Jew was a Yankee invention, dependent on money worship and religious orthodoxy. And I cannot picture a Jew without money maligned by Cummings. "IKEY(GOLDBERG)'S WORTH I'M/TOLD $ SEVERAL MILLION" (176: XV) is unacceptable, but it should not be misused. Perhaps the best one can say is that Cummings' hates are so catholic, so badly correlated with standard lines of allegiance, that we can only ("if we are a gentleman") try not to call the round peg square because the hole is.

At any rate, reading such political obscenity as poem 46 (454) in *XAIPE* helps those not repelled by his sexual references to realize how hard it has been for others to take calmly and with pleasure this *enfant terrible* of all the conformities. In itself a side issue, the treatment of race in Cummings' work illustrates perfectly his lack of self-censorship. Following inclination wherever it may lead, with a consistency unrelated to ethics or politics, is part of a double principle upon which Cummings stands opposed to the increasing pressure which makes unpopularity a federal offense and every inimitable act suspect.

Because he was brave when he might have been silent, Cummings entered *The Enormous Room.* With a gesture left over from the gallantry of a world already past, he joined a world which prefigured the future, a world of endurance and defeat, where the only victories are moral victories, victories of resistance.

John Aldrich points out, in *After the Lost Generation,* the place of endurance in Hemingway's work, the sense of impending catastrophe in Fitzgerald's, of inevitable defeat in Dos Passos'. Nevertheless, choice remains: Jake, Brett, Gatsby, Charley Anderson, all take an active part in their own destinies, no matter how handicapped they may be or how surely their struggles are doomed to failure. But from *The Enormous Room* choice is missing, except, significantly, the first choice, the choice of honor above safety. The only active role the prisoner can take is that of asserting in the face of all the circumstances which deny it his existence as a human being. If it assures him that he has yet a will which is his own, any act, however trivial, is in itself a major triumph.

Imprisoned for an attitude, not an act, without the rights of a citizen, and under the conditions of horror we have since learned to expect, Cummings was exposed early to a kind of experience that was to mark the consciousness of modern times.

Was it this that gave him his prophetic warning and inspired him to spend his life and talent celebrating just those things which totalitarians love least? Or did he choose this subject for his first book because he knew already just what heavy artillery would be turned on his new moons? I think neither of these is true in any important way. *The Enormous Room* was neither cause nor effect, except in the very different sense that he chose the subject by choosing the event by committing the crime of nonconformity. In other words, both things stem from the fact that he is himself, which gives us a more solid base for speculation than if they were influenced by outside events.

It would seem natural, then, to classify *The Enormous Room* with Arthur Koestler's *Scum of the Earth* and Jean Malaquais' *Journal de Guerre*. What is it that removes this book into another realm? It is a style vibrant with life and its own power, expressed in electric detail, accentuated contrasts, incongruous terms to evoke felt incongruities, a style which is joy, which is poetry in the Gertrude Stein sense of being in love with each incredible event and with every eccentric personage whose existence assures him that uniformity is not yet our world. The style takes its resistance first, of course, from the writer's personality, but more particularly from the abnormality of such an experience in *his* world, from his grounding in a world which gave to such methods no countenance. If his imprisonment had lasted for years, with the knowledge that family and friends were imprisoned also and all Europe being run like La Ferté Macé, we must surely have had, even from Cummings, a less buoyant account of his sufferings.

Even more than *The Enormous Room, Eimi* is a clue to the development of a poetic style out of a very special kind of social consciousness.

Cummings found the U.S.S.R. far more depressing than La Ferté Macé. There is nothing perverse or even obscure about that. Conceding first two things: that the French prison was French, which gives it an unfair advantage in the comparison, and that the validity of Cummings' judgment on Soviet society is limited by his refusal to use even the little he knows about Russian history and geography—we must nevertheless see in this preference, which contradicts common sense, the intended lesson that a tyranny is more dangerous in the long run with the acquiescence of its victims, and is made even more dangerous by the real advantages it may offer, since these may persuade people to write off their losses.

That abomination of a prison, La Ferté Macé, could claim no loyalty from its inmates, and its oppressions were of a savage and unsystematic kind likely to reinforce resistance and deepen eccentricity, and furthermore to lay bare the stupidity and futility of officialdom. But a nation dedicated to collectivism, and too hard-pressed to waste a single unit of energy, forces its citizens to internalize the official will, and the damage becomes permanent.

Eimi is another assertion of existence. It is in response to this fact that it becomes the bursting satchel of minor inventions that it is. The cumulative impression of unlife reaches such an unheard-of total that superlatives are left behind. There has to be a new invention to bring such sums within our manage, much as the concept of light-years enables us to talk about astronomical distances. The more rigid the external order, the more complex and deep a resistance style must convey.

IV

The most extreme form of such resistance will seem at first glance to have been Dada. This movement which desired not to make sense did make sense in one sense: it pointed to the meaninglessness of the meaningless. And Dada sanctions play, absurdity, and exuberant free association for their own sake, the frivolous necessities of art that abound in Cummings and may cause as much academic distaste as any single element in his work.

But if Cummings' poetry has some of the Dada spirit, it does not have the Dada method. One way to mock the meaningless is to be still more meaningless. Once done that is done. Cummings could never be faithful to Dada because he loves the world too much to stop with denial. By showing vivid and precise meaning in a way that seems obscure or senseless, he embodies his rejection of the prevailing conception of order, and he substitutes an insistence on a seemingly chaotic surface in order to indicate a stability so profound and inner that it needs no artificial props. Freedom, for him, is order, though it is an order which no one man can control, even in the sense of being able to know and understand everything. The individual must not demand for himself what seems like a manageable or systematic world. He must take his chances on the broad directions of flow, willing to endure the confusion of myriads of idiosyncratic beings and events, which are absolutely necessary if we are not to press toward conformity and sameness. "You and I wear the dangerous looseness of doom and find it becoming" (331).

Growth and risk emerge as the cardinal principles of Cummings' anarchistic freedom. The safety of perfection, of absolutes, of scientific precision, may be necessary, but can never be loved. "Mostpeople fancy a guaranteed birthproof safetysuit of nondestructible selflessness" (331). One cannot help despising a little those who in any aspect of life will never take a chance. One suspects a major defect of the spirit, underlaid by deficiencies of intellect or physique or money or position or education, which command one's sympathy in varying degrees. That major defect is the base of authoritarian systems of all kinds. Without risk there cannot be growth, only "the murdered finalities of wherewhen and yesno,impotent nongames of wrongright and rightwrong; . . . never to rest and never to have:only to grow" (332).

Cummings' own poetry is true to this theory. It sets an example of risk-taking under ideal conditions. He has the strength to take his chances, takes them willingly and joyfully, takes them for himself and not for others, does not always win, but when he wins makes something that is worth all the failures, even worth looking a bit ridiculous at times.

Eliot and Pound took calculated risks. Anything which might have made them look crass, vulgar, naïve, they avoided by ironic turnings. They put *nil admirare* on the banner. For the training the 17th Century gentleman received from the cradle, which allowed his cool eye to look out without falseness from a passionate interior, they substituted a quick leap from the Middle West, followed by extreme circumspection ever after.

Of course this did not prevent them from being poets of great accomplishment, originality and power, but it did mean that a certain boisterous, low, full-blooded element was squeezed out, leaving us sometimes with a pinched and bleak feeling. Misprizing the modern world, they reject gin, adultery, neurosis, slang, prostitution, meanness, urbanism, as though they did not know that all the flowers of a more elegant past sat upon just such stems. Like so many other textbook phrases, "rejection of the modern world" confounds two distinct elements between which the differences may be more important than the similarities. The self-pity of the man who wonders why he was born too late "into an incredibly vulgar detention camp swarming with every conceivable species of undesirable organism" (331) leaves him too weak for compassion. For Cummings, anger begins in compassion, because he is one of the strong.

Something more important than dignity has been lost to Cummings in writing by the principles of risk and growth. It is the thing that is usually called growth in a writer, meaning progress toward a more accurate and inclusive portrayal of the world. Growth should perhaps be called by some more architectural or purposive name. This is one of the chances Cummings took that led to a kind of failure, but we have to be grateful for that failure.

This century has seen many writers deliberately develop themselves into a new and improved product and lose in the process the best of what they had before. Hemingway and Silone are among them. Only a few artists in any field could, like Picasso, Stravinsky, and Joyce, find a new vision instead of merely a changed point of view. Eliot is an example of the poet who can extend his achievement, but this demonstrates the importance of an intellectual approach to life in achieving this kind of development.

It is hard to imagine beginning with lyricism, passion and insouciance, and then "developing." In certain directions, Cummings has taken lyric to a complete expression:

> multiplied with infinity sans if
> the mightiest meditations of mankind
> cancelled are by one merely opening leaf
> (beyond whose nearness there is no beyond)
>
> (421: LII)

When Van Wyck Brooks, as part of the post-war criticism of American culture, attributed the absence of any major literary figures to a failure of self-creating and self-sustaining powers, he was laying the blame only indirectly on society. "To be, to feel oneself a 'victim' is in itself not to be an artist, for it is the nature of the artist to live, not in the world of which he is an effect, but in the world of which he is the cause, the world of his own creation." Surely Cummings, with his independence and vigor, is closer to this definition of the artist than most of his contemporaries. Yet he does not become a major figure as Mann does, or Gide, though he does surely create a world of his own, which he keeps within smaller compass, closely drawn about himself, as though one could not create out of the materials available a broadly valid social universe. If the form in which he works is one explanation, it must be secondary to some other. If, that is, the criteria given us by Tate and Brooks are important ones, we must admit that Cummings has some of the attributes of greatness which best balance each other in the formation of a major talent. If he nevertheless falls short of that kind of achievement, it may mean that this time and this place do not permit it. Perhaps all such large accomplishments have sprung from a ripe society and a literary tradition matured in long and careful use. On this question, it may be wise to take refuge in Cummings's formula for continuity with the unknown:

> "Always the beautiful answer who asks a more beautiful question"
>
> (332)

The Meaning of Cummings

by Norman Friedman

By the "meaning" of Cummings I refer to the relationship between what he is trying to do (his means) and why (his ends)—between his techniques on the one hand, and his attitudes and vision of life on the other. And it sometimes seems to me that no modern poet has been so persistently misunderstood merely on this level as has Cummings. Although I am certainly not alone in regarding him as a serious poet, a common view still has it that he is a curious mixture of naughty-boy anarchist and Cavalier love poet, with a penchant for scattering type across the page and using nothing but lower-case letters. Those who favor or disfavor him on this basis are both missing the real point: that lyric and satire play a functional role in a serious view of life, and that experimental techniques cannot be understood—much less evaluated—apart from that relationship. We must turn, then, to a discussion of his vision before going on to explain the meaning of his art.

I

One of the central insights embodied in literature, and especially in modern literature, is the sense that reality exceeds the forms which man has devised for dealing with it. Systems, codes, and theories are always being threatened by what they have excluded; reality, like a wolf, when denied entrance at the door, tries to climb down the chimney. It is true, however, that we sometimes become so used to unreality that we can scarcely tell the difference, as when our society makes a virtue of acquisitiveness, for example, and a vice of pleasure. But a man is not a man until he can understand the difference, and a writer is not a writer until he finds a language for expressing this understanding. There is always more to learning than books, there

"The Meaning of Cummings." Chapter 1 ("Introduction") of *E. E. Cummings: The Growth of a Writer*, by Norman Friedman (Carbondale: Southern Illinois University Press, 1964), pp. 3–21.

is always more to love than marriage, there is always more to work than a job, and there is always more to culture than civilization. And it is with this "more" that many nineteenth- and twentieth-century authors have been concerned.

Let us, for the sake of getting Cummings' vision of life into clearer focus, define four possible attitudes which one can take to this "more." There is first of all the Philistine, who fears reality and consequently wants to strengthen the forms. For him, life is dangerous and in need of control. Very few literary examples of this type come to mind, but perhaps Herman Wouk or James Gould Cozzens will serve. There is secondly, and at the opposite extreme, the Anarchist, who feels that the forms are killing us and consequently wants to free life altogether from their icy grip. Perhaps Henry Miller is an example of this type, but I'm not sure that's all he is. Then there is, thirdly, the Reformer, who realizes life contains more possibilities than our forms allow and consequently wants to make them more flexible. Dickens is an example of this type. And there is, finally, the Utopian, who wants to abolish the old forms in order to make new ones and so get more of the reality into them. George Bernard Shaw is an example of this type.

But this scheme is much too simple, much too didactic. There are so many writers who take a more complex view, who believe that one extreme can only be reached by going to the other. And Cummings is one of these. Let us define a few more types, then. Regarding the extremes, there are the Paradoxers, those who say that freedom is achieved through order, and those who say that order is achieved through freedom. For the first, renunciation leads to salvation, and Hopkins is one of these. For the second, there is a natural order which can only be achieved by discarding the artificial orders which man is always trying to impose upon it, and Blake, Coleridge, and Wordsworth are of this type. Regarding the more intermediate positions, there are the Ambivalents, those who choose the orderly while loving the free, as Captain Vere does in Melville's *Billy Budd,* and those who choose the free while loving the orderly, as does Aschenbach in Mann's *Death in Venice.*

Cummings belongs with Coleridge and the Romantic tradition in seeing the natural order as superior to man-made orders. He, like Coleridge, views nature as process rather than product, as dynamic rather than static, as organic rather than artificial, and as becoming rather than being. And he, like Coleridge, believes that the intuitive or imaginative faculty in man can perceive this *natura naturans* directly, and so he is a transcendentalist. Specifically, he believes there is a world of awareness—the true world—which is outside of, above, and beyond the ordinary world of everyday perception. The ordinary world is a world of habit, routine, and abstract categories, and hence lies like a distorting film over the true world of spontaneity, surprise, and concrete life. The ordinary world is a world of two-dimensional surfaces, facts, and nouns—it is a second-hand world. The true world is a world of three-dimensional depths, truths, and verbs—it is the first-hand world. For Cummings, it is the poet's function to decry the ordinary world and exalt the true, to represent not what any camera can see but to imitate the "actual crisp organic squirm" itself ("Gaston Lachaise," *A Miscellany Revised,* p. 19). Cummings' transcendental vision, then, is of a spiritual world, a world where facts are saturated in values, a world of magic, miracle, and mystery. Nothing which is merely measurable is for him of the slightest significance.

Now there are several misconceptions about such a vision which need to be cleared away. Yvor Winters, for example, holds that the Romantic view represents an abandonment to impulse and disorder, but this is completely to ignore the Romantic metaphysic. If one regards the intuitively perceived world as having a natural order of its own, then an attempt to grasp it represents not an abandonment to disorder but rather a struggle to realize a higher order. But Winters, I suspect, is simply a very sophisticated Philistine who takes the Romantics as Anarchists.

Another misconception is that the transcendentalist vision is in reality too simple, that it fails to do justice to both worlds. The ambivalence of Yeats, for example, is a case in point. In one poem he yearns for an escape from the ordinary world, and yet in another he vows allegiance to it. His work is shot through with the tension of trying to sustain a balance, and when he achieves transcendence, as at the end of "Dialogue of Self and Soul," it has been earned.

It is true, of course, that there is more passionate turmoil and self-doubt in the poems of Yeats than in those of Cummings, for Cummings begins, as it were, where Yeats leaves off. And it is true that many contemporary critics can say with a certain show of plausibility that Yeats's vision is more tragic, more noble, more mature. It is also true, however, that these differences could be taken to imply a difference in kind rather than of quality. Without for a moment suggesting that Yeats is not a great poet, can we not suggest that he and Cummings are attempting different things? For he is an Ambivalent while Cummings is a Paradoxer.

There is no need to ask a Paradoxer to be an Ambivalent, nor should we criticize a freedom-Paradoxer for not being a discipline-Paradoxer. It is, however, easy to confuse Cummings with the Anarchists and I myself have been in the habit of postulating too clean a break in his work between the ordinary and the transcendent worlds. I see now, though, that their relationship is more complex than I had thought. It is, first of all, a discipline to achieve transcendent insight, and here is where the two sorts of Paradoxers meet. For both, renunciation brings salvation, surrender brings freedom—except for the discipline-Paradoxer it is freedom which is surrendered, while for the freedom-Paradoxer it is the ordinary world which is surrendered. What Cummings would have us renounce is not our intuitive life but rather our desire for security, for success, for stability, for comfort. And for most of us, this would be a struggle indeed.

There is, furthermore, the mystery that the spiritual ideal needs the ordinary world as an arena in which to fulfill itself. Not only does love transform unlove; it needs that unlove in order to come into being. In fact, the more powerful the ordinary world happens to be, the more this living ideal becomes itself. This paradox is what Cummings calls "the ultimate meaning of existence," "The truth of truths" ("A Foreword to Krazy," *A Miscellany Revised,* pp. 323–28). And it explains such phrases as "All lose,whole find" (398: XVI), and "the most who die,the more we live" (401: XX). May we not say, then, that for Cummings the transcendental world, although outside of, above, and beyond the ordinary world, is vitally connected with that ordinary world, and indeed depends upon it for its very existence?

But a third objection is not so easy to meet. It can be said that in many poems the unlove of the ordinary world is not transformed but rather hated. It is one thing to decry false values and another to hate those who hold them, and sometimes it seems that Cummings is too good a hater, turning even in the midst of a love poem to pour scorn on nonlovers. He himself has cited with great approval the passage in the New Testament where Christ forgives the woman taken in adultery (*i:Six Nonlectures,* pp. 66–67), and consistency with his own doctrine of transformation would require that his castigations of "mostpeople" be tempered with love. There is some evidence that they are so tempered, but there is too much evidence on the other side. Too often, when a brick hits this Krazy Kat the result is not love but rage. Perhaps this is because the one throwing it is Offissa Pupp (Society) rather than Ignatz Mouse (the individual). And for Cummings the mob is a gang, and so is not to be treated as if it were human. But the fact remains that there is a bit more spiteful peevishness and defensive boasting than we could wish in a poet who has a world of love to offer. I take this to be his main weakness and I want to face it honestly, not so that his detractors may have ammunition but so that they may come to see his flaws in the broader context of his strengths.

Let us conclude this section, then, by summing up Cummings' mature transcendental vision. This may be done under four related headings: the nature of the true world, knowing it, acting in it, and depicting it. Technically, these refer to his metaphysic, his epistemology, his politics, and his aesthetic. The true world, to begin with, is for him the natural world, the world of natural cyclical process. It is, furthermore, a timeless world of the eternal present—not that Cummings denies the past and the future, but rather that he denies that hope or regret, fear or nostalgia should usurp the living moment. This is a mystic concept, even a Zen concept, but it can be explained in simple terms: since time involves the sense of sequence, you are living in the world of timelessness when you eliminate your consciousness of sequence—when you destroy, that is, the memories and hopes which would distract you from what is happening in the moment. Thus is it that to live purely in the here and now is to live in the timeless world. The true world is, finally, an actual world, and paradoxically, a world of the dream. I think Cummings intends by this to mean that it is a world of imagination, of our deeper selves. And the opposite or ordinary world is, contrariwise, the artificial world, the world of time, and the merely real or logical world.

How do we know the true world? Here Cummings is not so much antirational as he is nonrational. Knowledge, which is rational and belongs to the ordinary world, is the same thing as unlearning ignorance. But it is not wisdom, for wisdom, like love, is a spiritual gift: not fact but truth is the goal. Now there's nothing wrong with knowledge—except when it's confused with wisdom. And, indeed, the most rational man must admit—and if he doesn't, he's hardly being rational in committing what Whitehead has called the fallacy of misplaced concreteness—that there is an area of ultimate values which lies beyond our logic. Logic itself, like geometry, rests upon axioms which cannot be proved; the physicist in his laboratory cannot simply gather data, for he must frame hypotheses and make assumptions in order to make any sense out of these data. How much more so is it in the practical field of human actions that unprovable first assumptions lie behind everything. And it is here, where desire and will rather than reason and proof are the determining factors, that Cummings lives. Moral choice is based on the ultimate image we have of what we are and want to become, a commitment rather than a demonstration. Values are the basis of logic rather than its product. And in order to "know" them we must get out of the categories and dare to face ultimates directly, intuitively, and spontaneously.

Cummings' politics may be summed up in two words—love, and the individual. Let us consider the individual first. Since truth can only be grasped intuitively at first hand, it follows that one cannot get it from others but must experience it for himself. If one is to "know" at first hand, it follows that one must live at first hand, refusing to be dominated by one's institutional and societal roles. One must live directly and spontaneously, freely and responsively. Hence the individual is a lover, an artist, a tramp, a clown—even an adolescent, for the adolescent has not yet been integrated into society—anyone who has managed to escape the categories. Now the problem is that Cummings seems to have no sense of community, of how people can be more than just individuals and live creatively together. For him, all groups of more than two are gangs, and collectivism of any kind—fascist, communist, socialist, liberal—is anathema. Only the personal is real, and happiness can happen only to people. Institutions can harm us, or they can at best enable us, but they cannot give us what we want. Thus, for the individual, "all/history is too small," and for lovers, "exceedingly too small" (412: XXXIX).

What may be said in defense of this attitude? That in criticizing society he is addressing himself to actual societies and not to an ideal community? Well, yes: this explains a lot. The police state is the prime fact of our time, and it's hard to believe that one can say too much against it—wherever it may be found and under whatever guise. But Cummings is not a Reformer or a Utopian, and he has no institutions to suggest in place of those he criticizes. A defense, however, can be built in favor of the Anarchist, even if Cummings is not simply an Anarchist. He takes his stand from a point outside our world, and we need him if only for the perspective on ourselves which he affords us. Material progress and welfare are simply not part of his scheme of values, since they belong to the world of fact and knowledge rather than of truth and wisdom. He warns us continually not to take means as ends, and all his emphasis is on the side of ends.

And what of ends? What he calls love is the answer, and he intends by this more than erotic romance, although this is certainly a part of it. What he means by love is simply perfect givingness, giving without thought of return, illimitably and openly and freely. As he says in his essay on Krazy Kat, love hasn't a why or because or although; there are no conditions, no strings attached. And because only a person who has achieved perfect selfhood can give freely, only a true individual can love. On the other hand, when a person has no faith in himself, he needs someone else's love to give him this faith, and so he gives his love in return for this faith. But since his need for security is bottomless, his need for love becomes insatiable and he sucks the life out of his beloved (something like this was troubling D. H. Lawrence, was it not?). The beloved is being asked to do for him what he can't do for himself: she is being asked to give over her soul, and this is a desire for power and not love. So self-sacrifice becomes one more way of gaining power over someone: give to me because I have given, repay me in kind. And love degenerates into a power-struggle, one manipulating the other for the sake of his own need, his weapon disguised under unimpeachable banners. But real love makes no demands, asks for no rewards, does not seek for control, and covets no possession. It is not something you acquire, like property, and the beloved is not something you own.

And what is love's relation to society and the individual? The individual, tending to be naturally selfish, tries to destroy love. Society, tending to be institutionally altruistic, tries to protect love by restraining the individual. Although neither of them understands her, she fulfills herself only when society fails to suppress the individual. It is his hate which she transforms, and his hate is intensified by the collectivist benevolence of society. The individual needs society, therefore, just as love needs the individual. Out of this struggle the ideal is born. Cummings seems to envision a society, then, in which love is realized out of the dialectic play between the Anarchist and the Philistine. Its essential condition is freedom, for if there were no individuals left no one would ever have any genuine feelings again. The role of the Philistine seems to be essentially negative: he exists to be thwarted, but his existence is essential to the individual as a spur. And he is attacked by Cummings when he is too successful. It is useless, then, to try to put a label on Cummings' politics: he is neither a liberal nor a reactionary, neither a Democrat nor a Republican.

The view of art which follows from this metaphysic, this epistemology, and these politics is, accordingly, Romantic. Art imitates nature, and since nature is dynamic, spontaneous, and concrete, art tries to achieve the miracle of the verb rather than the deadness of the noun. A poem should not be *about* something, it should *be* something. Nor does this imply an anarchistic abandonment of intelligence, and those wild men are mistaken who believe that poetry is written "spontaneously" without thought or care. Cummings is one of the most painstaking of craftsmen. Intelligence, for him, is essential, but it is "intelligence functioning at intuitional velocity" ("Gaston Lachaise," *A Miscellany Revised,* p. 17). A truly primitive view is not self-consciously childish, for it requires of us "an intelligent process of the highest order, namely the negation on our part, by thinking, of thinking"—it does not deny the intelligence but rather digests it (p. 18). And this brings us to a consideration of Cummings' own art, of the means used to achieve these ends and embody these attitudes.

II

Technically and stylistically, we would expect Cummings, in view of all that has been said, to be unconventional, an experimentalist. But here again we must not forget that we are dealing with a Paradoxer or we will miss the large and essential body of tradition in which he works. And not merely the obvious traditions of rhyme and meter—and even here how often does the common view fail to notice his sonnets and his quatrains—but also the more subtle tonalities of the Elizabethan song, the eighteenth-century satire, the nineteenth-century lyric, the remembrances of Campion, Jack Donne, Dryden, Blake, Wordsworth, Keats, Emerson, Whitman, Dickinson, and Thoreau. In being unconventional, Cummings is not being antiliterary. He was an educated man, and spoke with pride of his Latin and Greek. It is equally mistaken to be surprised at the catholicity and traditionalism of his literary tastes as it is to be amazed that a naughty-boy satirist can be a cavalier love lyrist. These are contradictions only to those who have tried to put Cummings in too narrow a category to begin with.

But his technical innovations are many and spectacular. Not anarchistic flauntings of sense, they are best understood as various ways of stripping the film of familiarity from language in order to strip the film of familiarity from the world. Transform the word, he seems to have felt, and you are on the way to transforming the world. Cummings' technical and stylistic devices are means of unlocking the kernels of aliveness within the husks of convention. I once said that the quality of his work should be defined in terms of modernist techniques for approaching traditional subjects, and one critic took this as evidence for concluding that Cummings has nothing new to say and so must wrap it up in gaudy packages to make it appear new. This inference can make one despair of reviewers, for I said "subjects" and not "insights"—but let that pass. The real problem here is the assumption that the worth of a poet is somehow directly connected with the newness of what he has to say. But surely it is a respectable theory which holds that the poet's function is to make us *realize* what we already know. And isn't it also plausible that the *way* something is said somehow alters *what* is said, or at least gives it its particular meaning vis-à-vis the reader? I am sure, for example, that the explanation I have given of Cummings' vision, although I hope it is informative, is hardly moving, however new that vision might be. It is the poet's job not so much to *have* a vision of the world as it is to touch it into life for us. What Keats said about truth being tested on our pulses applies here, and what happened to Shaw's English Chaplain after he saw Saint Joan burn at the stake illustrates the point. In our own experience we can hardly "know" something until we have *felt* it somehow; so too in poetry the poet must make us feel what he is saying before we can understand it.

And that is where his technical and stylistic devices come in. I leave it to the reader to judge whether what Cummings has to say is "new" or not—although I doubt whether it can be said too often—and concern myself with the ways in which he attempts to make us feel it. Language is a two-edged weapon: it clarifies our experience for us and helps us master and extend our world, but at the same time it removes us from the very reality we are attempting to come to grips with. I refer the reader to Muir's "The Animals," Graves's "The Cool Web," and Auden's "Their Lonely Betters." And both of these effects are products of the same cause, namely the abstracting and systematizing powers of language. Language cannot serve its purposes without conventions, but it can also serve these purposes only too well. The all-too-frequent result is sterility, deadness, and lack of felt significance. Words become counters to be manipulated instead of seeds of meaning. Anyone familiar with modern criticism will immediately recognize T. E. Hulme and Ezra Pound behind this paragraph, and hence will recognize that the problems faced by Cummings are those faced by most modernist writers: how to reverse the drag of language toward deadness without losing intelligibility altogether; how to "make it new" without destroying it.

Clearly, the answer is that they must somehow distort the normal conventions without breaking them, and paradoxically they must face the problem afresh every time one of these distortions becomes a convention in its turn. And, indeed, most experimenters must acknowledge inevitable failure at the outset, for if they succeed in establishing an innovation on an intelligible basis so that it does communicate, then it is more than likely that both they and their readers will begin responding to it automatically and without feeling. Thus does manner deteriorate into mannerism. Nor has Cummings escaped this fate. And who has?—Eliot, Pound, Stevens, Auden, Frost?

But this is a relative matter. Very few poets can remake themselves three times over as Yeats did. It is enough for a poet to create one genuine innovation in a lifetime, even if he doesn't go beyond it himself. And, I might say, even if it never succeeds in influencing anyone else: it is another curious doctrine that a poet's value is somehow directly related to his influence, as if bad poets don't influence others, or as if good poets don't have a bad influence. It is enough for a poet to devise one way of making us see one truth, and no amount of repetition can undo this good work once it has been achieved. This Cummings has done—and more. Although some of his early poetry is wild with typographical distortions, and some of his middle and later poetry is clogged with his own peculiarly twisted diction and syntax, it is not true that he doesn't grow and develop—in these as in other matters. Sometimes he repeats himself, sometimes his devices fall into place with a mechanical regularity, and sometimes his oddness is tiresome. But any experimenter by definition takes more chances than the ordinary writer: so long as he wins more often than he loses, his failures are worthwhile. This Cummings has done—and more. When he wins, he wins like no one else: his best poems are of such a miraculous purity, so precise a feeling, so fresh a vision, that he can be forgiven his losses. His growth represents not so much the perfection and abandonment of one device after another as the gradual discovery and mastery of a group of devices. Those who see no growth here have simply not troubled to look.

And what are these devices? Where Hulme and others found their answer in the miracle of metaphor, Cummings found his chiefly in the magic of the word itself. Concerned less with the interplay of ambiguities than with the vitalizing of movement, he has coined a vocabulary in which nouns are made out of verbs, thus preserving sense while at the same time creating motion. The knife-grinder who "sharpens say to sing" (443: 26) is also a poet who puts a keen edge on words. By means of this grammatical shift, the word has a noun husk but a verb kernel—what is needed is a noun, but what is meant is a verb. Not merely is there an aesthetic pleasure here in recognizing old friends in new disguises; there is also a significant insight produced as the reader makes the connection in his mind between meaning and function, between content and form. And this insight is that the mind can only grasp the truth of what is being said by means of motion. As the mind moves back and forth between the recognition that this is a noun and the discovery that it was once a verb, somewhere along the arc of insight it perceives the truth of what is being said: that the knife-grinder achieves a mystery of transformation in turning prose into poetry—he "sharpens say to sing." The mind perceives this because it has been asked to participate in the very process of transformation itself. This must be what Cummings means when he says that art is not *of* something, but rather *is* something; it imitates nature, and the reader becomes not a passive spectator but an active protagonist. The grammatical shift imitates the meaning, and in the resultant interplay something like a metaphor is produced—except that the two terms are not tenor and vehicle but rather noun-function and verb-meaning. Laborious analysis, however, should not obscure the rapidity, the delicacy, and the delight with which the reader senses all this.

Nouns are also made out of prefixes, interrogative pronouns, conjunctions, and so on. Similarly, coinages are created by analogy by adding adverbial suffixes where you least expect them ("happeningly"), adjectival suffixes ("neverish"), and noun-endings ("muchness"). These are Cummings' true trademarks, the devices that the critics, imitators, and parodists are bound to miss in their anxiety to fasten upon the more obvious typographical pyrotechnics. Also more characteristic are his distortions of syntax, and these too are missed by the readers who run.

But the typography deserves discussion. I, for one, like it in most instances; it seems to me just, useful, and right. But I recognize the possibility that I may simply be used to it. I also recognize the force of the argument which says these devices are not organic or functional because they can rarely be pronounced. And I understand furthermore that they often succeed in irritating people. Let me try, however, to say what can be said for them.

To break lines and words on the page, to use capitals and lower case letters where they don't belong, to insert parentheses anywhere and everywhere, to scatter punctuation marks apparently at random—what uses can these serve? There is, first of all, what I suspect is a heuristic function for the poet: it was simply helpful for Cummings to do these things as he tried to write a poem. And as such, we should be willing to accept them. But, of course, we could argue that he might just as well have gotten rid of them after the poem was written. So let us look for better reasons. There is, secondly, the "feel" of the poem as it lies on the page. To me at least there is a pleasurable tactility in these devices, a sense of visual structure as in a painting. Does not a reader of conventional poetry take a similar pleasure in the look of a sonnet or of a blank verse paragraph? This may have nothing to do with the meaning involved, but it is present and affective nevertheless. The third is the best reason, for it is here that the charge of inorganicity can be met: typography may not be pronounceable but it does affect the way we read. Pause and emphasis are supported by these devices; the meaning of words and lines is underscored; but, most important of all, meanings are created as the reader's mind is slowed in its progress through the poem and forced to go back and forth, thereby becoming aware of the meanings in an immediate moment of perception. This is what any good poem asks of the reader and Cummings is simply extending this request by making it explicit. Nor is it necessary to scorn a device which enables the poet to get two words for the price of one, as Cummings does, for example, when he splits "nowhere" into "now" and "here" (*95 poems*, #4). When he said he was fond of that precision which creates movement (Foreword to *is 5*, p. 163) he was in fact announcing the fundamental tenet of his aesthetic.

III

To explain the meaning of Cummings' work—to show the relationship between his devices and the vision they serve—is in a sense to meet one charge regarding its significance. For it is not uncommonly said that there is no meaning here and that therefore there is no significance. I would feel satisfied if this one point were to be finally recognized by all those who are concerned with modern poetry: that Cummings' experiments, his love poems, and his satires all play a functional role in a serious view of life—or, at least, a *view* of life, for its seriousness must be discussed separately. No one can honestly read these poems and conclude that Cummings is a trifler; no one can honestly read his better critics and say that Cummings' poetry has no meaning. A Campion, a Herrick, a Prior, a Landor, a Dowson may be consummate artists, and we may cherish them for their perfection of style and language, but a case can reasonably be made against them for not having anything much to say. Not necessarily anything *new* to say, but anything *much* to say. Cummings, however, is not one of these.

But it's the seriousness of his vision which, even if it be admitted to exist, may be questioned. Well, I have already discussed what may be said against it and have tried to answer certain objections. Cummings' view of life is nonrational, and he sometimes sees himself as the Fool, the Outcast, the Clown, and so on, vis-à-vis ordinary society. He is more interested, as Walter Pater was, in experiencing life than in theorizing about it, but for a rather different reason—Pater's moments of crystallization were precious because nature is always dying, while Cummings' are precious because nature is always just being born. He is interested in what is alive and growing, in what is therefore immeasurable and mysterious. Now there always have been and there always will be those who disagree with this attitude, and that is their privilege. But this is no necessary reason to discount its value as a serious poetic vision; indeed, it may be claimed that it is *the* poetic vision of most great literature since Blake, if not earlier. It has, at least, a certifiable literary history. And I for one think no truly rational man will deny the importance of a nonrational view of certain aspects of life—those in which Cummings is most interested.

It is unfortunate, however, that as many Romantics have misprized reason as there have been Rationalists who have misprized the imagination, and Cummings has not avoided this error. Nor has he avoided the error of demolishing all institutions in his anxiety to attack the evil ones which are still sucking the life out of us. But he may be defended against both charges on the grounds that his destructive work is needed and is therefore healthy, for there are times when going to extremes is required by the extremity of the evil to be corrected. And these are extreme times indeed: most of what he attacks has gotten worse instead of better during the course of his lifetime; and more and more, recent history is proving him right about what's wrong with the world.

Of course, one may have a serious view of life and still not be a significant poet. So the question must also be discussed as to whether Cummings' means are suitable to embody his ends—suitable, that is, in relation to what other poets have done regarding similar ends. For I hope I have already shown that his means are appropriate as ways of creating the freshness and motion and vitality which his vision calls for. If we ask of a poet that he not merely achieve his goal but also that he achieve it in an original and unexpected way, then Cummings fills the bill. There is nothing tame, nothing passive, nothing easy about his solution of his artistic problems: he is an innovator, an experimenter, a questioner. It is of the essence in the transcendental view never to rest content with any formulation of life's truth for long, and so it is necessary that transcendentalist writers be odd, cranky, even perverse. It is nonsense, therefore, to complain that Cummings hasn't influenced anyone—even if this were true.

We also have the right to expect of a poet that he know and revere the traditions of his art even as he is violating them. If Cummings says "welcome the future," he also says "honour the past" (*95 poems*, #60). He knows there is nothing which is merely new; he knows and understands more about language and its responsibilities, I suspect, than the critics who have complained of his whimsicality and arbitrariness. If my first point is that Cummings has a serious vision of life, my second point is that both it and his art are firmly rooted in tradition. No artistic experimenter can be significant who is not so rooted.

Or, it may be agreed that all I have said about Cummings is so, but that other transcendentalist poets—or at least poets whose view of life is framed by spiritual or imaginative insights—have done it better. I have tried to explain this point by distinguishing between the Paradoxers and the Ambivalents, and by suggesting that we need not limit our appreciation to the Ambivalents. Why not? The Ambivalents are characterized by self-doubt, and Cummings is surely not one of these. When they achieve a joyful moment of release, it is always at the end of their poems; Cummings begins where they leave off. In Aristotelian terms, their personae are people like us, while Cummings' persona is one who is better than we are. Theirs is an art of struggle, his of achievement. Naturally theirs is more flattering to us, his less. But does not their art encourage complacency in us, especially when it is written by the fashionable imitators whose ambivalence is a literary pose rather than a felt experience? As if to say that joy is a remote thing and we are in the swim if we feel despair. How much more difficult it is to write a really affirmative piece—more difficult than one would suppose—for it is so much harder to fake. False enthusiasm is easier by far to spot than false gloom.

An interesting light is thrown on these remarks by Cummings himself, in a letter to Allen Tate (Mr. Tate informs me that he thinks the "self portrait" refers to an early draft of his poem, "The Eye," which he wrote in 1947):

> Dear Allen—
> I am deeply touched by the self portrait
> (enclosed herewith) which you were so
> generous as to loan me. But (this is
> my own perfectly biased opinion)
> tu as tort in one respect: he who
> serves La De'esse Qui s'apelle "l'art"
> hath luck beyond rubrics n + 3 . . .
> Whereas (I feel) you've almost
> pretendedyourself into sadness-extraneous,
> tristesse-irrelevant, and grief-worldly.
> Bien sûr, l'existence est difficile
> (et comment!) for each him who
> desires La Vie; quite as difficile
> as it's facile for all unartists.

The value of Cummings' stance is in part a function of its rarity in twentieth-century poetry.

The Whole E. E. Cummings

by Patricia Buchanan Tal-Mason Cline

I

in time's a noble mercy of pro-
portion/. . . his wisdom cancels
conflict and agreement/. . . . *95 poems,* #11

Time has given a new proportion to E. E. Cummings' work. The lyric excesses and typographical scandals that distracted earlier critics have become simply the varied textures of an interesting whole. The changing evaluation of Cummings in the last decade has reflected an awareness of his timeliness, and through the efforts of a number of editors and commentators an almost Blakean figure, emanating love and human indignation, has been established.[1] Yet as appreciative as his "critics" have become, they have not sufficiently come to grips with Cummings' insistence on a holistic experience of life: the drawing together of separate areas of experience into a unified whole.

The poet has prepared a guide to the thought underlying his work in *i:Six Nonlectures,* the published title of his Charles Eliot Norton lectures at Harvard (Cambridge, 1953). Yet, as Cummings himself points out, the organizing of this developmental—but unconnected—series of ideas is left to the reader: "I shall take these expressions chronologically . . . letting you draw your own (if any) conclusions.

"The Whole E. E. Cummings," by Patricia Buchanan Tal-Mason Cline. From *Twentieth Century Literature* 14, 2 (July 1968), 90–97. © 1968 by IHC Press. Reprinted by permission of the publisher.

[1] Following Charles Norman's biography, *The Magic Maker: E. E. Cummings* (New York, 1958), a number of appreciative studies of Cummings' work have been published: Norman Friedman, *E. E. Cummings: The Art of His Poetry* (Baltimore, 1960) and *E. E. Cummings: the Growth of a Writer* (Carbondale, 1964), Barry Marks, *E. E. Cummings* (New York, 1964), and Robert Wegner, *The Poetry and Prose of E. E. Cummings* (New York, 1965). S. V. Baum, in *E. E. Cummings and the Critics* (East Lansing, 1962), has edited a collection of critical articles dealing with the poet; George Firmage in *E. E. Cummings: A Bibliography* (Middletown, 1960) has prepared a bibliography through 1959. Mr. Firmage has also edited and recently revised Cummings' uncollected essays in *E. E. Cummings: A Miscellany Revised* (New York, 1965).

Over- and under-standing will make their appearance later. . . ." (*i*, p. 63). Stripped of its rhetoric, the thought in *i* can be condensed, and the conclusions to be drawn from it provide a new "over-standing."

In *i,* Cummings predicates two realms of existence: a real "world" of growth and decay in time and matter and an ideal "world" of timeless and immeasurable absolutes (pp. 52–53). The natural world and the human beings in it exist in the real realm, yet they are invested with "mystery" because they are related to the ideal realm through love—"the mystery-of-mysteries who creates them all" (p. 43). This integration of the real and the ideal by love is perceived by the individual at the moment of self-discovery, during which the two realms are reconciled into a "homogeneous duality" (a seemingly paradoxical phrase which is the key to Cummings' holistic ideal, the simultaneous awareness of real and transcendent existence). This re-association of the sensibilities, with body and mind uniting to produce spirit, is the condition of the *whole* human being, who is capable of love.

The self-found man "Is"; he participates in Being. But beyond this wholeness lies the possibility—for certain "fated" people—of Becoming. Growth, to Cummings, is the active striving toward contact with the absolute, "to die in time and be reborn in timelessness," through love. Artists, lovers, worshippers, anyone who succeeds in a loving and total identification with matter, man or God, transcends his former self and grows (pp. 81–82).

The growth of the artist in the self-transcendent moment of creation is illustrated in *i* by a passage from the play *Him*. There on a high-wire, with no net, the solitary individual reminds himself of his potential (an artist), his condition (a man), and his imperfection (a failure) and demands of himself that he "MUST PROCEED." Passionately aware and concentrated, the individual kicks those three facts—artist, man, and failure—out from under himself and stands on air above the wire which was his former limitation. In other words, the man discards his conscious roles and concentrates his awareness in a "timeless moment" of oneness with the thing that he loves, a moment of relationship which seems eternal, therefore is outside of time. Through this experience the individual realizes his own illimitability and strives to PROCEED again and again. He grows.[2]

Although, Cummings points out, egocentricity is the fundamental human fact, the centered self is only whole if it can love, and through love relate to all of love's mysteries: the natural world, the created world of art, and the world of other loving human beings: "A givingly eternal complexity . . . a naturally and miraculously whole human

[2] Of the critics mentioned, Norman Friedman most thoroughly explores Cummings' transcendental vision, although he does not attempt to reconstruct the Platonic base.

being—a feelingly illimitable individual; whose only happiness is to transcend himself, whose every agony is to grow" (*i*, p. 111).

The classical model for the vision in *i* is obvious. In Plato's *Symposium,* Diotima depicts love as the contact between phenomenal and noumenal worlds—the way to knowledge of the ideal. And Plato provides Cummings with his major symbols, although the poet fuses basic Platonic dualism. In the autobiographical section of *i,* Cummings describes his first awareness: "& my father gave me Plato's metaphor of the cave with my mother's milk" (p. 9).

From the beginning to the end of his work Cummings platonizes—most directly in *Anthropos: or the Future of Art* (1930), which retells the parable of the cave, with a difference. But the lover in Cummings' lyrics most consistently embodies the poet's re-interpretation of the world of *Symposium.* The beast with two backs from Plato's dissertation of love, halved into male and female by Zeus, in his infinite wit, is a serious metaphor in Cummings' love poems. Wandering uncertainly between "Realities" and "Unrealities" in his early work, the poet/lover is seeking the actuality found in completion: "who's myself's Antimere?" Finding his "metamere" ends his quest (*Poems: 1923–1954* [New York, 1954], p. 286: 12); beginning with *ViVa,* in 1931, a unified experience of love is expressed, in "somewhere i have never travelled" (263: LVII), reappearing fully in the later *One Times One* (1944):

> one's not half two. It's two are halves of one:
> which halves reintegrating,shall occur
> no death and any quantity. . . . *Poems,* 398: XVI

This image of mutual interpenetration carries direct sexual connotations; Cummings' love *is* a fusion of the mind and flesh of two people, the relationship of *1 x 1.*

The striving toward reintegration of the self with the other is typically Romantic; yet it is important to be aware that Cummings' emphasis is not on the escape from the self into the other, but on the expansion of the self's potential through *complete* meeting with the other. Here the experience of Being is put to the uses of Becoming. The Romantic obsession with the eternal (that which is out of time) and the *fin de siècle* obsession with the moment (time's crystallization) is extended by Cummings' formula of growth-through-the-experience-of-time-lessness into an unfolding awareness. Cummings' end is the fruit of the experience—a more comprehensive self—not the experience itself. He modifies the Platonic cosmos to provide a version of the perennial philosophy of transcendence which can work in an era which demands that man be solely man. Diotima's route to the absolute via Eros is given to any fully human being who reaches out to things or people or God in a superfluity of love. This kind of self-transcendence does not rise above human life but, rather, raises human life above itself. Cummings simply brings Platonism a step further in the direction in which it had been headed in the latter part of the nineteenth century.

He is not alone—in the twentieth century—in his re-platonizing. The poet was aware, early in his development, of Freud's theory of the unconscious; he refers to it in several of his *Vanity Fair* essays.[3] Freud's Eros is essentially the same as Plato's, although expressed in biological terms. Yet Cummings' goes beyond the simply biological, envisioning a potential of transcendence within the "real," organic world.

In Cummings' holistic reworking of Platonism, transcendence exists within the individual along with his biological existence; it is up to the individual to reconcile the two. He bears the responsibility of relationship to other human beings, and to nature, even to his own unconscious. If he does not succeed in relating, he cannot love; he is isolated.

II

One may trace the stigmata of isolation and despair and the slow establishment of his means to affirmation in Cummings' writings, beginning with his references to himself as a child who was nurtured on the parable of the cave and who grew to adolescence in Cambridge. There, as he later remarks in *i,* he observed his real and ideal realms "bitterly struggling for dominion" (p. 53).

In his first experience of France—in an ecstatic moment of self-finding—he saw the struggle temporarily reconciled. As one reads *The Enormous Room* (New York, 1922), which chronicles the events taking place directly after this self-discovery, one finds, however, that the elation produced by that reconciling of opposites is heightened by an accompanying sense of the absurd. Things are described as "blague," "absurd," and "ridiculous." The events of the months to come first intensify, then sober, and at last destroy that elation, leaving only the absurdity. The author is arrested for a non-existent crime, imprisoned, and reduced eventually to despair. Yet he finds in the prison that there are men who do not fall victim to the filth and misery of their environment in any way: the main characters of the book are four men who are so integrated within their own personalities that prison cannot touch them; in a sense, they are free. Our hero, on the other

[3] See *E. E. Cummings: A Miscellany Revised,* G. J. Firmage, ed., for the author's early essays. Freud is mentioned as early as 1926, in "The Adult, The Artist and the Circus," p. 111.

hand, although he is "Happier in prison than words can pretend to express," is crushed by the experience. He loses, in fact, his mental stability.[4] The protagonist knows that he has a mind, feels that he has a body, and is aware that mind and body are unified in his self. But the concept of reality which Cummings has formed up to this point *does not work* in the prison at Ferté Macé. When he is freed, he is "born again," but his problem is not solved. An authentic approach to existence remains to be found.

Judging from the subdivisions of his first volumes of poetry, Cummings' early "reality" was bleak. In *Tulips and Chimneys,* 1923, and in *&* [AND], 1925, the reality sonnets deal with a gross level of experience. Most of the characters are prostitutes, unsentimentalized. "Unrealities" is the heading of a group of tremulous, spiritual, love poems; "Actualities" is concerned with a blending of physical and spiritual awareness. Finding a way of existing at the level of "actuality" seems to be the poet's problem in his early years.

There is a ten-year period between the despair after *The Enormous Room* and the affirmation that begins in *ViVa.* During this time, Cummings struggles to find a meaningful basis for his commitment to love. His poetry of this period reflects the search, as does his play, *Him,* published and produced in 1927–28. The poet is an alive, aware, and loving individual during these years, and even in the face of self-rejection he is capable of poetry; yet marks of despair appear in his work in the late 1920's and early 1930's.

Concomitant with despair is the thought of suicide. There is some evidence in his work that this thought crosses Cummings' mind during this troubled period. In *Him,* the protagonist threatens his mirror image with a pistol, wishing to destroy the symbolic self which the heroine loves—yet realizing that the act would be absurd, he cries "Quelle blague!" (I, iv, p. 23). A similar situation occurs in a poem: *Poems,* 243: XXIX. (It is interesting to note that the suicide is male, blond, and small of hand, a description vaguely resembling the poet.)

in a middle of a room
stands a suicide
sniffing a Paper rose
smiling to a self

"somewhere it is Spring and sometimes
people are in real:imagine
somewhere real flowers,but
I can't imagine real flowers for if I

[4] *The Enormous Room* (New York: Modern Library, 1934), p. 314.

could,they would somehow
not Be real"
(so he smiles
smiling) "but I will not

everywhere be real to
you in a moment"

In both play and poem, the self which is being destroyed is only a mirrored reflection. Still, "nothingness" is in conflict with being during these years, and in at least one poem it is preferable to existence (*Poems,* 156: VIII):

come nothing to my comparable soul
which with existence has conversed in vain,
O scrupulously take thy trivial toll,
for whose cool feet this frantic heart is fain. . . .

But Cummings is not merely passively aware of the doubtful value of existence; he is actively looking for meaning:

will out of the kindness of their hearts a few philosophers tell me
what am i doing on top of this hill at Calchidas, in the sunlight?

. . . . . .

(here the absurd I; life, to peer and wear clothes.
i am altogether foolish, i suddenly make a fist
out of ten fingers. *Poems,* 202: V

The only answer which keeps him alive is love; but love is not enough to erase his awareness of the absurdity of his life. An "absurd fraction in its lowest terms," still he can lean out of the window and will not fall to the street below for the simple reason that he believes in love (*Poems,* 212: XII). The thing is to temporize in the absence of any program except to live, "to eat flowers and not to be afraid" (189–90: XXXIII). Self-destruction is incompatible with hope.

In spite of the self-doubt and despair expressed by the hero of *Him,* birth and rebirth are the central themes of the play. The repeated obstetrical imagery indicates that something is coming to life, perhaps "Him" himself.[5] The play turns on the problem of Him's integration of his three selves: artist, man, and failure. His identity is not yet truly authentic, as he confesses to the heroine in the last act. It cannot be inferred from the play that Cummings' own problem of self-integration is solved, but the idea of birth which lends unity to *Him* emerges

[5] This point has been thoroughly treated by Mr. Robert Maurer in his article, "E. E. Cummings' *Him,*" *Bucknell Review* VI (May 56). [Reprinted herein, pp. 133–55. —Editor's note.]

in a paean in *Eimi,* his "miscalled novel," as the answer to the problem of being.

The working out of his own salvation and rebirth is the central drama in Cummings' "descent into Russia." Although Cummings has claimed *Eimi* to be no more than a true transcript of his Russian diary, its relationship to the *Divine Comedy* of Dante, both in plot and in direct reference, suggests a larger scope. As the grey world of Moscow closes in on the author, his reactions against its oppression and negation grow more emotional and intense. His own identity takes shape; it defines itself against the "unworld" which he is experiencing. Simply because of his one value, he refuses to accept the possibility of the success of such a system:

> something . . . is sure,I feel;something's certain:Eros wins. Eros wins;always: through a million or a trillion million selves,musically which are 1 who always cannot perish. . . . therefore;he(whatever his creed)who would subvert Eros,the form,shall become shadow.
>
> *Eimi* (New York, 1933), p. 116

The Inferno becomes more confused: Cummings' homosexual Virgil, his first guide, gives way to a Beatrice; ideological bickering is replaced with lyrical self-affirmation:

> We of whom Is partakes,only to whom our deaths are births—savagely makers beneath docile time(and beyond conquerable space travellers)who are not contained or comprised,who cannot fail in wonder. . . .
>
> *Eimi* p. 187

It is here in *Eimi* that Cummings uses the language of his self-transcendental belief. Here he speaks of "the Self's full perfect doom of imperfection" and of "timeless deep unspace,the single poem,which builds unconsciousness" (pp. 187–8). Without an understanding of his concept of artistic creation—through the seeming transcendence of time and space, in moments of total relationship—this amazing rhetoric is almost incoherent.

His lyric excitement increases as the journey proceeds. At the lowest point in his travels he goes down into the tomb of Lenin, confronting the "human god" only to find it a "fake reality" (pp. 240–4). Cummings does not find the god-in-man in Russia; divine humanness does not appear until the end of his journey. The Inferno past, the last stages of the trip may be read as a telescoped *Purgatorio-Paradiso.* As the poet returns from Russia he becomes increasingly aware of the divinity which he has found within himself. To the "metal steed" which is rushing him back to his love, he addresses an impassioned oration against all the "itgods" which it represents: he prophesies the victory of the still small god in man (Poietes, "only Whose language is silence") over "equally every purveyor of impotence and alikeness to mankind" (*Eimi,* p. 418). Pitting himself against all the itgods of a mechanized world, Cummings *becomes* the god-in-man speaking, uttering the lines from the *Tao Te Ching* which exalt man to the Universal.

Eimi was written in 1931; *ViVa,* a collection of poems published that year, provides transition between the shifting of values from *Him* to *Eimi.* In spite of a shaky self-concept:

> a clown's smirk in the skull of a baboon
> (where once good lips stalked or eyes firmly stirred)
> my mirror gives me,on this afternoon;
> i am a shape that can but eat and turd
> e'er with the dirt death shall him vastly gird,
> a coward waiting clumsily to cease
> whom every perfect thing meanwhile doth miss;
> a hand's impression in an empty glove,
> a soon forgotten tune,a house for lease.
> I have never loved you dear as now i love (259: LI)

there is a tentative movement toward affirmation in *ViVa.* A new self is growing through a new experience of love, in the beautiful lyric "somewhere i have never travelled" (263: LVII) and in:

> be unto love as rain is unto colour; create
> me gradually . . .
>
> Wait
>
> if i am not heart,because at least i beat
>
> *Poems,* 267–8: LXIII

Images of rebirth through love and self-transcendence appear more often in *no thanks* (1935). The scattered sonnets in this collection speak constantly of birth and "dying" in a timeless moment of creation. By 1938, the theme of rebirth has become so central to Cummings' thought that it is the topic of his introduction to *Collected Poems* in which he cries:

> . . . We can never be born enough. We are human beings;for whom birth is a supremely welcome mystery,the mystery of growing:the mystery which happens only and whenever we are faithful to ourselves. . . .
>
> *Poems,* p. 331

This cycle of self-demanded growth and rebirth provides man with a means for spiritual development within the organic framework of human life.

III

Cummings meets existence as a man alone, yet he embraces it positively. In his prison experience, he had encountered total isolation in the face of a world of "inhuman unfeeling"; the rest of his life is devoted to the effort to be fully human and to completely feel.

Cummings' search for a self which he could wholly accept bridges the years between *The Enormous Room* and *Eimi.* Throughout these years, his need to be "whole," which leads him in his satiric poems to define his identity by rejecting the "unliving" nonexistence of most people, is guided by his commitment to love. Only through love is relationship—the opening of the self to "immeasurable" nature, man, and art—possible. Love synthesizes the dichotomies. But the question is, where can one find enough love?

His answer lies in growth. Cummings' acceptance of an expanding pattern of self-transcendence and rebirth orients him toward the future.

After *Collected Poems,* 1938, the themes of love, timelessness, and growth through rebirth are maintained in Cummings' poetry, even in the posthumous *73 poems,* 1963. That "love is the every only god" (*Poems,* 378: 38) is established by 1940, in *50 POEMS;* it is infinite: ". . . imagined,therefore limitless (*Poems,* 409: XXXIV); it is immortal—". . . only love/immortally occurs beyond the mind" (*Poems,* 410: XXXVI):

> being to timelessness as it's to time,
> love did no more begin than love will end;
>
> . . . . .
>
> love is the voice under all silences,
> the hope which has no opposite in fear;
> the strength so strong mere force is feebleness:
> the truth more first than sun more last than star
>
> . . . . .

95 poems, #94
[New York: Harcourt Brace Jovanovich, Inc., 1958]

Through love, humans can be fully, organically human, as was "anyone" who "lived in a pretty how town" (*Poems,* 370–1: 29); through love a man can become more than human, as in "my father moved through dooms of love" (*Poems,* 373–5: 34).

Lovers can escape time—they are immortal: "true lovers in each happening of their hearts/live longer than all which and every who . . ." (*Poems,* 410: XXXVI); they can escape the "colossal hoax of clocks and calendars" (*Poems,* 461: 61). Gaining emphasis in *95 poems,* as in "stand with your lover on the ending earth," #71, the "eternal now" of love is a major theme in *73 poems.* There lovers are "(hosts of eternity;not guests of seem)"; poets, children, and lovers cannot tell time (*73 poems,* 45). And in the last sonnet:

> your lover(looking through both life and death
> timelessly celebrates the merciful
> wonder no world deny may or believe *73 poems,* 73

It is in this moment of relationship that time dies and growth occurs:

> —we(by a gift called dying born)must grow
> deep in dark least ourselves remembering
> love only rides his year.
> All lose,whole find
> *Poems,* 398:XVI

Lovers can continue to outgrow themselves (*Poems,* 409: XXXIV):

> . . . but our doom is
>
> to grow(remember
>
> this my sweet)not
> only
> wherever the sun and the stars and
>
> the
>
> moon
> are we're;but
> also
>
> nowhere *95 poems,* 14

Life's final challenge, death, involves him very little in his later work. The organism that stops growing begins to die; Cummings is aware of this, as he is aware of the annual cycle of birth and growth and winter, in the natural world which he celebrates. His youthful Gothic fear of death is left behind in his mature works. In the late poems, death is associated with the white peace of winter:

> that white sleep wherein
> all human curiosity we'll spend
> (gladly,as lovers must)immortal and
>
> the courage to receive time's mightiest dream
> *95 poems,* 3

Growth and rebirth are the final answers to Cummings' search for identity: through love the self experiences "timeless" contact with the other, and realizes its potential for growth. The human being transcends his "real" nature and incorporates his "ideal" nature—becoming newly whole and finding new possibility of growth. Only in terms of this "homogeneous duality" can Cummings' holism be fully understood.

His indignant satires attacking the forces which prevent growth and awareness—"mind without heart," stereotyping, mechanization—are merely the other side of the same argument. As he says, "love makes the little thickness of the coin" (*Poems,* 381: 43).

E. E. Cummings [*ViVa*]

by Allen Tate

The quality of *ViVa,** being quite uniform with that of Mr. Cummings' previous books, imposes upon the reviewer no obligation to describe important changes, in this poet's work, of style, composition, or point of view. This fact alone is, of course, of no significance, but it brings to the reviewer a grateful feeling of relief; it permits him to write with a full sense of the merit of the three previous books of verse by this poet, a sense that corrects, as it should, a feeling of disappointment in the quality of *ViVa.*

It is not that the quality has fallen off. Cummings' faults are well-known, I believe, if not generally defined, and they are still essentially the faults of *Tulips and Chimneys* (1923). In that book it was not easy to distinguish his own quality, and thus his limitations, from the influence of other poets, Keats and Swinburne; but this influence has disappeared. The special quality of his talent stands forth without the misleading features of an unformed style. He has refined his talent, perhaps not to the point of which it is ideally capable, but at least to the point at which he is able to convey a particular kind of meaning that very properly obsesses any poet in contact with his medium.

His uniformity is not uniformity of style. The point could be labored, but I think it is sufficient to refer the reader of Cummings to the three distinct styles of poems XVIII, LI, and LVII in *ViVa.* He has a great many styles, and having these he has none at all—a feature of his poetry concealed by his famous device of distorted word and line. For style is that quality of a piece of writing which may be distinguished from its communicable content but which in no sense can be subtracted from it: the typographical device can be so subtracted by simple alteration either in the direction of conventional pattern or in the direction of greater distortion. The typography is distinct

"E. E. Cummings" (a review of *ViVa*), by Allen Tate. From *Poetry,* 39 (March 1932), 332–37; reprinted in *Reactionary Essays on Poetry and Ideas,* by Allen Tate (New York: Charles Scribner's Sons, 1936). Reprinted by permission of the author and the publisher.

* *ViVa* (seventy new poems). By E. E. Cummings. Horace Liveright, Inc., 1931.

from style, something superimposed and external to the poem, a mechanical system of variety and a formula of surprise; it is—and this is its function—a pseudo-dynamic feature that galvanizes the imagery with the look of movement, of freedom or fresh perception, a kind of stylization which is a substitute for a living relation between the images and the sensibility of the poet. Mr. Cummings' imagery reaches the page still-born.

This characteristic of his verse has been brilliantly analyzed by Mr. R. P. Blackmur, in his "Notes on E. E. Cummings' Language." * To that essay I refer the reader for a discussion of Cummings' replacement of stock poetic conventions with an equally limited set of conventions of his own. "By denying the dead intelligence and putting on the heresy of unintelligence," says Mr. Blackmur, "the poet only succeeds in substituting one set of unnourished conventions for another." Again: "As if sensation could be anything more than the idea of sensation . . . without being attached to some central body of experience, genuinely understood and *formed* in the mind." And Mr. Blackmur summarizes his view: "So long as he is content to remain in his private mind, he is unknowable, impenetrable, and sentimental."

These statements reach to the center of Cummings' problem, but I believe that Mr. Blackmur takes too seriously the "heresy of unintelligence"; it is rather the heresy of supposing that personality, as such, outside the terms of something that is not personality, can ever be made known.

Now in addition to the typographical mechanism there is another that grows out of it—the mechanism of emotionally private words that are constantly overcharged into pseudo-symbols. This has two aspects. There is the repetition of single words (Mr. Blackmur, in his comprehensive study, examines in detail the personal *clichés:* "flower," "petal," "bloom," etc.); and there is the headlong series of miscellaneous words that attempt to imitate the simultaneity and shock of fresh sensation. Mr. Blackmur shows that the weight of the series cancels the sensory value of its single items. Both this device and the distorted line probably proceed from the poet's sense of the insufficiency of his style: there is something wrong, something obscure that demands a superimposed heightening for effect.

Without this external variety we get, in Cummings, the uniformity that I have mentioned, but it is rather a uniformity of meaning, of reference, than of conception. No single poem introduces the reader to an implicit body of idea beneath its surface, a realm of meaning detached once and for all from the poet. We go on to the next poem,

* *The Double Agent: Essays in Craft and Elucidation.* By R. P. Blackmur. New York: Arrow Editions, 1935.

and from the aggregate of Mr. Cummings' poems we return to the image of his personality: like all poets he seems to say "more" than the explicit terms convey, but this "more" lies in the origin of the poem, not in the tension of its materials. From "To His Coy Mistress" we derive no clue to the existence of such a person as "Andrew Marvel"; from *ViVa* we got only the evidence of personality. And this is what Cummings' poetry "means." It is a kind of meaning very common at present; Cummings is the original head of an easily imitable school. This does not mean that he has ever been successfully imitated; no one else of his generation has written personal poetry as well as Mr. Cummings writes it. It is rather that he has shown the possibility of making personal conventions whose origin and limit are personality. It is a kind of convention that, given "talent," can make of any one a poet. It requires a certain interest in oneself, which permits one to ascribe to one's "feeling-tone" for words an objective meaning, a comprehensible meaning to the relations existing among those words. This stanza, by no means an extreme example of pure "feeling-tone," illustrates the process:

> your slightest look easily will unclose me
> though i have closed myself as fingers,
> you open always petal by petal myself as Spring opens
> (touching skillfully,mysteriously)her first rose (263: LVII)

There is sententiousness in excess of an occasion that remains "unknowable," and we are brought back to the poet who becomes the conceivable reference of an emotion in excess of what is said. But "Cummings" in that sense is an empty abstraction, and the fact that the poet Cummings leads us there, away from the poem itself, explains Mr. Blackmur's remark that the poetry exists only in terms of something that is "impenetrable" and "sentimental." It fails to implicate the reader with the terms of a *formed* body of experience. The poet asks us at last not to attend to the poem as poetry, but to its interesting origin, the poet who, the publisher assures us, has a "cheerful disdain for the approval of pundits and poetasters."

In Mr. Cummings' work there is much that amuses and much that one admires. A rigorous selection from his four books would give us some of the best poetry of the age. In &, the magnificent sonnet on death (117: II [?]), and the love sonnet ending "an inch of nothing for your soul" (121: X), though projected in Mr. Cummings' personal imagery, achieve a measure of objective validity by reference to the traditional imagery of such poetry, which he inverts, but by implication leans upon. His best verse is that in which he succeeds, perhaps unintentionally, in escaping from his own personality into a world of meaning that not even the "heresy of unintelligence" can let him ignore. For this reason he cannot forever be immune to the heavy hand of the pundits. If he finds their pretensions tiresome, he will agree with me that it is the fate of interesting personalities to be continually bored.

Review of *50 POEMS*[1]

by R. P. Blackmur

As E. E. Cummings' *50 POEMS* makes the sharpest contrast to Mr. Baker, let us proceed at once with the statement that Mr. Cummings' poems depend entirely upon what they create in process, only incidentally upon what their preliminary materials or intentions may have been. Thus, above all, there is a prevalent quality of uncertainty, of uncompleted possibility, both in the items and in the fusion of the items which make up the poems; but there is also the persistent elementary eloquence of intension—of things struggling, as one says crying, to be together, and to make something of their togetherness which they could never exhibit separately or in mere series. The words, the meanings in the words, and also the nebula of meaning and sound and pun around the words, are all put into an enlivening relation to each other. There is, to employ a word which appealed to Hart Crane in similar contexts, a sense of synergy in all the successful poems of Mr. Cummings: synergy is the condition of working together with an emphasis on the notion of energy in the working, and energy in the positive sense, so that one might say here that Mr. Cummings' words were energetic. The poems are, therefore, eminently beyond paraphrase, not because they have no logical content—for they do, usually very simple—but because so much of the activity is apart from that of logical relationships, is indeed in associations free of, though not alien to, logical associations. In short, they create their objects.

Now there has been a good deal of catcalling at Mr. Cummings, and lately there has been a good deal of indifference, general indifference which is meaningless and also the indifference of some of his

"Review of *50 POEMS*," by R. P. Blackmur. From *The Southern Review*, 7 (Summer 1941), 187–213. © 1941 by *The Southern Review*. Reprinted by permission of the publisher.

[1] [This review appeared in an omnibus review entitled "Twelve Poets" in *The Southern Review*. The section reprinted here is found on pages 201–5. The preceding paragraphs discuss Howard Baker's *A Letter from the Country*. Blackmur found the poems in this book conventional, abstract, and unmodern: "Mr. Baker's poetry is not heuristic, it does not seek to discover something which is a product of its parts working together; it creates nothing for itself." The review of Cummings follows. —Editor's note.]

admirers who have taken him scot-free of attention: all good, all operative, all part of the canon, and this indifference is the worst injustice of all. There is, for the poet, no discipline like the justified reservations of his admirers, and this should be especially the case with a poet so deliberately idiosyncratic as Mr. Cummings. I have been one of his admirers for twenty-one years since I first saw his poetry in the *Dial;* and it may be that my admiration has gone up and down so many hills that it is a little fagged and comes up to judgment with entirely too many reservations. Yet I must make them, and hope only that the admiration comes through.

First, there is the big reservation that, contrary to the general belief and contrary to what apparently he thinks himself, Mr. Cummings is not—in his meters, in the shapes of his lines, in the typographical cast of his poems on the page—an experimental poet at all. In his "peculiar" poetry he does one of two things. He either reports a speech rhythm and the fragments of meaning punctuated by the rhythm so as to heighten and make it permanent in the reader's ear—as famously in "Buffalo Bill" (50: VIII), but just as accurately elsewhere as, for example, in poem 27 (368–9) in this volume—or in trying to do so he makes such a hash of it that the reader's ear is left conclusively deaf to the poem. I assume he is attempting to heighten sound in the failures as well as the successes; if he is not, if he is trying to write a poetry in symbols which have no audible equivalents—a mere eye poetry—then he is committing the sin against the Holy Ghost. My belief is that the high percentage of failures comes from his lack of a standard from which to conduct experiments, and without which experiment in any true sense is impossible; so that in fact many of his oddities are merely the oddities of spontaneous play, nonsense of the casual, self-defeating order, not nonsense of the rash, intensive order. There is no reason he should not play, but it is too bad that he should print the products, for print sheds a serenity of value, or at least of "authority" upon the most miserable productions which are very deceptive to the innocent.

It should be emphasized in connection with this that Mr. Cummings is an abler experimenter than most poets with rhythm and cadence and epithet; and that these experiments come off best when he is not engaged in false experiments with meter—when he is writing either heightened prose as in "Buffalo Bill," or when he is writing straightway meter of four or five iambic feet. Which is what one would expect.

My second reservation is less significant for most readers but more important for his best readers, and has to do with his vocabulary, which seems to me at many crucial points so vastly over-generalized as to prevent any effective mastery over the connotations they are meant to set up as the substance of his poems. I do not mean it is just hard to say, which is of little importance, but that it is hard to *know,* which is very important, where you are at in poems which juggle fifty to a hundred words so many times and oft together that they lose all their edges, corners, and boundary lines till they cannot lie otherwise than in a heap. But this reservation, formerly held to an extreme, does not now need to be; it is now but a cautionary reservation and applies to no more than half the new poems; for Mr. Cummings' practice has improved with his increasing interest, as it seems, in persuading his readers of the accuracy of the relationships which his words divulge.[2]

My third reservation is minor, and has to do with the small boy writing privy inscriptions on the wall; a reservation which merely to state is sufficiently to expound. Some of the dirt perhaps comes under the head of the poetry of gesture, and some perhaps is only the brutality of disgust. My complaint is meant to be technical; most of the dirt is not well enough managed to reach the level of either gesture or disgust, but remains, let us say, coprophiliac which is not a technical quality.

Beyond these reservations, which in this book of fifty leave ten poems free, Mr. Cummings' work is sufficiently admirable to allow for any amount of good will and concession and full assent to method, all warranted by the substance we are thus permitted to reach. Special attention should be called to the development of fresh conventions in the use of prepositions, pronouns, and the auxiliary verbs in the guise of substances, and in general the rich use of words ordinarily rhetorical —mere connectives or means of transition in their ordinary usage— for the things of actual experience. There are questions which may be asked of which the answers will only come later when the familiarity of a generation or so will have put the data in an intimately understandable order. How much of the richness depends on mere novelty of usage, the gag-line quality? How much depends on the close relationship to the everyday vernacular, the tongue in which Who and Why and How and No and Yes and Am, for example, are of supreme resort, and are capable of infinite diversity of shading? How much depends perhaps on Mr. Cummings' sense of the directional nubs, and the nubs of agency and of being, in his chosen words; a sense that resembles, say, the dative and ablative inflections in Latin? How much, finally, depends on the infinite proliferating multiplicity of available meanings in his absolute commonplaces made suddenly to do precise work? The questions would not be worth asking did not each furnish

[2] [In view of these remarks, it is strange that Blackmur kept reprinting his damning "Notes on E. E. Cummings' Language" (1931) at least as late as 1957 with the note, "There would seem little modification of these notes necessary because of *Eimi* or the subsequent volumes of verse." —Editor's note.]

a possible suggestion as to the capacity for meaning and flavor of his usage; nor would they be worth asking if there were not a major residue of his verse, as standard as death, which his oddities only illuminate without damaging.

I quote the first stanza of poem 34:

> my father moved through dooms of love
> through sames of am through haves of give,
> singing each morning out of each night
> my father moved through depths of height (373–5)

Latter-Day Notes on E. E. Cummings' Language

by Robert E. Maurer

The language that E. E. Cummings uses in his poems, no less than his more widely noticed experiments with typography and his sometimes startling choice of themes, is an expression of the fundamental basis of his life: he is aggressively an individualist, and, more than that, a protestant, as he makes clear in the autobiographical portions of his recent book, *i:Six Nonlectures*. The nonlectures themselves are an expression of his protestantism; when he was offered the Charles Eliot Norton Professorship of Poetry at Harvard for the academic year 1952–1953, he accepted only on the condition that he would not have to teach; and, though he was "extremely glad," as he said, to be giving the six "socalled lectures," he protested against the very idea of lecturing ("lecturing is presumably a form of teaching" [1]) by calling his talks "nonlectures," and by choosing to be autobiographical rather than professorial.

In the nonlectures he reveals that as a boy he reacted against the teacup society of his home in Cambridge, where his father was a professor at Harvard and later a clergyman, by making excursions into "sinful Somerville." His pattern of protest continued as he reacted against the well-scrubbed nice boys of Harvard by frequenting, in his college days, Boston's Old Howard burlesque house; against the authoritarianism of the Norton-Harjes Ambulance Corps, which he joined in 1917, by choosing to remain with a friend even though his steadfastness resulted in his going to a French prison; and, after he began to publish his writings, against polite society in general by glorifying the most abject of men and using prostitutes, stripteasers, and gangsters as the subjects of poems. An inveterate protestant almost automatically comes to sense in himself an aura of separateness, of

"Latter-Day Notes on E. E. Cummings' Language," by Robert E. Maurer. From *The Bucknell Review*, 5 (May 1955), 1–23. © 1955 by *The Bucknell Review*. Reprinted by permission of the author and the publisher.

[1] *i:Six Nonlectures* (Cambridge, Mass., 1953), p. 3.

aloneness; and because he wills himself a significant and very personal insight into all experience, it is understandable that, if he is a writer, he should want to fashion a language in keeping with the uniqueness of his viewpoint. Thus Cummings protested against "gentlemen poeds" (354–5: 6) and "Longfellow . . . dead" (58: I) by throwing away their linguistic principles and working out new ones of his own.

In this activity he was not alone. Cummings grew to artistic maturity in a period, the time just after the First World War, in which experimentation was not only common but almost expected of all serious young artists. Men who rejected all the ideological traditions and values of pre-war bourgeois society used artistic experimentation in a negative way as a means of destroying as many shibboleths as they could; positively, it enabled them to express their new-found individualistic relation to the world about them. The young writers of poetry were trying, as F. J. Hoffman and Charles Allen have expressed it in their book, *The Little Magazine,* to get rid of the poetic clichés that made meaning deceptively easy and to substitute for them an "awareness of complexity." Modern poetic language, they said, "violates . . . conventional recognition, and aims essentially to make the reader discard it altogether, to reform his attention and to reconsider his standards of acceptance." [2] Cummings, in working toward this aim, has used language with no concession to conventional recognition; he has always wanted his reader to drop all the accoutrements of the grammarian and the rhetorician that he may be wearing as protective clothing and to approach his poems, as it were, naked and unafraid. The reader should be free of preconceptions about English poetry, unafraid to "reconsider his standards of acceptance."

This is not to say, however, that Cummings does not know rules and tradition. He is instead a prime example of the old adage that an artist must know all the rules before he can break them. Cummings is no primitive, though he sometimes uses words as a child does; he is no Walt Whitman with a barbaric yawp, no untutored child of the prairie working in what is essentially an alien medium. He was writing poetry, according to his nonlectures, at the age of six—indeed, he was by then in his second poetic phase, in which he thought that a good poem is one that does good; his third phase opened when an uncle presented him with "The Rhymester" and he discovered verse forms—rondels, ballades, villanelles, rondeaus. Shortly thereafter Professor Josiah Royce, a neighbor, introduced him to the sonnets of Rossetti, and, as he says, "I've been writing sonnets ever since." [3] He learned Greek in public school. At Harvard he received "a glimpse of Homer,

[2] F. J. Hoffman *et al., The Little Magazine* (Princeton, 1946), p. 116.
[3] *i:Six Nonlectures,* p. 30.

a more than glimpse of Aeschylus Sophocles Euripedes and Aristophanes, and a deep glance at Dante and Shakespeare";[4] through his friends there he grew to love Sappho, Catullus, Horace, Blake, and Keats. His first book of poems, *Tulips and Chimneys* (1923), revealed the fact that he had had a classical education, although the poems in it that looked forward to his later writing were much more noteworthy than those which were traditionalist. And although he continues to work in the sonnet—perhaps his most memorable poetry is in this form—he long ago abandoned the language of Rossetti and Keats for one which fits his highly personal insight into experience. At its most highly developed state, in his later books, Cummings' language becomes almost a foreign one, usually possible to figure out for a reader who knows English, it is true; but he will get its full meaning only if he has read a great deal of Cummings and if he "knows the language."

It is unfortunate that most of the critical appraisals of Cummings' poetry were made early, shortly after his first books were published. Since those days—the twenties—were full of literary and artistic ferment, and a new poetic talent was to many people at least as exciting as a new baseball player, it is natural that he should have received a great deal of attention then; it is perhaps also natural that as the first shock caused by his poetry died down into acceptance of what seemed a fixed technique of an established poet, the critics should have turned their eyes elsewhere. Cummings, too, was somewhat out of the mainstream in the thirties. He was not popular with the New Critics because he was too personal and unintellectual; he did not think or write in their groove. Nor was he popular with the critics of the left who demanded their own variety of social consciousness in a writer. His "immorality" was too blunt for the Humanists, and his verse was too uncommunicative for the attackers of the cult of unintelligibility. When his last three volumes of verse came out, no one took the trouble to give Cummings the reappraisal that his poetry needed and deserved; very few people noticed the fundamental change of attitude which manifested itself in his growing reverence and dedication to lasting love; even fewer noted the development in his use of language.[5] Thus

[4] *Ibid.*, p. 47.

[5] One writer, James G. Southworth, in 1950 included a chapter on Cummings in his *Some Modern American Poets* (Oxford, 1950), and despite the fact that he then had before him (or should have had) all of Cummings' books of poetry except the most recent, *XAIPE,* he persisted in describing what Cummings "does" by describing what he did in *Tulips and Chimneys*. He paid some lip service to the later books, but justified his peculiar emphasis on a poet's first efforts by saying that ". . . as is now generally recognized by most of his readers, no important changes have occurred in his methods since his early work" (p. 141).

in 1955 an essay, "Notes on E. E. Cummings' Language," by Richard P. Blackmur,[6] written in 1930, remains the only extensive treatment of the subject; and too many people think of his language, as they think of the subject matter of his poetry, as if it were all of a piece, which it most emphatically is not.

The man who in 1923 could publish such an echo of poets immemorial as:

> i like
> to think that on
> the flower you gave me when we
> loved
>
> the far-
> departed mouth sweetly-saluted
> lingers.
>
> (from *Tulips and Chimneys,* "Amores," VI: 36)[7]

in 1944 was writing:

> what if a dawn of a doom of a dream
> bites this universe in two,
> peels forever out of his grave
> and sprinkles nowhere with me and you?
> Blow soon to never and never to twice
> (blow life to isn't:blow death to was)
> —all nothing's only our hugest home;
> the most who die,the more we live
>
> (from *1 x 1,* XX: 401)

The progression is tremendous, not only of language but of thought, of rhythmic patterns, of density, of originality. These examples are not taken out of context merely to make a point; almost any poem from *Tulips and Chimneys* could be set alongside almost any poem from *1 x 1,* in which the latter verse appears, and the contrast would be just as great.

In 1952 Mr. Blackmur appended a note to his republished essay saying, "There would seem little modification of these notes necessary because of *Eimi* or the subsequent volumes of verse," [8] but this statement is an oversimplification. Many of the things that Mr. Blackmur

[6] Reprinted in *Language As Gesture* (New York, 1952), pp. 317–40.

[7] References to Cummings' poems will give the original volume in which they appeared and their number in that volume, then, following the colon, the page on which the poem is to be found in the new collection of Cummings' *Poems 1923–1954* (New York: Harcourt, Brace and Company, 1954).

[8] "Notes on E. E. Cummings' Language," in *Language As Gesture,* p. 317.

said are still accurate descriptions of some of the phenomena of Cummings' language; the trouble is that his remarks are incomplete. They do not consider Cummings' later practices of using one part of speech as another, of leaving out words so that the resulting condensation is so dense as to be almost impenetrable, of thoroughly scrambling English word order with the same effect. Mr. Blackmur was instead occupied with such things as Cummings' tough-guy attitude and his romantic egoism, with his overuse of certain favorite words to which he seemed to assign private meanings, and with the question of whether such diction did not make his poetry impenetrable. Mr. Blackmur concluded unequivocally that it did; and, if in 1952 he saw no need for modification of his notes, one assumes that he still thinks so.[9] He does not mean to say that Cummings is isolated in his fault, however; he puts him in the company of Surrey, Crashaw, Marvell, Burns, Wordsworth, Shelley, and Swinburne, and he asserts: "Most of their work, most of any poet's work, with half a dozen exceptions, is tenuous and vague, private exercises or public playthings of a soul in verse."[10] Since the work of these poets, tenuous and vague though it may be, has been studied with profit, it may not be amiss to give some attention to what is a great obstacle to complete perception of Cummings' poetry, his use of language.

Cummings, a man who admires paradox enough to utilize it constantly in his work, has a knack for unconsciously exemplifying it himself. Although his language, especially in the later books, is intricate and difficult, what he asks of his reader is, as always, the frank approach of a child; and it is this attitude which he himself takes to his mother tongue and to its tenets and rules. Of course, such an approach is consistent with that most salient feature of his viewpoint, his glorification of the child (or the "maturely childish" adult); he is, when he fashions language as a child would, merely practicing what he preaches. It is doubtful whether he ever said to himself, "I shall form and use words as if I have not completely mastered the idiom of the English language, although I know its rules"; but this is precisely what, in his first ventures into unusual language, he began to do. He divested himself of the literate adult's prejudices against such things as double negatives, redundant superlatives and comparatives, and non-dictionary words.

A child will construct his language by means of analogy, forming the past tense of irregular verbs by adding the *-ed* suffix (*runned, swimmed,* and so forth), and forming all comparatives or superlatives

[9] [See preceding essay. —Editor's note.]
[10] *Ibid.*, p. 326.

by adding the normal *-er* or *-est* (*beautifuler, chiefest*), or stepping up the power of a word such as *last,* which is already superlative, and saying *lastest.* Intent on making his point clear and only half certain of the niceties of grammar, a child will repeat negatives or superlatives in triple measure, and so will Cummings. A line from one of his poems, "somebody might hardly never not have been unsorry,perhaps" (from *ViVa,* XXVII: 242), rivals if it does not outclass in bristling negatives such famous lines as Chaucer's "He never yit no vileineye ne sayde" and Shakespeare's "Nor what he said, though it lacked for a little,/Was not like madness." That Cummings has not outgrown his childish technique of word forming is shown by his comparisons in the following fragment, which match those of any child who is determined to make his admiration amply known:

which is the very
(in sad this havingest
world)most merry
most fair most rare
—the livingest givingest
girl on this whirlingest
earth?
          why you're
by far the darlingest   (from *1 x 1,* L: 420)

His creation of *havingest, livingest, givingest,* and *whirlingest* carries the child's habit of adding *-est* to all adjectives one step further: he has added the suffix to words which are rarely if ever used as adjectives at all—*having* and *giving*—thus not only creating a non-dictionary superlative but changing the part of speech of his base word. *Living* and *whirling,* of course, are often used as adjectives; but they are not normally compared.

He uses a similar technique in the following passage, in which he is pointing out the spiritual quality of the moon:

whO perfectly whO
flOat
newly alOne is
dreamest   (from *no thanks,* 1: 277)

By making an adjective out of a word that is normally a noun or a verb, *dream,* he exercises his habit of assuming that the cubbyholes into which words are put are flexible; by doing so he is enabled to express concisely an idea which in English has no one-word equivalent: that a natural phenomenon can contain the quality of dreams to a great degree. The same kind of part-of-speech derangement may be seen in his use of *wonderful* in this passage:

And if somebody hears
what i say—let him be pitiful:
because i've travelled all alone
through the forest of wonderful,

(from *XLI POEMS,* "Sonnets," XII: 158)

Here he is giving unusual weight to a normally overused and colorless word by changing its grammatical classification. The "forest of wonderful" he speaks of is the beauty of his loved one; the line might have read "through the forest of her wonderful beauty," in which case the figure would have been the same but the surprise of language would have escaped. Similarly, he combines the "childish" technique of using redundant comparatives with the highly sophisticated element of paradox in the following lines:

love is more thicker than forget
more thinner than recall

(from *50 POEMS,* 42: 381)

Sometimes, in the simplest of his word coinages, he merely creates a new word by analogy as a child would without adding any shade of meaning other than that inherent in the prefix or suffix he utilizes, as in the words *unstrength* and *untimid,* which appeared in his first book. The meaning of *unstrength* is not precisely different from that of *weakness,* although the latter has certain derogatory connotations which the former may lack (possibly this is the reason why Cummings coined it for the particular passage in which it is used); but certainly *untimid* is no different from *not timid,* although it is less complimentary than *brave.* The chief advantage of the coined words in such cases is that they add a bit of freshness to a poem. In a later book, however, Cummings took the same prefix, *un,* and added it to a word in such a way as to form a pun: in *manunkind* (397: XIV). Here attention is focused on what is not present, as it was in *unstrength;* but by placing *un* in the middle of the word he in effect changed the suffix *kind* to the adjective *kind* and ended with the quite normal adjective *unkind* modifying *man.* The result is not merely a coined word; it is a new idea, which happens to be an apt and concise expression of one of Cummings' convictions.

Less startling, perhaps, than his extensions on a child's way of forming language is his habit of combining two or more words to form a single new one. Quite often these combinations are little more than normally hyphenated words without the hyphen, or a mere printing together of two or more words to give an effect of wholeness, of one quality, as when he describes a color as *yellowgreen* or *yellowandbluish,* or when he describes a movie actress as *muchmouthed.*

Sometimes, however, the printing of several words together adds a commentary on the words: by saying "*poorbuthonest* workingman" (181–2: XXV), for instance, Cummings is scornfully implying that the words have become a cliché. Or he may print words together in order to regulate the speed of reading and come closer to the nature of the action being described, as when he writes "and break onetwothreefourfive pigeonsjustlikethat" in imitation of Buffalo Bill's phenomenally rapid shooting (50: VIII).

Such word coinages as have been mentioned so far are only slight digressions from the conventions of good English, but they do help to give Cummings' writing the distinctive stylistic character it has had practically from the beginning. Thus in *Tulips and Chimneys,* although the greater part of his language is conventional and sometimes even banally "poetic," one find such unusual usages as *unstrength, purpled, Just-spring, eddieandbill, puddle-wonderful, almostness, greentwittering, quiveringgold, flowerterrible, starlessness, fearruining, timeshaped, sayingly.* Except for *sayingly* and *almostness,* which are among the first examples of his changing one part of speech into another, and *unstrength,* there is nothing very startling about most of these words. The mere printing of two words together, as in *greentwittering,* might be considered more a typographical technique than a linguistic one, although it is apparent that when Cummings combines two words to form one adjective he usually creates a new concept by the juxtaposition of two unlike descriptives: *flowerterrible, timeshaped.* (It is such language as this that Mr. Blackmur objects to; he would say that it is impossible to determine the exact meaning of such words as *flowerterrible* and *timeshaped,* and undoubtedly he is is right.) *Tulips and Chimneys* abounds with such words and with phrases that are made up of conventional words in unconventional juxtapositions, such as "the convulsed orange itch of moon" (67: V), "little accurate saints thickly which tread" (66: IV), "a skilful uncouth prison" (65: II), "a polite uproar of knuckling silent planes" (56: V), "brittle towns" (53: I), "chattering sunset" (53: I), "the square virtues and the oblong sins" (37–8: VII).

These phrases that (one must agree with Mr. Blackmur) convey a thrill but not a precise impression swarm through the book but are not able to occupy it exclusively. In contrast to them are many images which depend for their power upon the unexpected but which manage to convey an accurate reproduction of the poet's thought, which show, indeed, that the poet *had* a thought and not merely a rush of words. Such a poem as "La Guerre," II (39–40), shows Cummings in control of his images and his words:

O sweet spontaneous
earth how often have

the
doting
        fingers of
prurient philosophers pinched
and
poked
thee
, has the naughty thumb
of science prodded
thy

    beauty   . how
often have religions taken
thee upon their scraggy knees
squeezing and

buffeting thee that thou mightest conceive
gods
      (but
true

to the incomparable
couch of death thy
rhythmic
lover

      thou answerest

them only with

                    spring)[11]

Cummings is in control, too, in the three "Chansons Innocentes" (pp. 21–23), and in the sonnet whose first line Mr. Blackmur quotes in rare approval: "the Cambridge ladies who live in furnished souls" (p. 58); although, as Mr. Blackmur points out, the last four lines of this sonnet go off into one of his thrilling but not precise metaphors:

> . . . the Cambridge ladies do not care, above
> Cambridge if sometimes in its box of
> sky lavender and cornerless, the
> moon rattles like a fragment of angry candy

The volume *Tulips and Chimneys* has been unavailable for a long time. One is surprised, therefore, upon going back to its full text as

[11] From *Poems 1923–1954* (Harcourt, Brace and Company), copyright, 1923, 1954, by E. E. Cummings.

reprinted in the new *Poems: 1923–1954,* to find that Cummings' first volume of poems, though it has long been a famous book, is not a uniformly good one. It contains the tired romanticism of "Epithalamion" and "Of Nicolette," the embarrassing lushness of "Puella Mea" and "Orientale," the unoriginal love thoughts of "Amores"; it is packed with original but probably imprecise images of the kind quoted above; it displays such juvenile sentiments as "your little voice/Over the wires came leaping/and i felt suddenly/dizzy" (p. 38) and "her heart breaks in a smile—and she is Lust. . . ./mine also, little painted poem of god" (p. 60). In short, the volume is the work of a young man whose taste is not yet impeccable nor his mastery of his medium secure. The poems are not, of course, dated; but some of them were written when he was in college, and almost ten years later he did not exclude them from his first collection. Many *were* excluded from his miscalled *Collected Poems,* which appeared in 1938, and today it comes as a shock to find that Cummings used to write lines like "Lover, lead forth thy love unto that bed" (p. 6), or "Eater of all things lovely—Time!" (p. 20), or ". . . right wildly beat/her heart at every kiss of daisy-cup" (p. 8). It is typical of the unevenness of *Tulips and Chimneys* that on the same page with the sophomoric "her heart breaks in a smile—and she is Lust. . . ." appears the fresh and well-stated image, "whose least amazing smile is the most great/common divisor of unequal souls" (p. 60).

The language of *Tulips and Chimneys,* then, like the imagery, the verse forms, the subject matter, and the thought, is sometimes good, sometimes bad. But the book is so obviously the work of a talented young man who is striking off in new directions, groping for original and yet precise expression, experimenting in public, that it seems uncharitable to dwell too long on its shortcomings. Edmund Wilson, who, although a year younger than Cummings, seemingly never was immature as a critic, wrote, shortly after *Tulips and Chimneys* came out, ". . . a master is precisely, as yet, what Mr. Cummings is not. . . . A poet with a real gift for language . . . he strikes often on ethereal measures of a singular purity and charm . . . but he never seems to know when he is writing badly and when he is writing well. . . . his emotions are familiar and simple. They occasionally even verge on the banal." But Mr. Wilson concluded: "for the fact that, though not yet fully grown, he is a genuine lyric poet at a time when there is a great deal of writing of verse and very little poetic feeling—Mr. Cummings deserves well of the public." [12]

Mr. Wilson was not speaking of Cummings' language as distinct

[12] "Wallace Stevens and E. E. Cummings," in *The Shores of Light* (New York, 1952), pp. 50–53.

from the other elements of his poetry, but what he had to say applies to Cummings' linguistic usages in *Tulips and Chimneys* and in the two books which soon followed it *&* [*AND*] and *XLI POEMS*. These books were published within three years and are fairly much alike (although the typographical distortions that reach extremes in *&* [*AND*] were barely hinted at in the first book); in style and in subject matter the three books are the work of the same youthful poet. Although his control over his material is firmer in *XLI POEMS* than in *Tulips and Chimneys,* and although his mature style begins to be suggested, *XLI POEMS* still contains such lines as "i will wade out/till my thighs are steeped in burning flowers" (p. 139) and such conventionally "poetic" thoughts as "my soul slowly which on thy beauty dreamest" (p. 152) and "Time shall surely reap,/and on Death's blade lie many a flower curled" (p. 154).[13]

All three books, however, are indelibly the work of Cummings; in one of the first poems in *Tulips and Chimneys,* for instance, appears this double-barreled hint of his later style and of one of the first principles which are to underlie all his work:

each is a verb, miraculous
inflected oral devious,
beneath the body's breathing noun

(from "Puella Mea": 19)

When Cummings refers to something as a "verb," he means that it is alive, vital; this is the highest compliment he can pay, just as he indicates the quintessence of individuality in a person by calling that person an "is."

Although, as Mr. Blackmur points out, the early books are punctuated with favorite words (*thrilling, flowers, utter, skillful, groping, crisp, keen, actual, stars,* etc.)[14] almost as copiously as another author would use commas, an awareness of these words is not unrewarding if one wishes to understand Cummings. The words *flower* and *stars* are, as he uses them, not mere substantives representing a thing in nature but are metaphorical shorthand for concepts which Cummings finds admirable: the flowers, for example, representing growth, being, aliveness; the stars standing for the steadfastness of beauty in nature.

Such adjectives as he continually uses (Mr. Blackmur lists a great many), though they are admittedly overworked in the early books to the point of tiresomeness, are nevertheless indicative of his viewpoint:

[13] It is interesting to note that there is almost no satire in the original *Tulips and Chimneys,* and what there is seems strangely mild. In *&* [*AND*] appears the first of his sharply barbed poems, "here is little Effie's head/whose brains are made of gingerbread" (p. 95), and in *XLI POEMS,* "Humanity i love you" (p. 151).

[14] *Language As Gesture,* p. 321.

he admires phenomena that can be described as crisp, keen, actual, gay, young, strong, or strenuous, and dislikes the groping, the dim, the slow, the dull. In reading the early poetry, it is often necessary to know which of Cummings' words are, in Hayakawa's terms, "purr words" and which are "snarl words" in order to get any meaning from the poem. As Cummings progressed, he outgrew his penchant for such expressions as "thy whitest feet crisply are straying" (p. 11) and grew into his mature style, which is something infinitely more precise, often more concrete, and which relies more on such straightforward words as nouns and verbs than on piled-up adjectives for its effects.

To refer, however, to Cummings' words as nouns and verbs is to make things sound much simpler than they are, for the one outstanding characteristic of his mature style is his disrespect for the part of speech. It would be more accurate instead to say that he *uses* words as nouns, for instance, which are not normally so; it would be hard to find any one of his later poems which does not utilize a word in a sense other than its usual one. *Yes* is used as a noun to represent all that is positive and therefore admirable, *if* to stand for all that is hesitating, uncertain, incomplete. The style thus becomes spare; the later books contain many poems written in extremely short lines, lines which, utilizing the simplest words, say a great deal. For instance, these two fragments from *1 x 1*:

yes is a pleasant country:
if's wintry
(my lovely)
let's open the year (from XXXVIII: 412)

who younger than
begin
are,the worlds move
in your
(and rest,my love)
honour (from XXXV: 410)

It is possible, of course, to argue that in the above stanzas *yes, if,* and *begin* do not convey precise meanings; that, since they are not used within their historical framework, no one but the poet can possibly know exactly what he meant to convey. This is an objection that, if it is accepted, is unanswerable; and the person who reads with such an assumption by his side will never make any sense out of Cummings' poems. But again, by accepting the fact that the poet may be saying something worthwhile and may be seriously trying to convey both truth and beauty as he sees it, one will try to look through the poet's eyes. To understand Cummings fully, more so than in understanding most other poets, it is necessary for one to have read much of Cummings. To a reader familiar with his techniques such a statement as "yes is a pleasant country" is as penetrable as a deep, clear pool; it might, however, seem more opaque to one reading him for the first time. Such words as *yes* and *if* take on a historical meaning within the body of his poetry, a meaning not divorced from their traditional ones but infinitely larger: *yes,* for instance, conventionally is used in a particular situation; as Cummings uses it, *yes* represents the sum of all the situations in which it might be used. And such a technique as "who younger than/begin/are" is not too complicated to be used by some practitioners of the art of writing for mass consumption, as witness the first line of a very popular song from *South Pacific*: "Younger than springtime, you are."

One of Cummings' most universally liked poems, "my father moved through dooms of love" (*50 POEMS,* 34: 373–5), is extremely dense linguistically as a result of its suffusion with such words as *sames, am, haves, give, where, here, which, who, why, begin, pure, now, beyond, must,* and *shall* used as nouns. Again, it is helpful, if not necessary, to know the basic assumptions of Cummings, to know what he likes and what he dislikes, in order to interpret these reincarnated words. The following couplet will serve as an example:

> and should some why completely weep
> my father's fingers brought her sleep: (p. 374)

A word such as *why* in an otherwise simple, straightforward passage such as this calls attention to itself at once; it causes a linguistic shock. Its startling effect is not due merely to the fact that it is used as a noun, since *why* does sometimes function in this fashion, in such expressions as "get to the *why* (bottom) of the situation," or "there is a terrible *why* (enigma) involved in this." However, it is immediately obvious that such normal substantive meanings of the word are not called into play in Cummings' couplet, and the reader must use his own resourcefulness in exploring the possibilities of new meaning.

In these two particular lines *why* actually presents no difficulty, for it is placed in the context of a concrete dramatic situation that is perfectly understandable: the *her* in the second line indicates that *why* is the substantive antecedent of the pronoun and that it can therefore be assumed to represent some feminine noun of a general character, such as *girl* or *woman.* If, however, *girl* or *woman* should be substituted for *why,* the startling quality of the first line would surely be lost, as would much of Cummings' meaning, which is ascertainable as much from the nature of the word *why* itself as from its use in context. In normal interrogative usage *why* presupposes an unanswered question and a mind searching for answers. If these conditions are fitted into the dramatic situation that is portrayed in the couplet—a girl weeping and given peace through sleep—the elements fit together: she is mentally puzzled, unable to answer the questions in her mind, miserable because she is mixed up. So that without further extensions the passage conveys an exact meaning, if not all that Cummings intended.

Just as do *yes, if,* and *begin* in the passages quoted above, *why* takes on an aura of meaning within the body of his poetry, a meaning that it is impossible to illustrate from this single example. Babette Deutsch has described Cummings' use of these words as follows:

> His later poems make words as abstract as "am," "if," "because," do duty for seemingly more solid nouns. By this very process, however, he restores life to dying concepts. "Am" implies being at its most responsive, "if" generally means the creeping timidity that kills responsiveness, and "because" the logic of the categorizing mind that destroys what it dissects. Here is a new vocabulary, a kind of imageless metaphor.[15]

Why, Miss Deutsch might further have explained, generally means to Cummings a state of uncertainty, a searching for direction from sources outside oneself, an unspontaneous demanding of reasons and causes in the face of life. A person who is a *why* is generally a subject for ridicule, being, like an *if,* a timid creature who thinks, fears, denies, follows, unlike an all-alive *is.* However, in the couplet above the measure of Cummings' father's compassion and stature is that he sees this particular *why* as a pitiful creature, to whom he brings solace through love.

Right though she is in assigning meanings to Cummings' *am's, if's,* and *because's,* Miss Deutsch does not get to the root of the technique used in these words when she describes them as examples of "imageless metaphor." Metaphor has as its base the use of comparison and analogy, of the verisimilitude within dissimilitude that exists between two images, actions, or concepts. Actually, a closer insight into the real nature of these words is found in Mr. Blackmur's study, though, in contrast to Miss Deutsch's commitment to the technique, his definition of the process comes within a general attack on Cummings' language. He says at the end of his essay that all of Cummings' "thought" (the quotes are Mr. Blackmur's) is metonymy, and that the substance of the metonymy is never assigned to anything. "In the end," he concludes, "we have only the thrill of substance."[16] Metonymy is based on reduction rather than comparison: an object associated with a thing is substituted for the thing itself (as *crown* for

[15] *Poetry in Our Time* (New York, 1952), p. 113.
[16] *Language As Gesture,* p. 340.

king), or a corporeal object is used to represent an abstract concept or idea (as *heavy thumb* for *dishonesty*). When Mr. Blackmur says that Cummings' metonymy contains only the "thrill of substance," he means that in the case of such a word as *flower,* one of Cummings' favorite metonymical vehicles, the substance—flower—is there but the idea of which it is a reduction is neither present nor ascertainable. If the reader receives a "thrill" from such a word as *flower,* well and good; but Mr. Blackmur asserts that a thrill is all he will receive.

It must be remembered that Mr. Blackmur's essay was written after only the earliest of Cummings' books had appeared; none of them exemplify his mature style—in those days *flower* and *star* were about as far as he had gone in the direction of metonymy. In his use of *why,* however, he has extended not only the uses to which a particular word can be put but also the accepted limits of metonymy: he has taken an abstract word and made it stand for a host of ideas, the negative characteristics mentioned above. Mr. Blackmur's "thrill of substance" is therefore not applicable to Cummings' present use of metonymy, for such words as *why* do not represent a substance and certainly, if they are isolated, convey no thrill. That it is possible for *why* to induce a thrill is seen in the lines quoted above, but the thrill comes not from the "substance" of *why* but from the uniqueness of its use; perhaps also there is a thrill of comprehension which comes when the implication of the metonymy strikes the reader.

Again, if one accepts Mr. Blackmur's argument it is unanswerable; he would say that to derive an implication from a metonymical concept is not enough, that the idea or object which the "substance" represents must be precisely known. However, there must perhaps have been a day when *heavy thumb* was not a universally accepted reduction for dishonesty; the person who created this particular metonymy must have been doing a rather original thing, and his created expression must have had to go through a process of recognition into acceptance before it came to be unquestioned. That Cummings' metonymical usages are unlikely to go through this particular process is immaterial; such metonymies as *why* and *yes* are a little too subtle, too closely based on a poet's private convictions, to find a place in ordinary language. It should not be concluded, however, that their meaning cannot be understood—that their substance cannot be assigned—just as readily as was the meaning of *heavy thumb* by a person who was willing to apply to the metonymy the knowledge that he possessed about butchers, green-grocers, and bakers.

To understand a Cummings metonymy, one can bring his plain common sense to bear first, and, in the case of such expressions as "who younger than/begin/are" or "and should some why completely weep," common sense is often enough to establish a correct meaning.

But the reader who can apply to the metonymy not only his judgment but his experience with Cummings will have an advantage in that he will have in his mind an accumulation of meanings for such a word as *why* and will therefore be able to identify a complete, rounded concept whenever he comes upon the "substance." *Why,* as the couplet above illustrates, is a reduction for the puzzled, questioning state of mind. In another context, one much more indefinite than that of the couplet, another meaning is suggested:

> doubting can turn men's see to stare
> their faith to how their joy to why

(from *1 x 1,* XL: 413)

Without knowing the complete metonymical function of *why,* the reader of this passage can come to a common-sense understanding of its meaning—here *why* refers to the joylessness that comes from lack of faith—even though the lines contain three other reductions: *see, stare,* and *how.* And when the reader has penetrated the following use of *why,* which is much the most difficult of the three examples, he is well on his way to recreating the larger body of meaning of which *why* is a reductive part:

> proudly depths above why's first because
> (faith's last doubt and humbly heights below)
> kneeling,we—true lovers—pray that us
> will ourselves continue to outgrow
>
> all whose mosts if you have known and i've
> only we our least begin to guess

(from *1 x 1,* XXXIV: 409)

Here in a passage saturated with metonymical words and paradoxical combinations Cummings' meaning is clear enough: proudly true lovers will continue to grow to a far greater extent than all those who are limited by their timidity and unresponsiveness, who do not continuously transcend themselves as lovers mysteriously do; lovers are beyond the restrictions of niggling reason, which is represented in these lines by the words *why* and *because.* Hence, from the three fragments which have been studied, *why* takes on its full metonymical meaning: in the first quotation it is associated with the troubled mind, in the second with the mind that lacks faith, in the third with the reasoning, unintuitive mind.

In short, his technique in creating new uses for such words as *if, why, because, which, how, must, same, have,* and *they* on the one hand and *now, am, yes, is, we, give,* and *here* on the other is to accumulate meanings for each of them that total up to the same kind of positive and negative oppositions that are set against each other throughout his work: tulips and chimneys, as he put it in the title of his first book of poems; beauty and ugliness; love and hate; the one and the many. As in the three examples cited for *why,* he makes each of these words self-subsistent in terms of the context in which they appear, and, by varying the meanings in each usage, makes the words metonymical reductions for a whole set of concepts. In a way he is creating an easy cipher of meaning, penetrable but not completely so at first sight. And is this not also the case of any author who utilizes a few dominant symbols in order to express his special insight into experience, who must make each use of a symbol function in its context and yet adds to its meaning with each repeated use? (Hawthorne's repeated use of light and shadow in his works might be cited as an example of this method.) The success of a metonymous or symbolic system of this sort depends partly upon the degree to which the poet objectifies and clarifies his conception of the world, partly upon the effects of freshness and vitality his language produces; when one comes across such lines as the following there can be no doubt that Cummings is successful in both respects:

> she laughed his joy she cried his grief
> bird by snow and stir by still
> anyone's any was all to her
>
> (from *50 POEMS,* 29: 370)

Using a traditional rhetorical pattern in the second line (*little by little* serves as a model for it), he superimposes a metonymous structure: *bird* and *snow* are reductions of summer and winter; *stir* and *still,* of all manner of activities. The net result of such a line is a new and delightful sense of linguistic invention, precise and vigorous.

To say that Cummings is successful in objectifying his conception of the world and in achieving a freshness and vitality of language is not to diminish the difficulty of many of his poems. Nor is it meant to say that his metonymical usages are not overworked, just as were his favorite adjectives in *Tulips and Chimneys.* What was originally a fresh idea, and what still has great power if used with discrimination —his utilizing abstract words to be the "substance" of a metonymy— can become boring, tiresome, and even meaningless if called upon constantly to carry the whole weight of a poem. Just as the word *flower,* which obviously was a symbol for something, when used in every poem became a mere word, to be accepted and passed over, so a constant succession of *which's* and *who's* and *why's* and *they's* begins to roll off the tongue too quickly for the mind to make the transference from the "substance" to the idea for which it stands; and the force of the metonymy is lost. A poem written almost exclusively in these words loses, too, its beauty and grace; one-syllable abstract words are not particularly melodious, and a poem in which they are not frequently interspersed with words which are more interesting in themselves, or more concrete, is likely to plod along (like Pope's "And ten low words oft creep in one dull line"), one metonymy after another, never skipping or dancing or singing.

However, at the same time that Cummings developed the metonymy to its ultimate use he was growing in another direction: many of his poems became much more, not less, musical than his earlier ones. In the earlier books he had placed his dependence upon the sonnet form, often upon a grand manner, and sometimes upon free verse; but he very seldom wrote a poem which cried out to be sung, which could be read only with a joyous, pronounced rhythm. Such poems as these occur frequently in the last three books. Cummings has given up being grand and derivative and become simple and himself. If he utilizes old verse forms, they are more likely to be of the nursery rhyme than of the Spenserian stanza. His lines, as has been mentioned, are often short; his meter is usually iambic; his words—when they are not metonymies—are colloquial. As a result, one can read these poems with a sense of the child's pure delight in poetry; Cummings himself has become more maturely childish as he has grown.

The rhythmical poems do utilize the typical abstract word metonymies—it is a rare poem in his later books which does not; even his satires make use of them to some extent—but the metonymies are likely to be placed in the context of concrete words and lively happenings. Such a poem as the following, from *1 x 1,* in which the metonymies are made to stand alone with only a little help from such semi-abstract words as *hell, paradise, eternal,* and *distinct,* becomes the exception rather than the rule:

as any(men's hells having wrestled with)
man drops into his own paradise
thankfully
                    whole and the green whereless truth
of an eternal now welcomes each was
of whom among not numerable ams

(leaving a perfectly distinct unhe;
a ticking phantom by prodigious time's
mere brain contrived:a spook of stop and go)
may i achieve another steepest thing—

how more than sleep illimitably my
—being so very born no bird can sing
as easily creation up all sky

(really unreal world,will you perhaps do
the breathing for me while i am away?) (XVIII: 399)[17]

In contrast to such an unfocused plethora of metonymies (it is interesting to note that this poem falls back on some of the old favorite modifiers: *eternal, perfectly, distinct, steepest, illimitably,* and loses force because of them) is the next poem but one in the same volume. Here is the new joyous rhythmical manner in a poem in which metonymies are contrasted to such concrete *things* as wind, leaves, sun, hills, sleet, snow, and to such forceful verbs as *bloodies, yanks, blow, hanged, drowned, flays, strangles,* and *stifles.* The final stanza of this poem has already been quoted in the introduction to this article; for purposes of specific illustration of the techniques that have just been studied, it is well to note the first two stanzas also:

what if a much of a which of a wind
gives the truth to summer's lie;
bloodies with dizzying leaves the sun
and yanks immortal stars awry?
Blow king to beggar and queen to seem
(blow friend to fiend :blow space to time)
—when skies are hanged and oceans drowned,
the single secret will still be man

what if a keen of a lean wind flays
screaming hills with sleet and snow:
strangles valleys by ropes of thing
and stifles forests in white ago?
Blow hope to terror ;blow seeing to blind
(blow pity to envy and soul to mind)
—whose hearts are mountains, roots are trees,
it's they shall cry hello to the spring (XX: 401)[18]

In the third stanza of this poem Cummings becomes personal; he speaks of "me and you," and the last couplet is triumphantly affirmative of the power of two people—two lovers—to live despite whatever may happen to "this universe":

[17] From *Poems 1923–1954* (Harcourt, Brace and Company), copyright, 1944, by E. E. Cummings.

[18] From *Poems 1923–1954* (Harcourt, Brace and Company), copyright, 1944, by E. E. Cummings. The final stanza of this poem is quoted on page 82.

—all nothing's only our hugest home;
the most who die,the more we live

This progression from the external to the personal, from the outer world of "mostpeople" to the inner world of "us," finds its expression, sometimes quietly, sometimes with childish innocence, sometimes with a dauntless courage, in poem after poem in the volume *1 x 1*. Cummings concludes the book with

we're anything brighter than even the sun
(we're everything greater
than books
might mean)
we're everyanything more than believe
(with a spin
leap
alive we're alive)
we're wonderful one times one (from LIV: 423)

And, as he begins one of the most beautiful of his sonnets: "one's not half two. It's two are halves of one:" (XVI: 398). This whole conception of i-you-we (or my-your-our) becomes one of Cummings' most frequently used metonymies. Its impact, to anyone who knows that "two are halves of one," is immediate. When Cummings starts out a poem:

o by the by
has anybody seen
little you-i
who stood on a green
hill and threw
his wish at blue (from LIII: 422)

and then continues:

blue took it my
far beyond far
and high beyond high
bluer took it your
but bluest took it our
away beyond where

the reader does not have to be told why "our" should be "bluest." In the i-you-we metonymy the whole is greater than the sum of its parts, and the metonymy itself becomes a prime example of Cummings' ability to use the simplest words as a shorthand for concepts which represent his own convictions. It is fitting that his most musical poems should be the ones, like those from which the last three quotations were taken, in celebration of i-you-we; for to Cummings love is still the most joyous of all things. Mature love to him becomes not more sober and settled but more intensely lyrical, less tortured, more a thing for singing and dancing and child-like delight. *We* takes its place along with *yes* and *now* and *is* as the metonymies for all that is best in this "really unreal world."

Lower Case Cummings

by William Carlos Williams

To me, of course, e.e.cummings means my language. It isn't, of course, mine so much as it is his, which emphasizes the point. It isn't primary, english. It isn't at all english. Not that superb inheritance—which we both, I am sure, stand before in amazement and wonder knowing the dazzling achievements of which it is the living monument. We speak another language; a language of which we are so jealous that we won't even acknowledge that we hold it in common.

Esoteric is the word the englishers among us would give to the languages we americans use at our best. They are private languages. That is what cummings seems to be emphasizing, a christian language —addressing to [sic] the private conscience of each of us in turn.

But if, startlingly, each should disclose itself as understandable to any great number, the effect would be in effect a veritable revolution, shall we say, of morals? Of, do we dare to say, love? Much or even all cummings' poems are the evidences of love. The french say you can't translate his poems into french: just so many words. A curious sort of love, not at all french, not at all latin. Not, above all, anything even in the faintest degree resembling the english.

I think of cummings as Robinson Crusoe at the moment when he first saw the print of a naked human foot in the sand. That, too, implied a new language—and a readjustment of conscience.

We are inclined to forget that cummings has come *from* english to another province having escaped across a well defended border; he has remained, largely, a fugitive ever since. I don't think he should be held too closely to account for some of his doodles, his fiddling with the paraphernalia of the writing game. He has been for a good part of the last twenty years like the prisoner in solitary confinement who retained his sanity by tossing a pin over his shoulder in the dark and spending long hours searching for it again.

Without the least question cummings is a fugitive; a fugitive from the people about him whom he irritates by telling them they are hu-

"Lower Case Cummings," by William Carlos Williams. From *The Harvard Wake*, 5 (*Cummings number*—Spring 1946), 20–23. © 1946 by Harvard University. Reprinted by permission of Seymour Lawrence.

man beings subject to certain beauties and distempers they will not acknowledge; a fugitive as well from the university where the bait of official recognition has brought down many of his former fellows.

cummings, who is not robust, is positively afraid of physical violence if he goes out of his rooms. For, a species of Americans and certain other wild animals are prone to attack a man going alone. Imagine the armed bands of the intelligentsia which roam Greenwich Village by day and night—the belligerently convinced—that a poor lone man like cummings would have to face to survive if he went so much as to the baker's for a dozen breakfast rolls. It is frightening. Important. But he hasn't run away. Just the opposite.

It would be all right if e.e. were himself more gregarious, more, what shall we say, promiscuous—at least less averse to the pack—even to very nice packs certified by the very best teachers in the very best schools here and abroad. But he isn't. He feels that among those curious things called americans there isn't one, in this inarticulate jungle, to whom he can say more than—How do you do? Was that your footprint I saw in the sand this morning?

Imagine if the startled black should turn on him and say in reply, Swing low sweet chariot! That wouldn't be it. That wouldn't be it at all. cummings would be completely defeated, and cummings cannot afford to be defeated! why he's a member of the strongest nation on earth—bar none. He's in a very tight squeeze every day of his life, Year in, year out, holding to his supplies, finding what shelter is possible to him. Writing. Isn't that the thing to do? Write.

He paints also—but I don't like his painting. I think it represents the worst of his style; an insistence that any artist will fall into when he is sick of his proper medium and of those defects which he, better than anyone else, is conscious of, and which yet he tries still to put over by a shift in direction to flout the world. But maybe he paints just because it rests him—a minor matter.

Words are his proper medium, the specific impact of words, which give them in his work such a peculiarly unhistoric, historical new world character. A toughness which scorns to avoid fragility.

When I say "new world" I do not mean american. That is just what cummings says over and over again, that's what he lives; that, too, is what makes him solitary. Not "american," sensual. I almost want to say, that that, which deprives him of academic as well as popular understanding or effectiveness in argument, makes him at the same time a good deal like the steeple of one of these New England churches facing the common up there, so strangely remote an effect. I avoid speaking of the clipper ships. I avoid speaking of Moby Dick.

No, it is something very much older and very modern too. Cotton Mather? Yes, he had a library. If it goes back to the King James version of the Bible, and it does, it goes there solely for what that *says* to the Christian conscience. It says, Ignore the dress in which the Word comes to you and look to the Life of which that is the passing image.

cummings is the living presence of the drive to make all our convictions evident by penetrating through their costumes to the living flesh of the matter. He avoids the cliché first by avoiding the whole accepted modus of english. He does it, not to be "popular," God knows, nor to sell anything, but to lay bare the actual experience of love, let us say, in the chance terms which his environment happens to make apparent to him. He does it to reveal, to disclose, to free a man from habit. Habit is our continual enemy as artists and as men. Practice is not a habit though it must be watched lest it become so.

The drunk, the whore, the child, are typical cummings heroes. (Is that Deacon Cummings speaking? Probably.) At the start, right out of the Greek of his college days, he threw the whole of the english department armamentarium out the window—a sort of Cambridge Tea Party.

Then he began to speak of rabbits, mice, all the sprites of the native pastures—as though he had just got sight and were afraid he was going to lose it again—with infinite tenderness, with FEELING. He wanted to feel. He wanted to see, see, see! and make the words speak of what he saw . . . and felt. For it must not be forgot that we smell, hear and see with words and words alone, and that with a new language we smell, hear and see afresh—by this we can well understand cummings' early excitement at his release. If a woman came into the picture early she vanished in favor of women: he got them badly mixed up. He didn't know what the thing meant—much. It wasn't, in effect, art. He was sure of that.

Now women, that's different. That's a subject that has some meat to it. You can love women. But how in almighty heaven can you love a woman and be free to embrace the world in new and unaccepted terms?

Then he left his entire early mountain world. Went to France and landed—The Enormous Room. That doesn't need explanation; but it is, for cummings, today, an annoyance. There he was and he wrote what he had to say about it, superbly. One remembers (if vaguely now) those spirits, ghosts—lost souls—victims of whom do you think? The Japs? No, by God, the French! Can you imagine the impertinence of smelling a french stink? But cummings merely smelled it.

Finally he came, with finality, to New York. The express elevators ran up and down inside him for a while—until they busted and—stopped.

To adopt the ballad forms of nursery rhymes—merely emphasizes in a primary manner . . . the continued necessity for reappraisals in the arts: and the preeminence of the lyric. The best of cummings' lyrics seem as if they had been taken from something else, a series of fantastic plays which he never wrote—for it would have represented an actual world which never existed save in his imagination. It is a new world—the only clue to its substantiality being the language cummings uses. It may have been Atlantis—which he knew to exist since he could tell very definitely that his father had been there also.

He lives today in a second Enormous Room, this time of the imagination—so real it is.

I don't see how you can avoid speaking of cummings in this way, dangerous as it surely is. You are likely to go off into a Never Never Land which is so much froth. But if we lay the fact of cummings against that background we see better than in any other way how bitterly he has persisted with his revolution in the language and to what planned effect.

He has fixed it, too, that he can't be imitated. You've got to learn the *basis* for his trapeze tricks. When you have done that you'll be able to do tricks of your own—as the masters did in the past. Not before. In that he's our best schoolmaster in the language; the kind that you just don't avoid.

What fools critics are who try to make him a painter with words. With cummings every syllable has a conscience and a specific impact—attack, which, as we know now.;';—is the best defense.

Perhaps, at some time in the future, though it is extremely unlikely, we'll be able to shed the lower case and embellish the new language with Caps. But for the moment cummings has the right idea.

E. E. Cummings: The Technique of Immediacy

by S. V. Baum

Since the publication of his first book of poems, *Tulips and Chimneys,* in 1923, E. E. Cummings has served as the indispensable whipping boy for those who are outraged by the nature of modern poetry. Each time a protest becomes necessary, several lines are wrenched from a poem by Cummings to furnish conclusive proof that his is the work of a trickster who delights in offending sense; the poetic sample offered for examination is invariably a jumble of disjointed words and scattered punctuation. The accusers contend on the basis of such evidence that Cummings must bow to punishment and that with him must bow the rest of the "obscurantists."

The difficulty in judging the whole output of a poet by a fragment of a part does not seem to discourage castigations directed against Cummings in particular. He has been singled out for attack again and again. A glance at any Cummings volume suggests the advantages of using him in preference to any of his so-called confreres. Each printed page discloses such violation of order that the reader is shocked: words are stretched out vertically and horizontally; capital letters jump up where they do not belong; punctuation marks intrude irregularly; lacunae appear within and between lines. Because order has been violated, it is concluded that meaning, in its dependent variable, has been destroyed at the same time. And a poem without meaning is nonsense.

This disruption of established order, from the beginning, has been the focal point of the disapproving attitude toward Cummings. The substance of his poetry has been well understood and appreciated, but the typographic disarrangement characteristic of his writing has been condemned as extraneous to the matter involved. In reviewing *Tulips and Chimneys,* Harriet Monroe, at that time editor of *Poetry,* pref-

"E. E. Cummings: The Technique of Immediacy," by S. V. Baum. From *The South Atlantic Quarterly,* 53 (January 1954), 70–88. © 1954 by *The South Atlantic Quarterly*. Reprinted by permission of Duke University Press.

aced her critical reception of his poetic exuberance with: "Mr. Cummings has an eccentric system of typography which, in our opinion, has nothing to do with the poem, but intrudes itself irritatingly, like scratched or blurred spectacles, between it and the reader's mind." A later review of the same book commented:

> His typography is so perverse that the reader is scared off before he has gone very far. The puzzle of his punctuation is not even an amusing one; it certainly is not worth solving.

This attitude, which separates form from matter in Cumming's poetry, has persisted in varying degrees among critics. Yet an overall examination of Cummings's work reveals his denial of external authority in its many aspects, for from every point of view and in every style he expounds the basic idea of individualism, the ultimate value in all his writing. Cummings began his re-evaluation of language in *The Enormous Room* (1922), when he defined the personality of the Zulu as an IS. In him existence was suddenly viewed as a vital function independent of doing; IS, then, is a celebration of the self. It is relevant to Cummings's later poetry that in this prose passage he transformed one part of speech into another. *Is,* regularly a verb, was converted into a noun, just as *perhaps* in the phrase, *the prerogative of perhaps fairies,* has an adjectival force. Yet both words manage to retain some of the original function. This violation of the laws of grammar, whereby Cummings shifts the parts of speech at will, is apparent in much of his poetry: *what if a keen of a lean wind . . ./ . . . stifles forests in white ago* (401: XX); *he sang his didn't he danced his did* (370–1: 29); *and should some why completely weep/my father's fingers brought her sleep* (373–5: 34); *he sharpens is to am/he sharpens say to sing* (443: 26). In all of these Cummings searches to express existence, being, by developing a noun out of any other part of speech in the language.

This theme of "to be" was developed even further by Cummings in 1933 with the publication of *Eimi,* the travel journal of the poet's thirty-six-day stroll through the great Marxist experiment. He documented his objection to this gigantic political insistence, not with an array of statistics, but rather with a progression of fiercely personal *instantés.* By Cummings's own declaration, "Eimi is the individual again; a more complex individual, a more enormous room" ("Introduction" to Modern Library Edition of *The Enormous Room* [1934], p. viii). The very title of the book is a statement of his credo, by which he waves the banner of individual joy in the face of the Soviet Union, shouting his delight in Being. *Eimi,* present indicative first person singular of the Greek verb "to be," is an eloquent reassertion of his belief.

This theme of "one times one" has been repeatedly sounded by Cummings in his poetry from *Tulips and Chimneys* to *XAIPE* (1950). All experience has been ordered according to his moral standard and has consequently been reduced to two groups. The first is that of the lyric affirmative, equations of IS which make for this individual joy —the bird, the bud, the love of two human beings. While asserting the truth and beauty of these qualities which [signify] total aliveness, he has also been tasked to express the falseness and evil of the sterile negatives which threaten to despoil the store of individual lyricism and so to reduce being to not-being. In this way he has set himself up in firm opposition to the negative pronunciamento of tradition, governments and political ideologies, advertising agencies—in each case challenging and violating convention and the established order. In defense of this vital quality of being, Cummings has had to evolve a manner of writing which would communicate concrete sensations and perceptions in all the immediacy with which they are experienced.

In perceiving the world with full awareness, each man stands in momentary relationship with life, for everything whirls past him in never-ending change. When the moment has passed, it will never be repeated and can never be exactly matched. The poet's responsibility is to set down without falsification this single fragment of time. The difficulty arises in the poet's grappling with the experience of the poem so as to make it as concentrated and intense as possible and yet to produce the immediacy and directness which one would draw from the experience itself. The very use of language creates an unfaithfulness, for conventional syntax is historical, that is, it is based on an arrangement of thoughts, feelings, and sensations already completed. When the poet uses words, he enters into the confinement of time, and temporal order is imposed upon the experience of the moment, destroying the simultaneity of its complex. There is no order to the momentary perception; it is a sudden explosion during which all one's senses are attacked at once. To arrange the elements of this explosion in some sort of chronological sequence would be a serious breach of honesty. Campaigning against the prosaic characteristics of existence, what he calls *un-ness,* Cummings has felt compelled to violate the conventions of language as well: the stereotypes of syntax and parts of speech, which are symbols of submission to language. Most of all, he has felt a need to put punctuation and typography to fresh use so that they fulfill a dynamic function by approximating the sensations being recorded. This manner of expressing his insights and intense feelings has become so peculiarly his own that Marianne Moore in speaking of his poetry was reminded of "the corkscrew twists, the infinitude of dots, the sumptuous perpendicular appearance of Kufic script."

The general critical discussion accorded Cummings has concluded that his idiosyncratic use of language and typography has resulted, at best, in ideographic picture-writing. Yet from the beginning there has been a small but slowly growing group who have given him consideration and acute evaluation to determine what purpose and effect the poet was seeking. The first such examination, "Syrinx," was published in 1923 by Gorham Munson in the little magazine, *Secession*. Munson recognized Cummings's reorganization of punctuation and typography as an attempt to make them active instruments for literary expression, and in defense of his opinion catalogued some of the means the poet employed to display his accuracy and to indicate tempo. By 1926 Marianne Moore had aligned her sympathies with Cummings in full appreciation of his purpose in "(shaping) the proggress of poems as if it were substance." The major show of understanding came in 1926 with the publication by Laura Riding and Robert Graves of *A Survey of Modernist Poetry,* which enthusiastically sought to validate the innovations practiced by Cummings. By analyzing poem 25 in *Collected Poems—stinging/gold swarms/upon the spires* (43: V)—the authors established their belief in the poetic values gained by his intentional disorganization of language. The last two decades have brought increased understanding and appreciation to Cummings's poetry with only occasional objections to the "purposelessness" of his technique of expression. The full extent of this esteem can be estimated by reading the contributions of contemporary literary figures to the Cummings number of *The Harvard Wake,* published in 1946 and "devoted, with care, to the sincerity of E. E. Cummings." If one recalls the early comments made in *Poetry* on the subject of Cummings's unorthodoxies, there is a note of poetic justice in the fact that in 1950 the University of Chicago awarded him the Harriet Monroe Poetry prize, endowed by the late editor and director by terms of her will in favor of writers with progressive tendencies.

In his essay, "Notes on E. E. Cummings' Language," which measured the effect of Cummings's choice of vocabulary in his poetry, R. P. Blackmur paused to consider the poet's partiality for typographical eccentricity:

> Excessive hyphenation of single words, the use of lower case 'i,' the breaking of lines, the insertion of punctuation between the letters of a word, and so on, will have a possible critical importance to the textual scholarship of the future, but extensive consideration of these peculiarities to-day has very little importance, carries almost no reference to the *meaning* of the poem. . . . No doubt the continued practice of such notation would produce a set of well-ordered conventions susceptible of general use.

With the growing awareness of purpose in Cummings it is now apposite to reconsider Blackmur's suggestion as a serious proposal, to extend Munson's original catalogue. To extract "a set of well-ordered conventions" from the body of Cummings's poetic mannerisms is an assignment equal to founding order within disorder. Such an attempt bears an ironic content, for of all modern poets Cummings most virulently objects to the rash intruder who weighs and measures the lines of his poetry, pointing out examples of instances. And yet the paradox exists whereby Cummings has found his greatest share of appreciation among the scrutinizers rather than among readers innocent of literary sophistication. The factor most likely bearing weight against the poet is determined resistance to his unfamiliar technique. Consequently, the only measure which can relieve this opposition is to probe the body of his poetry in search of the *how* and *why*, systematically grouping instances of violation until such disorder assumes the shape of order and regularity. In the following catalogue quotations have been drawn from all of Cummings's published work with occasional reference to poems as yet uncollected.

In his use of space alone Cummings applies the devotion of a virtuoso. Stanzaic divisions, line breakage, and word relationships are freely varied for the indication of auditory rhythms. Ordinarily, formal indentation can be either a guide to rhyming pairs of words or else a sign that the first part of a line is missing. Under Cummings's direction such indentations denote musical rests of varying value:

(A) the moon looked into my window
. . . .
she went creeping along the air
                                        over houses
                                                roofs
And out of the east toward
her a fragile light bent gatheringly (205: I)

(B) the queer
old balloonman whistles
far   and   wee (21–2: I)

In this example Cummings carefully spaced the last line so that the whistle sounds are heard intermittently and shrilly, so shrilly that the final sound of the word *wide* in *far and wide* is lost in the high-pitched note of *wee*. When the purpose of his poem so demands, Cummings will isolate a word in naked exactitude and emphasis from the rest of the poem. In (C) the positional detachment of the second last line is an enforcement of its satiric intensity:

(C) "from the Loggia where
are we angels by O yes
beautiful we now pass through the look

girls in the style of that's the
foliage what is it didn't Ruskin
says about you got the haven't Marjorie
isn't this wellcurb simply darling"
O Education:O
thos cook & son (183–4:XXVII)

In a discussion of Cummings's use of space one must also consider his practice of fragmentizing a word so that its parts are spread over several lines. Frequently, punctuation marks will be inserted as additional controls. The total effect of such word breaking is to slow up the tempo of reading, an application of his complex system of pauses and rests:

(D) the green robe
o
p
e
n
s
andtwoare

wildstrawberries (437: 16)

(E) . . . a star's
nibbling in-

fin
-i-
tes-
i
-mal-
ly devours

darkness the
hungry star
which
will e

-ven
tu-
al
-ly jiggle
the bait of
dawn . . . (41–2: III)

In (E) the poet has wiredrawn the duration of time by breaking the two adverbs into monosyllabic bits. Occasionally Cummings will use one of the word-fragments as a separate whole. In such a case, not only has the word been broken in order to serve as a time-control, but one or more of its parts stands as an independent attributive with much the same function as that of a pun. In example (F) the first syllable serves to qualify the scene descriptively:

(F) dim
i
nu
tiv

e this park is e
mpty (*95 poems*, 24)

(G) nobody
ever could ever

had love loved whose his
climbing shoulders queerly twilight
:never,no
(body.

Nothing (353–4: 4)

Just as Cummings has special purpose in mind when he breaks words, so, too, there is a reason for his neglecting to observe spacing. The compounding of words acts to quicken the tempo as in (H), where the gradation of increasing volume is expressed with the compression of time by the expedient of running words together and by making the explosion leap up in capital letters:

(H) jolly shells begin dropping jolly fast you
hear the rrmp and
then nearerandnearerandNEARER (193: IV)

(I) Buffalo Bill's
defunct
who used to

. . . .

. . . break onetwothreefourfive pigeonsjustlikethat

(50: VIII)

More frequently, the use of compound words expresses telescoped imagery. It is this device which Cummings used so often in *Eimi* to secure the vividness of the passing scene:

(J) (past now float he-shes chiselled from darkness.
slicesofnight with greyrockfaces—also)once,
a spoolhat priest with a bellhat(all got up fit

to,why it's . . . with redder than orange than
redorange petticoats)bride. (p. 415)

(K) . . . out

of the black this which of
one street leaps quick
squirmthicklying lu

minous night
mare (355: 7)

Sometimes this imagery is telescoped so tightly that a portmanteau word is the result, as in *untheknowndulous s/pring,* which combines *unknown spring* with the sheen and movement of *undulous spring.* As in example (F) where the broken word was used for purposes of punning, Cummings may also use the compound word in double sense:

(L) five

(are all dancesing singdance all are

three
with faces made of cloud dancing (364: 21)

It has been seen that when Cummings wishes to provide a major check to the tempo of his poem, he gains a long pause by spacing. The presence of punctuation marks in his poetry is important in the same sense as well. The poet has commonly been charged with punctuating his verses with a pepper shaker, but all of these marks act as minor time-controls, as has already been noted in conjunction with the word-fragmentation of (E). The parallel relationship of spacing and punctuation is verified by consideration of the final two lines of (M):

(M) . . . in the battered
bodies the odd unlovely
souls struggle slowly and writhe
like caught.brave:flies; (46: III)

One cannot predict what marks Cummings will use to retard the tempo, for in this respect all are employed with undifferentiated effect:

(N) l oo k-
pigeons fly ingand

whee . . . .
. . . l-
ing all go BlacK wh-eel-ing (99: 1)

(O) (the;mselve;s a;nd scr;a;tch-ing lousy full.of.rain
beggars yaw:nstretchy:awn) (317–18: 57)

(P) I heard laughter(stunned,whisper;to stunned)
Really? (won.der-ing)
. . . Will you sit with me in the garden?(to a shadow
says a child)
(won : der : ing-l ; i ; s ; t-e, n, i, n, g) "avec plaisir monsieur"
(*Eimi,* p. 339)

In order to use part of a word in separate sense Cummings may insert a mark of punctuation to break the reading; this acts in the same way as the word-fragment which became a descriptive qualifier:

(Q) i sing of Olaf glad and big
whose warmest heart recoiled at war:
a conscientious object-or (244–5: XXX)

(R) o

the round
little man we
loved so isn't

no! w (433: 8)

Overpunctuation of a line sometimes serves to increase the excitement, giving it a breathless quality:

(S) . . . . Streets
glit
ter
a,strut:do;colours;are:m,ove (318–19: 59)

One of the most important elements in Cummings's technique of immediacy is the set of parenthetical marks. Because of his extreme honesty as a poet he has been compelled to describe the complex unit of experience without the presence of falsifying temporal order. Perception of the moment involves many impressions, none complete in itself; instead, they blur and overlap one into the other. In order to catch the effect of "all-at-oneness," Cummings inserts some part of the experience within the boundaries of parentheses and so suggests the simultaneousness of imagery. Examination of (N) in its complete form shows the nature of this experiment. By splitting the word *wheeling* in half and by putting the description of the sprinkling between the halves, Cummings destroys all chronological sequence. The experience of seeing the pigeons is now divorced from time:

(N)   l oo k-
          pigeons fly ingand

     whee(:are,SpRiN,k,LiNg an in-stant with sunLight
     t h e n)l-
     ing all go BlacK wh-eel-ing   (99: I)

(T) . . . meanwhile comes,through almost-night bumping,
an antedeluvian(a crammed with tovariches)camion
and(ree-ling)lurch-es,along quailess,and(arriving
finally beside Frenchless Marine)halts — outspill-
ing every which(tovariches)way tumbling who all
sprawl(revealing I tranquil large iron disk).   (*Eimi*, p. 353)

At times Cummings will interrupt his thought to register an aside. This word or phrase is marked off by parentheses and is easily construed as a whisper or a comment made *sotto voce:*

(U) it's over a(see just
over this)wall
the apples are(yes
they're gravensteins)all
as red as to lose
and as round as to find.   (390: III)

(V) in
Spring comes(no-
one
asks his name)

a mender
of things   (462: 62)

This *sotto voce* pronunciation is sometimes indicated within the word itself when the letters parenthetically enclosed are marked for emphasis of sound or of meaning. In (W) the word *he* is whispered as a final sad reminder that he has rolled into nowhere, taking all the *gay of a brave and . . . true of a who* with him:

(W) a gay of a
brave and
a true of a

who have

r
olle
d i

nt

o
n
o

w(he)re (433: 8)

Cummings ordinarily uses parentheses in pairs, but he will occasionally set down only the opening or closing mark. This incompletion creates the impression that the poem is but a recorded fragment of a larger continuum, most of which has been deliberately omitted. In this way, he brings the suggestion of the unsaid into the poem:

(X) —tomorrow is our permanent address

and there they'll scarcely find us(if they do,
we'll move away still further:into now

(412: XXXIX)

(Y) nobody loved this
he)with its
of eye stuck
into a rock of

forehead. (353-4: 4)

Objection has frequently been made to Cummings's "indiscriminate" use of capital letters. Academic procedure obligates the poet to capitalize the initial letter in every line and the pronoun *I* wherever it may occur. Along with other modernist poets Cummings feels justified in rejecting the initial capital letter on the basis that he may not necessarily wish to give that word the poetic emphasis such capitalization implies. And if he were to observe this academic regulation, how might he emphasize the first word in a line if it had already been burdened with a capital? Hence, a capital letter is to Cummings another mark of emphasis which he may use even within the body of a word to point out part of its action and to give it new force and vigor:

(Z) Nobody wears a yellow
flower in his buttonhole
he is altogether a queer fellow
as young as he is old (213: XIII)

(AA) chairs wait under the trees

Fields slowly Elysian in
a firmcool-Ness taxis, s.QuirM

and, b etw ee nch air st ott er s thesillyold
WomanSellingBalloonS (84–5: XIV)

By rejecting the pronoun *I* Cummings assumes a casual humility. The detachment of *i* is much more to his liking; it dissociates the author from the speaker of the poem, leaving him free to assign emphasis where he feels it truly belongs. When *I* does appear, however, as in (CC), there is a shadow of irony lurking behind it:

(BB) Christ(of His mercy infinite)
i pray to see;and Olaf,too

preponderatingly because
unless statistics lie he was
more brave than me:more blond than you.

(244–5: XXX)

(CC) . . . . A-
mer
i

ca, I
love,
You. . . . (167–8: II)

Real appreciation of Cummings's technique cannot result from such piecemeal consideration of verses as has been offered in the preceding catalogue. One must take the unit of the poem intact in order to determine how well the separate elements of this technique complement one another. This will be the case as three of Cummings's poems are examined in detailed exegesis. In this treatment any mention of word or words drawn from the body of the poem will be parenthetically identified by the number of the line which is being considered . . . :

ta
ppin
g
toe

hip
popot
amus Back

gen
teel-ly
lugu-
bri ous

                    eyes
LOOPTHELOOP

as

fathandsbangrag

Collected Poems, poem 52 (86: III)

This poem is the study of a jazz pianist, absorbed in the rhythm and sound of his music. Cummings has attempted to suggest the tempo of the music by starting off with short, staccato syllables (1-2) that catch the insistent rhythm to which the musician is beating time. The letter *g* (3) has been isolated to pound out a single harsh movement; whether this is a sudden pounding of the pianist's foot or a sudden harsh musical note is unimportant. As Cummings examines the jazzman, his eyes travel up from tapping toe to the bulk suspended in the chair. For him so far the most impressive part of this man is his *Back* (7); to show the relative measure of his attention he has allotted an initial capital to the word. The *Back* is qualified descriptively by the word *hip/popot/amus* (5-7), enough in itself to give the idea of overstuffed girth. But by breaking the word into parts, the poet has managed to provide applicable puns as component ideas. The *Back* is now visualized as *hip* (5) and as pot-shaped. Even better, the *Back* is so fully rounded that it is more than pot—it is *popot* (6).

The music, and with it the pianist's movements, become less sharp; now they flow with almost liquid assurance in longer and softer syllables (8–11). After a pause, Cummings' attention is pulled up to the eyes which control the whole face of the jazzman. The abrupt importance of the eyes is indicated by the fact that the word has been forced out of line over to the extreme right (12). The poem suddenly bursts into a frenzy of movement that intrigues Cummings, for he cannot resist the pianist's eyes as they roll ecstatically. The force of this feature of the man's personality is so intense that it controls the poem and, as such, it has been solidly capitalized (13). Furthermore, the unexpected boldness of the large eyes, the blacks rolling in white, can be felt somewhat by the appearance of these black capital letters set in abundant white space. The pianist's fingers slacken off for a moment as he gathers his strength for the final whirl of sound. Then with all his might he smashes down on the keys and quickly jams the sound into a rapid succession of notes. Notice how Cummings has chosen all emphatic one-syllable words to pack closely into line as expression of the musical tempo (15).

It is interesting to observe how the poem seems to be separated into parts by double-spacing. These divisions should be considered time spacers, which regulate the movement of the poem. The spacing between lines 4-5 and lines 7-8 delays the examination of the pianist as it proceeds up from toes to back. The unexpected space between lines 11-12 may serve to punctuate the shock of surprise coming in lines 12 and 13. And finally, as has already been indicated, the spacing above and below the word *as* (14) gives the pause of slackening before the last outburst of music.

1	a thrown a
2	-way It
3	with some-
4	thing sil
5	-very
6	;bright,&:mys(
7	a thrown a-
8	way
9	X
10	-mas)ter-
11	i
12	-ous wisp A of glo-
13	ry.pr
14	-ettily
15	cl(tr)in(ee)gi-
16	ng *XAIPE*, poem 34 (448)

The appearance of this poem is deceptively slight. On first reading, it seems the confused view of a Christmas tree which has been thrown away, a silver wisp of tinsel still clinging to the branches. For purpose of simplification the poem should be considered without any of the words which are set off parenthetically. This will exclude (/*a thrown a-*/*way*/*X*/*-mas*) . . . / . . . (*tr*) . . . (*ee*) . . . (6-10, 15) and so reduces the poem to a direct description of *It* (2), the importance of which is attested to by the use of the capital letter. It is significant that nowhere in the simplified lines is any definite identification made of *It;* instead, Cummings describes the bit of tinsel left clinging. This is the *some-*/*thing sil-*/*very*/;*bright,&:mys* . . . / . . . *ter-*/*i*/-*ous* (3-6, 10-12). The split writing of *sil*/-*very* (4-5) affords the poet the opportunity of using the second half again in further qualifying the tinsel as -*very*/;*bright* (5-6), while the glitter and his resultant feeling of awe are suggested by the overpunctuation surrounding the brightness: ;*bright,&:mys* (6). Since the parenthetical words are to be passed over in this initial examination, the next difficulty is found in the misplacement of *wisp A of glo-*/*ry* (12-13). *A* (12) provides the second capital letter encountered so far and serves to draw attention to the word and its reversed order. Obviously, the word's proper position would be before *wisp* (12), but by this misplacement Cummings has managed to distribute equally the force of his adjectival comment. Now because of its medial position the quality of *sil/-very/;bright, &:mys . . . / . . . ter-/i/-ous* (4-6, 10-12) identifies both *some/thing* (3-4) and *wisp . . . of glo-/ry* (12-13).

Surely, what has been examined so far makes a trivial poem, hardly worth the effort expended. But this is not all of the poem, for the parenthetical aside omitted in the analysis is its real heart. In the course of observing the part of his pleasure, the *some-/thing* (3-4), Cummings pauses to identify the whole of *It* (2) as *(/a thrown a-/way/X/-mas) . . . / . . . (tr) . . . (ee) . . .* (6-10, 15). And just as this parenthesis is the wholeness of *It,* it is at the same time the meaning of the total experience; for Cummings sees this as man's rejection of true life. The Christmas tree becomes *a thrown a-/way/X/ -mas)ter* (7-10), and man in having discarded *Christ* (9) the *master* (10) has lost the full glory his life might be. His only reminder is the wisp of glory he sees interwoven in the branches, still clinging here and there in the *(tr) . . . (ee)* (15). Notice the split parenthetical insertion which serves to duplicate the appearance of the silver tinsel.

The Christmas tree has always had the appeal of childlike wonder for Cummings. In one of his early volumes, *XLI POEMS* (1925), he wrote a poem to a little Christmas tree which is soothing with innocence. A comparison of this poem, number 104 in *Collected Poems* (141: II), and the more recent one drawn from *XAIPE* shows an increase of seriousness in the poet's tone. Cummings's capacity for pleasure is still very much alive; only now it is expressed with a twinge of gravity.

!blac
k
agains
t

(whi)

te sky
?t
rees whic
h fr

om droppe

d

,

le
af

a:;go

e
s wh
IrlI
n

.g

50 POEMS, poem 1 (351)

It is impossible to defend this poem line by line, accounting for each of the unconventional practices. This time the poem must be accepted as an entire unit, the structure of which has been determined by the subject and by Cummings' intent to produce the effect of immediacy. In prose sentence the experience under description would read, "Black against the white sky stand the trees from which a dropped leaf goes whirling." One immediately notices that some rearrangement as well as expansion of words has been required to make this fully coherent. Yet even with these adjustments the prose statement fails to approach the magnitude of the experience being considered. Cummings has taken the moment of a thunderstorm when a flash of lightning suddenly reveals the scene. In the prose version there is no suggestion that this is anything but a simple observation of the landscape; all the dramatic element is lacking. In the translation to poetry Cummings has added the enormous machinery of a thunderstorm, incorporating the excitement of sound and sight in an attempt to produce in the reader the immediate reaction of being physically present at the moment.

The misplacement of the exclamation mark in the first line succeeds in establishing excitement anticipatory to the event itself. This is the crack of lightning, sharp and definite, that illuminates the scene for its quick realization. The flash of broken vision appears in the parenthetical (*whi*) (5), its duration being so momentary that identity of the dark-massed shapes is still questionable. Thus, the use of the question mark in *!blac/k/?t/rees* (1-2, 7-8) is equal in effect to some such dubitative epithet as *perhaps*. Examples of this are available in Cummings's earlier writing: " . . . *with an effortless spontaneity which is the prerogative of perhaps fairies*" (*Enormous Room*, p. 231); "*Spring is like a perhaps hand*" (100: III). Here the poet has displayed his skill in infusing fresh color into the most neutral words, so that the elusiveness of identification is given a gracious quality. This is an unmistakable instance where Cummings has chosen to make punctuation substitute for words, resulting in more highly intensified suggestion. It is significant that half of this poem is concerned with movement

(10-20); as such, it is almost wholly composed of verbal forms: *droppe/d* (10-11), *go/e/s* (15-17), *wh/IrlI/n/.g* (17-20). By using punctuation and spacing Cummings has tried to control the reading of this part of the poem so as to approximate the slow-motion descent of a falling leaf, the eccentric, vertical motion of which is traced by the incomplete lines.

This is a moderate example of those elaborate word portraits in which Cummings embodies the subject's action in the form of the poem. Most extreme of these is the well-known "grasshopper' poem, number 276 in *Collected Poems* (286: 13), in which the poet has resorted to violent disarrangement of the word *grasshopper* in order to exhibit the surprise activated by the insect's unpredictable movements in the grass.

The Enormous Room and *The Pilgrim's Progress*

by David E. Smith

I

E. E. Cummings probably used Bunyan's *Pilgrim Progress* as an organizing principle of *The Enormous Room*[1] because he suspected that for most people in his generation its spiritual power and moral lessons were either forgotten or misunderstood. *The Enormous Room* is surely an intentional *Pilgrim's Progress,* with the striking difference that in a world made nauseous, in Hemingway's phrase, "as the result of untruth or exaggeration," where "all our words from loose using have lost their edge," Cummings chose a radical method to reinstate the truths of *The Pilgrim's Progress.* He was not immediately understood.

The Enormous Room shocked not only the complacent and the prudish in its generation of readers, but even contemporary reviewers who were otherwise quick to admire the youthful poet's verbal experiments. P. L. Masson, in the *New York Times,*[2] admitted with considerable reserve that "apart from its crudities . . . the book [was] quite worthwhile;" The *Detroit News* reviewer, D. K. Lamb, felt that "the author could have succeeded . . . without being so gratuitously filthy;" [3] and the reviewer for the *Boston Transcript*[4] contrasted the book's "exquisite finesse in portraiture" with its "brutal inchoate raving [dissolving] into a maze of meaningless word sounds." Two reviewers—John Dos Passos in *Dial* (July, 1922) and Ben Ray Redman in *Nation* (June 7, 1922)—praised the new book unequivocally. Dos Passos, a fellow-student in what Alfred Kazin has called "the finishing

"The Enormous Room and *The Pilgrim's Progress,"* by David E. Smith. From *Twentieth Century Literature,* 2 (July 1965), 67–75. © 1965 by IHC Press. Reprinted by permission of the publisher.

[1] Page references are to the Jonathan Cape edition, London, 1928. References to *The Pilgrim's Progress* are to the definitive edition of Wharey-Sharrock (Oxford: The Clarendon Press, 1960).

[2] 28 May, 1922.

[3] 4 June, 1922.

[4] 17 May, 1922.

school of the lost generation: the Norton-Harjes ambulance corps,"[5] compared *The Enormous Room* to DeFoe's *Journal of the Plague Year,* and Redman protected the author's prose style from the attacks of "certain nice-stomached gentry" who had "manifested nausea at Mr. Cummings' use of language."

A retrospective reading of the contemporary notices dramatizes the general response of reviewers that *The Enormous Room* was pretty strong meat. Readers felt compelled to take sides on the crucial issue of the book's "gratuitous filthiness." Yet it was not apart from its crudities, we feel today, that the book was "quite worthwhile," but because of them. Like a number of his younger contemporaries, Cummings had intuitively divined the efficiency of filth as metaphor, and like Swift before him, succeeded in conveying an excremental vision of life with unmistakable power. In addition, by ringing changes upon the allegorical structure of conventional pilgrimages, he evolved a Paradise within an Inferno, a Celestial City upon the ruins of the City of Destruction. In short, if Christian could no longer journey to the Delectable Mountains, Cummings would bring the Delectable Mountains to Christian.

II

For half its length, the narrator's journey resembles Christian's in *The Pilgrim's Progress.*[6] Only the obtuse would require the careful resume at mid-point in the narrative:

> In the preceding pages I have described my Pilgrim's Progress from the Slough of Despond, commonly known as *Section Sanitaire Vingt-et-Un* (then located at Germaine) through the mysteries of Noyon, Gré and Paris to the *Porte de Triage de la Ferté Macé,* Orne. (p. 130)

The parallel journey is spiritual, not literal, yet the identification of the narrator with Christian is illuminated at crucial instances in such a way as to reflect a fundamental dependence upon the earlier allegory. The prisoner's burden, consisting of a huge duffle-bag and a bed-roll, represents for him the same weight of sin, the same cumbersome con-

[5] *On Native Grounds* (New York, 1942), p. 345.

[6] Reviewers at the time generally failed to take note of Cummings' scheme, although it is obvious enough with such chapter-titles "I begin a Pilgrimage," "A Pilgrim's Progress," and "Apollyon." A recent critic of the novel, Kingsley Widmer, feels that "While the use of Bunyan and the pilgrimage is only partial, and probably could not justify the ingenuity of systemic exposition, it does give elements of order at several levels to the poetic narrative." "Timeless Prose," *TCL,* 4 (1958), 6. What I wish to suggest is that the spiritual pilgrimage actually begins in La Ferté Macé; that "timelessness" is of its essence; and that such a notion is not contradictory to Bunyan's allegory understood on its grander spiritual level.

science of the guilty man, as it did for Christian. When he is able to put the burden down, he is "himself." (p. 45) When he checks his burden at the end of the eventful train-ride to Briouse, he has arrived psychologically at the identical point at which Christian was relieved of his burden—he is at the Cross:

> Uphill now. Every muscle thoroughly aching, head spinning, I half-straightened my no longer obedient body; and jumped: face to face with a little wooden man hanging all by itself in a grove of low trees.
>
> The wooden body clumsy with pain burst into fragile legs with absurdly large feet and funny writhing toes. . . . About its stunted loins clung a ponderous and jocular fragment of drapery. On one terribly brittle shoulder the droll lump of its neckless head ridiculously lived. . . .
>
> For perhaps a minute the almost obliterated face and mine eyed one another in the silence of intolerable autumn.
>
> Who was this wooden man? Like a sharp, black, mechanical cry in the spongy organism of gloom stood the coarse and sudden sculpture of his torment; the big mouth of night carefully spurted the angular actual language of his martyred body. I had seen him before in the dream of some mediaeval saint with a thief sagging at either side, surrounded with crisp angels. Tonight he was alone; save for myself, and the moon's minute flower pushing between slabs of fractured cloud. (pp. 74–75)

Now the narrator is one of the Elect; and only from this crucial point may his spiritual progress be measured. Having lost his burden at the cross, Cummings enters into that terrifying Interpreter's House, The Enormous Room, which is to be transformed through human courage until it permits a view of the Delectable Mountains.

Like all initiates into the mysteries, the narrator is *Le Nouveau:*

> With the end of my first day as a certified inhabitant of [La Ferté Macé] a definite progression is brought to a close. Beginning with my second day at La Ferté a new period opens. [It] extends to the moment of my departure and includes the discovery of the Delectable Mountains. . . .
>
> (p. 130)

Cummings' rebirth into the Society of The Enormous Room shares superficially in the conventional religious symbolism of conversion: he is baptized (in a chilling *douche*); he partakes of a kind of communion; the room gradually fills with light; *Le Nouveau* is not immediately aware of the full significance of the mysteries. The pilgrim is confronted by an Infernal Trinity[7] symbolizing the world, the flesh,

[7] For the most comprehensive summary of the significance of the Infernal Trinity–"the captains of the hosts of hell which war against the soul"—see Samuel C. Chew, *The Pilgrimage of Life* (New Haven and London, 1962), pp. 70–78. The "instruments of [Apollyon's] power" in *The Enormous Room* were "Fear, Women, and Sunday." (p. 162)

and the devil. However, this traditional Infernal Trinity in *The Enormous Room* is overshadowed by the hovering presence of a farsubtler Trinity, one which has been ingeniously suggested (in other contexts) by Kenneth Burke:

> The substantial nature of imagery may often produce an unintended burlesque of substance, in drawing upon the ambiguities of the cloacal, where there are united, in a "demonic trinity," the three principles of the erotic, urinary, and excremental. . . . Images from the cloacal sources are basic to the "thinking of the body"; and we may expect their privy nature to complicate the capitalist rationale of private property.[8]

Whereas for Burke the "demonic trinity" often finds expression in the 'excremental' nature of invective or vilification (e.g., a writer heaping "verbal offal" upon his opponent), *The Enormous Room* manipulates the images of the erotic, urinary, and excremental to symbolize the most precious mysteries of Christian brotherhood. In not perceiving Cummings' extraordinary use of the "excremental," earlier critics of *The Enormous Room* have misunderstood its intention.[9]

Cleanliness is next to ungodliness in Cummings' ludicrously inverted

[8] Kenneth Burke, *A Grammer of Motives* (New York, 1945), pp. 300–303. Burke anticipated by well over a decade the provocative "studies in anality" of Norman O. Brown (*Life Against Death: the psychoanalytical meaning of history,* Wesleyan, Conn., 1959), which as yet comprise the fullest philosophical development of the concept. Compare Brown's view of the "anal character of Luther's Devil" with Cummings' Apollyon:

> Luther detects the Devil at work wherever he sees disguised (sublimated) anality, and conceives it to be the function of the Gospel to expose the disguise and reveal the anality behind the sublimation. "The Devil does not come in his filthy black colours, but slinks around like a snake, and dresses himself up as pretty as may be. . . ." Hence, Luther's grossly anal abuse of the Devil is not hysterical rhetoric but a correct exposure of his exact nature. (p. 225)

In Brown's view, Luther "sees civilization as having an essentially anal-sadistic structure, as essentially constructed by the sublimation of anality." (pp. 225–226) It is important for any view of Cummings to compare Brown's description of Luther's eschatology:

> Since in Luther's historical eschatology the world was going to get worse before it got better, he sees the approaching end of the world as taking the form of a "rain of filth." The Second Coming will reduce sublimations to the anality out of which they are constructed. The Devil turns cow dung into a crown, but "Christ, Who will shortly come in His glory, will quiet them, not indeed with gold, but with brimstone." And in this world, in line with Luther's new *theologia crucis,* though grace may keep the inward spirit clean, the Christian must surrender his flesh to the extremest assaults of anality." (p. 226)

[9] In his study of "Change in the Poetry of E. E. Cummings," *PLMA,* 70 (1955), 1913–33, Rudolph Von Abele noticed that "Cummings sensed the satiric potentialities of the interdicted imagery of sex and excrement" (p. 928), and that as a consequence critics have "perhaps inevitabl[y]" called him "infantile" and "adolescent" for it. Von Abele limits his discussion, of course, to Cummings poetry.

scheme of things. The only physically clean beings are the non-prisoners. The "very definite fiend," Apollyon, who is the director of the prison, is an impeccable dresser, a terrifying little monster whose most disgusting feature is his inhuman fetish for personal cleanliness. We see him "shaking a huge fist of pinkish, well-manicured flesh, the distinct, cruel, brightish eyes sprouting from their sockets," as he adjusts his cuffs and mutters horrible insults to the women prisoners: "PROSTITUTES and WHORES and DIRTY FILTH OF WOMEN." (pp. 173–74) It is a perfectly obvious irony that, behind his puppet-like façade of cleanliness, Apollyon is responsible for the filthiest of prisons.

Under such circumstances, human brotherhood remains possible only among the condemned. However, entrance into The Enormous Room is not by itself an initiation into the monastic community of the faithful, for there are some prisoners who resist conversion. A notable example is Count Bragard, the impostor.[10]

When Cummings first meets Bragard, he is not yet aware that the man is a hypocrite. Bragard is "immaculately apparelled in a crisp albeit collarless shirt, carefully mended trousers in which the remains of a crease still lingered, a threadbare but perfectly fitting swallow-tail coat, and newly varnished . . . shoes." (pp. 91–92) The "Count," who poses as a painter, claims friendship with Cezanne. He is disgusted with his fellow-prisoners, whom he regards as swine:

> 'This filth'—he pronounced the word with indescribable bitterness—'this herding of men like cattle—they treat us no better than pigs here. The fellows drop their dung in the very room where they sleep. What is one to expect of a place like this? *Ce n'est pas une existence'*—his French was glib and faultless. (p. 92)

It is immediately after his introduction to Bragard that *Le Nouveau* undergoes the "cleansing" experience of the icy, dirty bath—a kind of baptism into the filth of the "unmistakably ecclesiastical" Enormous Room.

The theme is at once revolting and transcendent: human excrement, normally the object of universal disgust, symbolizes human brotherhood and, eventually, Christian Salvation. The most prominent feature of The Enormous Room is its odor:

> As you stood with your back to the door, and faced down the room, you had in the near right-hand corner . . . six pails of urine. On the right-hand wall . . . a few boards tacked together . . . marked the position of a *cabinet d'aisance,* composed of a small coverless tin pail identical with the other six. . . . (p. 90)

[10] The Count's name carries out the book's general pattern of allegorical names. "Bragard" sounds like "braggart;" his initials, "F. A.," suggest *fanfaron.*

Le Nouveau painfully acquaints himself with those prisoner-friends who will become for him "Delectable Mountains'; even as he does so, he must reject the usual premium placed superficially upon general cleanliness. Finding himself in a comic, repugnant world which appears inexpressibly chaotic,[11] he must eventually arrive at the position of his friend "B" (a kind of Interpreter), who says, "Cummings, I tell you this is the finest place on earth!" (p. 85) *Le Nouveau's* friendships and loyalties develop to the degree that he is able to become one with the gaping, belching, trumpeting fraternity: he must be "swallowed by the Enormous Room." He must learn to consume, in company with his fellows, the "faintly-smoking urine-colored circular broth," (p. 113) and he must learn to trust this kind of communion while he rejects the hypocritical and even comical performance of the Holy Eucharist supervised by Apollyon:

> . . . a *planton* mounted to the Enormous Room and shouted
> *'La Messe!'*
> several times; whereat the devotees lined up and were carefully conducted to the scene of spiritual operations.
>
> The priest was changed every week. His assistant . . . was always the same. It was his function to pick the priest up when he fell down after tripping upon his robe, to hand him things before he wanted them. . . . At moments of leisure he abased his fatty whitish jowl and contemplated with watery eyes the floor in front of his highly polished boots, having first placed his ugly chubby hands together behind his most ample back.
>
> (pp. 186–87)

The conventional Mass reaches its ironical climax for the prisoners on a Sunday when a particularly thoughtless priest exhorts the forcibly assembled group—" *'Vous êtes libres, mes enfants, de faire l'immortalité . . . Le ciel est fait pour vous'*—and [Cummings observes] the Belgian ten-foot farmer spat three times and wiped them with his foot, his nose dripping; and the nigger shot a white oyster into a far-off scarlet handkerchief—and the Man's strings came untied and he sidled crab-like down the steps. . . ." (pp. 187–88)

Cummings' violent dismissal of the ordinary forms of things does not imply that he has rejected the ultimate spiritual meanings which the forms should symbolize. Civilization itself is unspeakably corrupt;

[11] I disagree with Kazin's interpretation: "The enormous room, by its very remoteness from war, mirrored and intensified its inherent meaninglessness; it became a maze in which men clawed each other to escape or to keep their reason. And the central theme of their imprisonment was chaos." *On Native Grounds,* p. 325. I do not deny that the "profoundly irrational" pervades the atmosphere of the enormous room, but I assert that a religious meaning must be assigned to it. Cummings' "vision of the universe" is not "surrealist," as Professor Kazin claims. It is incongruously Christian.

it is reflected in the injustices of governments, the ironies of power-struggles between nations, and the horrors of a chaotic and meaningless war. In the microcosm of The Enormous Room it is represented by *Le Directeur,* by the Black Holster (brutal chief of the *plantons*), and by the "Three Wise Men" and their Inquisition. Above all, civilization's least satisfactory product is the unthinking and insensitive American, the incommunicative, middle-class, self-satisfied average-man, represented here as "Mr. A.":

> "You boys want to keep away from those dirty Frenchmen. . . . We're here to show those bastards how they do things in America."
>
> (p. 27)

Cummings' "war-time" Mr. A.—section-chief of an Ambulance Service subsidized with Morgan money—reappears in the post-war poems in civilian clothes as the prototype unthinking-American immortalized, in all of his fastidiousness, in the cynically-portrayed subject of "POEM, OR BEAUTY HURTS MR. VINAL," defecating (with a hun-dred-mil-lion-oth-ers) on a "sternly allotted sandpile," emitting a "tiny violetflavored nuisance:Odor?/ono." (167: II)

What most disturbed Cummings in the immediate post-war years was a mass insensitivity to the distressing and, relevantly, stinking conditions of war (and, by extension, of civilization). Those who refused to use their noses except to avoid the actual smell of life became, like the Cambridge ladies of the sonnet, possessed of furnished souls and comfortable minds merely; their daughters, like their lives, were "unscented" and "shapeless." [12] (58: I) *The Enormous Room* was addressed to this unscented majority in the hope that it would be not merely shocked but would somehow sense, beyond its Wrigley's–Spearmint, Nujolneeding, Odorono values, that Christian brotherhood existed among human odors, not beyond them. The new Samaritan of the poem " 'a man who had fallen among thieves'," ignores the "frozen brook/ of the pinkest vomit" to save his victim:

> Brushing from whom the stiffened puke
> i put him all into my arms
> and staggered banged with terror through
> a million billion trillion stars [.] (184: XXVIII)

In choosing for his prototype fool an overcivilized, anal American with a supersensitive nose, Cummings discovered an essential symbol.

[12] Cummings' prepossession with olfactory images serves in part to explain his deliberate and early use of the sonnet form to describe prostitutes. The sonnet-sequences of *Tulips and Chimneys* bear more than a superficial resemblance to "Holy Sonnets." They are deliberately religious in tone while they turn repeatedly to subjects which are physically offensive. Cf. Brown, op. cit., note 8 above.

Inevitably, therefore, his own pilgrim would need to be able to smell his fellow-human beings in order to progress with them toward the Delectable Mountains. In contrast, the impostor Count Bragard, who cannot tolerate the stink of his fellow-prisoners, is clearly identifiable with the worst excesses of modern civilization: he prostitutes his art; his real god is not Cezanne, but Vanderbilt.[13]

A genuine communion of the brotherhood of prisoners is suggested by the imposed necessity of their acting together rather than as individuals. During a journey of several nights and days, four prisoners were handcuffed wrist to wrist, and "the handcuffs were not once removed. The prisoners slept sitting up or falling over one another. They urinated and defecated with the handcuffs on, all of them hitched together." (p. 247) In a ludicrous scene, Apollyon surprises some women prisoners as they are "carrying their slops along the hall and down-stairs, as (in common with the men) they had to do at least twice every morning and twice every afternoon." Cummings describes

> . . . five or six women staggering and carrying pails full to the brim of everyone knew what; five or six heads, lowered, ill-dressed bodies tense with effort, free arms rigidly extended from the shoulder downward and outward in a plane at right angles to their difficult progress, and thereby helping to balance the disconcerting load—all embarrassed, some humiliated, others desperately at ease. . . . (p. 172)

The sudden appearance of *Le Directeur* has its result:

> I saw once a little girl of eleven years old scream in terror and drop her pail of slops, spilling most of it on her feet; and seize it in a clutch of frail child's fingers, and stagger, sobbing and shaking, past the Fiend—one hand held over her contorted face to shield her from the Awful Thing of Things—to the head of the stairs; where she collapsed, and was half-carried, half-dragged by one of the older ones to the floor below, while another older one picked up her pail and lugged this and her own hurriedly downward. (p. 173)

On this occasion *Le Nouveau* declares that, for the only time in his life, he wanted to kill. (p. 174)

III

"In the course of the next ten thousand years," wrote Cummings after his return to New York, "it may be possible to find Delectable

[13] Count Bragard's hypocrisy is intensified when we recall that Cummings admired Cézanne and expressionism, his own role in *The Enormous Room* being that of a semi-abstract painter. Bragard, the false-painter, draws horses for money; Cummings, the true-painter, portrays a gallery of divine subjects. His "portraits" are drawn with the same nervous calligraphy evident in the line-drawings he was publishing at this time.

Mountains without going to prison." (p. 309) While he was in captivity, however, he found that communication was only possible with those "common scum" who had not been hopelessly indoctrinated by civilization. Bunyan's Worldly Wise-men, for Cummings, constituted the majority of the "monster manunkind." (397:XIV) "The Great American Public," he wrote, had "a handicap which my friends at La Ferté did not as a rule have—education. Let no one sound his indignant yawp at this." (pp. 308–9) Communication, then, in The Enormous Room, if it were to exist among the prisoners at all, had to be established upon some deeper principle than spoken language. The principle was that of a communion of the Elect. Words were inadequate:

> Things . . . which are always inside of us and in fact are us and which consequently will not be pushed off or away where we can begin thinking about them—are no longer things; they, and the us which they are, equals A Verb; an IS. The Zulu, [one of Cummings' intimates, a "Delectable Mountain"] then, I must perforce call an IS. (p. 239)

In speaking of this second of the four "Delectable Mountains," Cummings is careful to make the point that The Zulu spoke no conventionally communicable language, and yet "I have never in my life so perfectly understood (even to the most exquisite nuances) whatever idea another human being desired at any moment to communicate to me, as I have in the case of The Zulu." (p. 246) The secret of The Zulu's means of communication ". . . lay in that very essence which I have only defined as an IS; ended and began with an innate and unlearnable control over all which one can only describe as the homogeneously tactile." (p. 246)

The Delectable Mountains were those persons who embodied, for the pilgrim, all possible human values—notwithstanding a totally corrupt civilization which has unjustly attempted to destroy them. They were, like The Zulu, incapable of ordinary discourse, but like him, communicated upon a deeper and more intuitive level. The "third Delectable Mountain," for example, was Surplice. No one was certain about his nationality. His words were "trying hard to be and never [could] be Polish," (p. 262) Surplice was a fool. He was "utterly ignorant," "utterly curious," "utterly hungry." His name was so badly mispronounced that the Belgians and Hollanders referred to him as "Syph'lis." [14] Surplice is intended as a symbol for Christ: the imagery of the Chapter devoted to him is developed in a series of allusions to the Son of God. "Of nobody can he say My Friend, of no one has he ever said or will he ever say My Enemy." (p. 262) Surplice's departure was like our Lord's:

[14] The pun here conveys Cummings' central ironic intention.

> We did our best to cheer him; we gave him a sort of Last Supper at our bedside, we heated some red wine in the tin-cup and he drank with us. . . . We offered him a cup of wine. A kind of huge convulsion gripped, for an instant, fiercely his entire face: then he said in a whisper of sheer unspeakable wonderment. . . .: *'Pour moi, monsieur?'* (p. 272)

Surplice, or Christ, is more clearly and repeatedly identified with human excrement than is any other character. Some of the prisoners despise him for it. "Every morning he takes the pail of solid excrement down, without anyone's suggesting that he take it; . . . he has, in fact, an unobstreperous affinity for excrement; he lives in it. . . ." (p. 262) Surely, Cummings' deepest intention here is not merely to revolt the reader. This same Surplice, or Syph'lis, is "intensely religious, religious with a terrible and exceedingly beautiful and absurd intensity." (p. 262) Clearly, the only revolted persons are the superficially fastidious who are also, in this setting, the inhuman. "Mr. A," the section-leader of the Ambulance corps, had warned:

> "We gotta show we're superior to 'em. Those bastards doughno what a bath means. . . . If you want [privileges] you gotta shave and look neat, and *keep away from them dirty Frenchmen.* [Author's italics.] We Americans are over here to learn them lousy bastards something." (p. 86)

Implicit in "Mr. A's" attitude is the sniffy contempt which will characterize the provincial America of Cummings' post-war poems: we have deodorized ourselves out of existence.

The narrative of *The Enormous Room* concludes with *Le Nouveau's* departure from *La Ferté Macé.* (Actually, Cummings had been released from the French prison-camp largely through the deliberate efforts of his father, a Unitarian minister.) The emphasis, as in any rite of passage, is upon what the initiate has learned from his journey. In this instance, the maimed hero can never again regard the outer world (i.e., "civilization") without irony. But the spiritual lesson he learned from his sojourn with a community of brothers will be repeated in his subsequent writings both as an ironical dismissal of the values of his contemporary world, and as a sensitive, almost mystical celebration of the quality of Christian love.

IV

Even if we admit the ingenuity of Cummings' device in *The Enormous Room,* we may still ask if the enormity of the conceit, developed so fully as it is, succeeds. Until one returns directly to Bunyan's allegory, he may forget just how scummy the Slough of Despond actually was. Bunyan implies that a virtually inescapable condition of man's spiritual salvation is that he "wallow for a time," and become "grievously bedaubed." (p. 14) Christian cannot help wondering why the place is not "mended, that poor Travellers might go . . . with more security," and his companion of the moment, Help, explains:

> It is the descent whither the scum and filth that attends conviction for sin doth continually run, and therefore it is called the *Slough of Dispond:* for still as the sinner is awakened about his lost condition, there ariseth in his soul many fears, and doubts, and discouraging apprehensions, which all of them get together, and settle in this place; And this is the reason of the badness of this ground. (p. 15)

Help clearly implies that the Slough of Despond will always be where it is. It is a necessary part of the journey. Similarly, Cummings implies that The Enormous Room is "necessary," although he hopes that "In the course of the next ten thousand years it may be possible to find the Delectable Mountains without going to prison." (p. 309) We need only recall the ultimate plight of Bunyan's Ignorance, the erstwhile traveling-companion of Christian and Hopeful—who had entered the King's Highway unlawfully from the Country of Conceit—to realize the full significance of the Enormous Room as a purging-place. He and Cummings' "Mr. A.," in their smug complacency and self-confidence, are one-of-a-kind. Neither will enter the gates of the kingdom, although each thinks that he will.

There remains the question of obscenity in *The Enormous Room.* Could Cummings have succeeded, as reviewer D. K. Lamb put it, "without being so gratuitously filthy"? Had William Thackeray lived to read *The Enormous Room,* he would unquestionably have called it "filthy in word, filthy in thought, furious, raging, obscene," as he described *Gulliver's Travels* to a group of nineteenth-century ladies. But happily, such a view of "filthiness" has been demonstrated to be superficial, and despite the persistence of a few critics in reading Swift as personal history, Professors Landa, Ehrenpreis, and others, have taught us that to regard *Travels into Several Remote Nations of the World* as evidence of coprophilia in Swift is itself madness. Thus, while it is important to comprehend the meaning of the excrement in Houyhnhnmland, it is trivial to be offended by its odor.

Without insisting upon the parallel between the pilgrimages of Bunyan's Christian and Swift's ironic Gulliver,[15] I would nevertheless

[15] Calhoun Winton, in "Conversion on the Road to Houyhnhnmland," *The Sewanee Review,* 68 (Winter, 1960), 20–33, maintains that *Gulliver's Travels* "intentionally echoes. . . . *A* [*sic*] *Pilgrim's Progress.*" Gulliver, in his view, is "a sort of eighteenth-century English Everyman whose pilgrimage from a position of complete religious ignorance culminates with 'conversion . . .' to . . . the reasonable faith of the hyper-reasonable horses, in Houyhnhnmland's new Eden." Swift is not to be mistaken for Gulliver, whose conversion is to be understood ironically.

agree with Professor Monk,[16] who sees a "grim joke" in Gulliver himself being "the supreme instance of a creature smitten with pride."

The significance of such a view for readers of Cummings is this: Gulliver, in his rationalistic pride, is no longer able to smell his fellow human beings without experiencing a wave of nauseating disgust. Having lived in the super-rational "civilization" of the horses, he finds the odor of human beings altogether repugnant. Cummings' twentieth-century pilgrim provides us with an alternative. In a world of rationalistic, super-scientific, deodorized, Nujolneeding Gullivers, he found it necessary for his salvation to escape into a community of odorous human beings. He discovered them by being imprisoned among them in The Enormous Room.

[16] Samuel Holt Monk, "The Pride of Lemuel Gulliver," *The Sewanee Review,* 68 (Winter 1955), 48–71.

E. E. Cummings' *Him*

by Robert E. Maurer

In 1927 E. E. Cummings was, at the age of thirty-three, very much the rising young star in the literary firmament. He had published in rapid succession since 1922 an autobiographical book and four startlingly original books of poetry; his poems, drawings, and essays had been appearing in little magazines ever since he left Harvard, eleven years before. In November of 1927 the only full-length work for the stage he has ever written, a three-act expressionistic play called *Him,* came out in book form.[1] As was to be expected of a child of Cummings' pen, *Him* turned out to be frankly experimental; like his poetry, it was lively, robust, sometimes incoherent, sometimes indecent, often disrespectful, and often supremely lyrical. The play contained twenty-one scenes and a hundred and five characters.

In the game twenties this unorthodox literary property was issued by a commercial publisher[2] and became the object of serious consideration by able critics. Edmund Wilson, Genevieve Taggard, Conrad Aiken, Waldo Frank, Paul Rosenfeld, and S. Foster Damon reviewed it with a genuine desire to see what the author was trying to do; although some of them, notably Mr. Wilson, were most highly impressed by the play, they all assumed that because of its eccentricities *Him* would remain a closet drama.

The members of The Experimental Theatre, Inc., successor to the Provincetown Players, were a venturesome group, but even they failed to see how such an expansive production could be mounted on the tiny stage of the Provincetown Theatre. Cummings' play had been suggested to the group by Henry Alsberg as a striking work that

"E. E. Cummings' *Him,*" by Robert E. Maurer. From *The Bucknell Review,* 6 (May 1956), 1–27.

[1] His three other works written ostensibly for the stage are *Tom* (1935), a ballet based on *Uncle Tom's Cabin; Anthropos* (1930, 1944), an extremely slight dramatic parable; and *Santa Claus* (1946), a morality play.

[2] *Him* was published by Horace Liveright. All page references within this text refer to the Liveright edition (New York, 1927).

would be likely to refill the Provincetown's coffers and revive its energies and hopes. The play fired the imagination of the group's director, James Light, who went into consultation with Cummings and Eugene Fitch, a set designer, and produced a series of charts that convinced the group that the roles could be played by thirty people and the scenes be made to run smoothly.[3] *Him* opened on April 18, 1928, ran for twenty-seven performances, and precipitated both Cummings and The Experimental Theatre into one of the hottest literary fights of the twenties.

In his play Cummings had embodied some ideas about the stage that he had advanced two years earlier in *The Dial,* when for two issues he took over the job of theatre critic while Gilbert Seldes was on vacation. The reviews, more valuable as revelations of his own philosophy of drama than as guides to a potential theatre-goer, indicated Cummings' extreme dislike for the conventional, realistic drama of the twentieth century: he referred to the proscenium stage as a "pennyintheslot peepshow parlour;" he called the chorus "that long-idle, inexhaustible treasure;"[4] he said that the ideal of the drama should be "elastic space," and called it "a noble ideal, to misunderstand which requires the peculiarly insulting stupidity of 'critics.' "[5]

The "insulting stupidity" of critics, if such it was, was soon directed against Cummings' own practicing of what he had preached in his reviews. His play was a living protest against the purely decorative purpose of settings, the completely artificial separation of play area and audience, and the static quality of most drama that violates Cummings' basic tenet that a characteristic of all good art is movement. These ideas had already been put into practice by the German expressionistic theatre, and expressionism and experimental techniques of all sorts were common in little theatres at that time; but the American commercial theatre was still under the strong influence of the realism fostered by James A. Herne and David Belasco, and the men on the drama desks of New York newspapers in 1928 were apparently not able to accept a work that combined unorthodox settings with fantasy, poetic lyricism, burlesque comedy techniques, and scathing satire. Without exception, they disliked the play.

The surprising thing, however, is not that the play failed to impress them favorably but that it aroused an intemperate wrath that seemed almost unrelated to its stimulus. The disparity between the approach to *Him* of the literary critics and their dramatic counterparts, and

[3] Helen Deutsch and Stella Hanau, *The Provincetown* (New York, 1931), pp. 158–159.

[4] "The Theatre," *The Dial,* 80 (April, 1926), 343–44.

[5] "The Theatre," *The Dial,* 80 (May, 1926), 432–34. [For both these pieces, see *A Miscellany Revised,* pp. 141–48. —Editor's note.]

between the conclusions they reached, is hard to account for—certainly *Him* was no less revolutionary on the page than in the theatre. But only one of the daily theatre critics was able to write an intelligent appraisal of the play;[6] the reviews of his colleagues, such men as Alexander Woollcott, George Jean Nathan, Percy Hammond, Walter Winchell, and Brooks Atkinson, took on a hysterical tone.

Such notably volatile judges as Mr. Woollcott and Mr. Nathan doubtless were antagonized as soon as they reached the theatre and looked at the program of *Him,* for which Cummings had written one of his personalized instructions on how to approach his work:

> *Relax, and give this PLAY a chance to strut its stuff—relax, don't worry because it's not like something else—relax, stop wondering what it's all "about"—like many strange and familiar things, Life included, this PLAY isn't "about," it simply is. Don't try to despise it, let it try to despise you. Don't try to enjoy it, let it try to enjoy you. DON'T TRY TO UNDERSTAND IT, LET IT TRY TO UNDERSTAND YOU.*[7]

Having repeatedly been told to relax, Mr. Nathan tensed his muscles and expected the worst, which, according to him, is what he got:

> For utter guff, this Cummings exhibition has never been surpassed within the memory of the oldest play-reviewer operating in Manhattan. It is incoherent, illiterate, preposterous balderdash, as completely and unremittingly idiotic as the human mind, when partially sober, can imagine.[8]

Mr. Nathan's polemics have a thunderous roll that one cannot help admiring; it is a pity, however, that he never stooped to comment on the play itself. Against such an un-Aristotelian approach to the art object, forces were mustered to defend *Him.* Jacques Barzun, writing a reminiscence of *Him* for the Cummings issue of *The Harvard Wake* (1946), tells how students, in their newspapers ". . . shot barbed arrows over the college walls at the downtown press which, led by that sentimental Man-Mountain, Mr. Woollcott, imputed naughtiness and incompetence to the brave Cummings."[9] The Provincetown, after the storm arose, published an anonymous booklet, *him AND the CRITICS,* that contained an unsigned defense of the play by Gilbert Seldes, a number of scathing criticisms reprinted from the "downtown press," as well as some of the favorable reviews written when the book was published. Cummings, by producing a work for a group audience and actually presenting it to a public less conditioned to experimen-

[6] John Anderson, of the New York *Evening Journal.*

[7] From the program note of the first performance of *Him* [Cf. Charles Norman, *The Magic-Maker* (revised), p. 168. —Editor's note.]

[8] George Jean Nathan, quoted in Gilbert Seldes, "The Theatre," *The Dial,* 85 (July, 1928), 77–78.

[9] "E. E. Cummings: A Word About *Him,*" *The Harvard Wake,* 5 (Spring, 1946), 55.

tation than are readers of poetry, suddenly found himself a storm center, a position unique in his career.

He must have foreseen, of course, at least part of the antipathy that would greet any performance of *Him,* and his advice on the program was meant as more than mere defiance of the Philistines. Like all of his introductions, this one is intended to be a sincere attempt to minimize puzzlement by providing a theoretical foundation for approaching the work. Critics less irascible than Mr. Nathan found his advice not a sign of idiocy but a definite aid to enjoyment. Stark Young, writing in *The New Republic,* declared that "In an odd sort of fashion this [Cummings' introduction] is good advice for *him.* I found myself, letting the piece alone, listening to it as if I were listening to a piece of music . . . anything but bored, not until the last act, at least." [10]

Exactly what, then, were the ingredients that Cummings stirred into his brew for the relaxed and unwondering playgoer? First, a large portion of burlesque, a little Dada, and a soupçon of Surrealism. Second, a story which was not a story, two characters without real names, one character who played nine parts, a great deal of theorizing about love and art, much genuine passion, and an ending that might be regarded as tragic.

Cummings did not try to substitute an entirely new conception for the proscenium stage. He did, however, make it functional by having the four walls (including the invisible one which is between the actors and the audience) revolve in a clockwise direction for each of five scenes involving the hero and the heroine; and he had the actors perform as if the invisible wall were quite as tangible and furniture-supporting as the other three. For other scenes in the play he used variously a painted backdrop through which the heads of two actors emerged; curtains; or an absolutely bare stage, sometimes with a little furniture, sometimes not. In one scene there were neither props nor characters nor, needless, to say, actions; the curtain merely rose and fell again. It required an unusually open-minded and sympathetic critic to make a fair judgment of such a play.

Early in the first act Cummings has his "nonhero" Him say, "The average 'painter' 'sculptor' 'poet' 'composer' 'playwright' is a person who cannot leap through a hoop from the back of a galloping horse, make people laugh with a clown's mouth, orchestrate twenty lions" (p. 12). In other words, most pseudo "artists" (with quotation marks) are able to create only static effects, but the true artist, which Cummings—and Him—are striving to be, produces works that are analo-

[10] *"Him," The New Republic,* 54 (May 2, 1928), 325.

gous to a performance by a bareback rider, a clown, or a lion tamer—works that amaze by their daring, their precision, and their perfection.

When Cummings wrote *Him* he wanted to arouse within the spectator that feeling of aliveness, an extra-literary quality, that is the peculiar attribute of the drama and that effectively produces its results before intellectual analysis begins. Just as he uses typographical manipulations to re-create spontaneous, simultaneous impressions in his poems, so also he wants his playgoer to experience each movement as directly and unintellectually as he does the events of his life. Certain of life's entertainments might be placed at the zenith of non-intellectualism; Cummings is inordinately fond of two of these—the circus and the burlesque show.[11] He would be pleased if his audience would approach and accept *Him* in the same way as a spectator watches a circus: with a sense of wonder; of joy in sound and color and movement; with a readiness to laugh; above all, with no questions.

It may be well at this point to take a look at what happens on Cummings' stage to see just what was the "utter guff" that so incensed Mr. Nathan and his colleagues. The first scene showed a painted backdrop depicting a doctor anaesthetizing a woman; the heads of the two people pictured turned out to be living heads which emerged through two holes at the appropriate places. Facing this scene, in rocking chairs with their backs to the audience, sat three withered female figures, knitting and carrying on an absurd conversation. The viewer saw this kind of scene recur five times within the play (always either preceding or following a scene involving the hero and heroine); he learned that the names of the female figures were Miss Stop, Miss Look, and Miss Listen Weird, and, if he were perspicacious, he realized that these three "Weird sisters" were meant to represent, in a perverted sort of way, three fates, at the same time as they were utilized as the chorus Cummings admires so much. As for the patient and the doctor on the backdrop, the action of the former was limited to the closing of her eyes; the doctor withdrew his head from the hole and appeared on stage along with the play's hero, Him. When the three Miss Weirds got up one by one and turned around to be introduced to Him, it was revealed that they wore identical mask-faces.

The second scene revealed two people in an almost bare room: the three walls were, from left to right, solid, a door wall, and a window wall; the furniture consisted of a sofa on which lay a man's hat, a table holding a cigarette box, and, near the table, two chairs;

[11] See, for example, his essays, "Burlesque—I Love It!" *Stage,* 13 (March, 1936), 6; "The Adult, the Artist and the Circus," *Vanity Fair,* 25 (Oct., 1925), 51; and "You Aren't Mad, Am I," *Vanity Fair,* 25 (Dec., 1925), 92. [See *A Miscellany Revised,* pp. 292–7, 109–14, and 126–31. —Editor's note.]

the fourth, or invisible wall, held an invisible mirror, in front of which the heroine inspected herself and fixed her hair.

The two participants in this scene, Him and Me (who could be recognized as the patient of Scene I), did, at least, seem like real people, and the spectator must have judged that the plot of the play was to be woven about them. Although their conversation was somewhat difficult to follow, it must have been clear that Me and Him were involved in a love affair in which a completely satisfying union was unreachable, owing to Him's conception of himself as an artist and Me's inability to understand either Him's interests or her own attraction to him. When in Scene IV of Act I Me and Him appeared on the stage again, the room in which they conversed had made one clockwise revolution, so that the mirror wall was now to the left and the window wall invisible; and the revolutions continued with each scene until the room had described a full circle.

The nine scenes of the second act made up a play within a play; in this act Cummings let loose with all the satiric fun and deranged movement of which he was capable. The first scene, for instance, was pure Dada: the scene in which the curtain rose, revealing a bare stage, stayed up for one minute, and descended. Another scene, which dramatized the Frankie and Johnny ballad—complete with singing choruses and an allegorical representation of the ground—was meant to be a satire on the folk dramas that were especially prevalent in the twenties and on the Theatre Guild, which was fostering them; surprisingly enough, this scene was the only one in the whole play that found any favor with the unfriendly critics (perhaps this was due to its frankly ribald character). Another scene, which the knowing interpreted as a satire on Shaw's habit of bringing history up to date, showed Mussolini (or Caesar) as he might have been interpreted at the Old Howard burlesque house in Boston.

According to the rationale of this second act, Him is showing these scenes to Me as the play that he might write if he (or his other self) were to write a play to make money. The unfortunate Me, however, fails to find any meaning or any coherence in the scenes; indeed, she finds some of them repulsive. All she can think of to say after one comic routine is "What was that about?"

The last act was devoted mostly to two long dialogues between Him and Me (always in their room), although Cummings did insert one surrealistic and bitterly sarcastic scene showing American tourists in a Paris night club (this has been omitted from productions of *Him,* as adding unnecessarily to the length of the play and being not particularly relevant). The play ends as Me looks clear through the mirror wall and sees the "real people" outside, "pretending that this room and you and I are real" (p. 145).

After they had left the theatre, even the most sympathetic critics and the most receptive college students must have discussed among themselves "What was that about?" For there is meaning in Cummings' play, despite the fact that he refuses to help anyone discover what it is. (Notice that Cummings never says, "There is nothing to understand"; he merely says, "Don't *try* to understand it.") Twenty-five years later Cummings included *Him* among the works in which he finds his stance as a writer most clearly expressed.[12] A reader might almost put *Him* at the head of this list, for it is Cummings' sole work which is specifically concerned with the problems of the artist and his position *in society,* the artist and his relation to a loved one; and these are problems that must be of greatest concern to Cummings. In *Him* he not only poses the questions but gives a positive statement of the necessary position of the true artist who would also be a true lover.

"Our nonhero," as Cummings refers to Him, "calls himself an artist." As an artist, "One thing . . . does always concern this individual: fidelity to himself;" and yet "this incarnation of isolation is also a lover . . . a profoundly alive and supremely human being." Cummings has said, in commenting on the play, that there are "three mysteries: love, art, and selftranscendence or growing." [13] Confronted with what seem to him to be conflicting desires for self-transcendence through devotion to his art and through unselfishly surrendering at least part of himself in love for the heroine, Me, and afraid that the two means of self-transcendence are mutually exclusive, Him is forced to make a choice; and he is not able to make the one that would lead to a complete life. Cummings can say today that "we should go hugely astray in assuming that art was the only selftranscendence," [14] but twenty-five years ago his nonhero failed to make the proper synthesis of artist and lover and was forced to part from the lovely heroine. The inner turmoil of Him must have presented itself quite naturally to Cummings in dramatic form; he must have felt, and rightly, that the most forceful way of presenting such a conflict is to dramatize it.

Another attribute of the drama may have moved Cummings to work in that form—objectivity. Previously he had published an extremely subjective "miscalled novel," *The Enormous Room,* and a great deal of lyric poetry, which, of all literary forms, is likely to be most self-revealing. Cummings did not suddenly change his habit of self-expression; actually *Him,* like everything he has written, is intensely personal, but it is not apparently so. Even the playgoer who saw beyond the circus aspects of *Him* into its serious theme of the artist did not

[12] E. E. Cummings, i:*Six Nonlectures* (Cambridge, Mass., 1953), p. 4.
[13] *Ibid.*, pp. 81–82.
[14] *Ibid.*, p. 82.

necessarily see that the artist Cummings was writing about was himself, although at one point in the play he specifically says so.

Cummings, when *Him* was published, had perhaps reached a point of deep concern about the living of his own life. He must have wanted to clarify in his mind once and for all the way he, as an artist, should live: he had passed through the excitement of college discovery days, the disillusioning experiences of the First World War, the revolt against his family, America, and all tradition; and perhaps now he wanted to end the period of revolt and find the firm ground on which he would stand for the rest of his life. At any rate, in *Him* he stopped and took stock of himself. To move his problem far enough away from him so that he could look at it dispassionately, he embodied his concerns in a character whose very name suggests objectivity. There is a great deal of anguish in Cummings' play and a great deal of confusion, but by the simple device of creating a character and putting him on the stage he himself became, so to speak, a member of the audience, viewing the anguish and the confusion as if they were another man's and able to see where the other man failed. At the same time, by incorporating into his play a timeless statement of the necessary position of the artist, he gave the play a measure of universality higher than that achieved in any of his other major works.

Aside from the circus, burlesque, light and darkness, Negro choruses, bursting balloons, and fates, *Him* is a love story: the tale of two people, one of whom happens to be an artist, the other a woman meant to be the true or complete woman, who have had a deeply passionate affair; who find it difficult, as most people do, to understand each other; who fail, finally, as many people do, to resolve their differences of personality and fuse themselves into a perfect union. "Let it try to understand you," Cummings instructed; and that is just what the love story of *Him* and *Me* is trying to do; it tries to penetrate the heart of the vast "you" which is human beings, to understand it, and to show it to "you" as in a mirror. "This play of mine is all about mirrors," said *Him,* smiling (p. 29). *Him*'s play, which is the play Him's audience saw, is about the many mirrors in which the members of the audience could, if they wished, find themselves reflected.

That Him's play is a fantasy, the whole of it the expression of the dreams of Me while she is under ether, can account for and even make logical the wild scenes of the second act, the conception of the fates as three old women in rocking chairs, the long scene in the third act during which Me is exhibited before Him as one of nine circus freaks, and any other effect of fantastic motion with which Cummings cared to have fun. The device around which he built his play is the perfect one for his purposes: he is enabled to be as gay, mad, serious, or terrifying as he wishes and no one can say that what he is doing does not have verisimilitude, for who can say what would not be in a dream, or what meaning a dream would not have?

The spectator of Cummings' play who was used to modern literary devices might have guessed at once, after seeing Me being put under an anaesthetic, that the rest of the play was to be a dream sequence; and if he were attentive to Me's remarks in the first scene he would have guessed that she was receiving these ministrations because she was about to give birth to a child. Me is obviously full of anxiety and uncertainty and fears; one gathers that there are many unresolved difficulties between her and the father of her child. The scenes between Him and Me in the play, although they are part of her delirium, must be taken as largely the remembering kind of dream; she recapitulates what has happened between them to lead to their parting; and the spectator or reader who gives his full attention to these scenes can reconstruct the course of their affair, learn what they are like as people, and see himself perhaps reflected.

Nevertheless, even the most enthusiastic critics were somewhat disappointed by the total effect of *Him,* not only because of its inordinate length, but because the play lacked a sense of order, of development and climax, all of which would have been necessary to fuse with the brilliant vitality of the technique to make clear the lasting human significance of the work. The twenty lions were always on stage, these critics declared, but where were they orchestrated? There is no doubt that the unifying element for which the critics were searching was actually present in *Him,* but Cummings chose, by emphasizing his embellishments, to veil the main theme (the part that would require "understanding") so thoroughly that even an acute playgoer would be likely to miss it. Many of them failed to get even what "story" there was, and to realize that the first scene, showing Me being anaesthetized, was the key to the play.

At no time until Eric Bentley published an extended interpretation of *Him* in 1952 did anyone attempt to unravel in detail the meaning of each scene; and Bentley, who thought highly enough of *Him* to direct it at a drama festival he organized in Salzburg in 1950, confessed: "Even when I came to know the whole text almost by heart I still was not sure of the sequence of events in Him and Me's relationship: there is attraction, intimacy, estrangement, departure, return, but in what order, with what results?" [15] It seems, however, the order and the results of the Me-Him incidents *are* ascertainable

[15] Eric Bentley, *From the Modern Repertoire; Series Two* (Denver, 1952), p. 487.

from a study of the four scenes between the lovers that make up the heart of the play. Actually, as will be seen from the following synopsis, the four scenes are in proper chronlogical order.

On the first reading it might appear that there is no "sequence of events," since in each scene Me and Him merely occupy the room and talk to each other. The action is virtually limited to their sitting down on the sofa and standing up again, looking in the mirror or out the window; no one ever makes an entrance, no one ever leaves until a scene is over. The play, then, is obviously open to the charge of being talky; but the talk is so marvelously definitive that it lays bare the souls of two people as has hardly ever been done on the stage. Whether the conversations of Him and Me are partly remembered and re-created or whether they are entirely a product of Cummings' sensitive imagination, they are remarkable and unique in dramatic literature.

What Cummings often does is to scrap conventional dialogue, in which each speech serves a dramatic purpose, and to concentrate on the way in which people, especially a man and a woman, do talk when they are trying to communicate with each other. He is not afraid to "waste" a speech, to include a line that has no *raison d'être* except that it might have been said in such a situation. While other writers usually have their men and women reply logically to every remark of the other, Cummings realizes that people talk mainly to themselves. One person makes a remark, the other says something, which is often not a reply, the first then proceeds with his original thought, and so on. Even when two people are striving hardest to understand each other, their capacity to use words is often so limited and so faulty that the person spoken to, unless he intuitively listens beyond the words, is likely to misunderstand what has been told him. This is particularly true of two people who are intimate enough to try to tell each other more than surface pleasantries. At one point Him says to Me: "We are married"; and when she asks him, "Why do you say that?" he replies, "Isn't that the way married people are supposed to feel?" (p. 15)

As the play opens Him and Me, in the manner of married people or familiar lovers, are paying no attention to each other. Each is involved in an activity that typifies his own personality: Him is writing in a notebook while Me is fixing her hair before the invisible mirror. Me is voicing her own thoughts, which seem to be rather worried ones, while Him merely wants to go on writing in his notebook. She succeeds, however, in drawing him into a conversation, in which it is revealed that he is writing a play, that she is upset about their relationship because she feels that she can't be interested in what interests him, and that he feels they are "in love" and that's enough.

The beginning of this scene is actually quite conventional "first five minutes of the play" exposition, although Cummings chooses to distract from it by having Him recite some pure Dada dialogue. It is obvious that they *are* in love; Him is very tender with her, and they carry on the kind of bantering, loving conversation that reveals infinitely more than it says. Him is likely to let his high spirits run away with him and at any moment burst into some pure nonsense; Him uses this Dada talk not only as an expression of good spirits but also as the kind of protective covering so often used by shy, sensitive people.

Suddenly, however, in the midst of their banter, Him starts talking to himself about his problems as a playwright (which seem to be similar to Cummings' problems): "And here am I, patiently squeezing fourdimensional ideas into a twodimensional stage" (p. 12). Me comments lightly and he, not hearing her, goes on more seriously to talk about his conception of the artist (the "average 'painter' 'sculptor' . . ." speech quoted [on page 136]) and his feelings about himself as an artist:

> . . . I feel only one thing, I have only one conviction; it sits on three chairs in Heaven. Sometimes I look at it, with terror: it is such a perfect acrobat! The three chairs are three facts—it will quickly kick them out from under itself and will stand on air; and in that moment (because everyone will be disappointed) everyone will applaud. Meanwhile, some thousands of miles over everyone's head, over a billion empty faces, it rocks carefully and smilingly on three things, on three facts, on: I am an Artist, I am a Man, I am a Failure—it rocks and it swings and it smiles and it does not collapse tumble or die because it pays no attention to anything except itself. (*Passionately*) I feel, I am aware—every minute, every instant, I watch this trick, I am this trick, I sway—selfish and smiling and careful—above all the people. (*To himself*) And always I am repeating a simple and dark and little formula . . . always myself mutters and remutters a trivial colourless microscopic idiom—I breathe, and I swing; and I whisper: "An artist, a man, a failure, MUST PROCEED."
>
> (pp. 12–13)

The key word in the passage above is "selfish." Him does not use it in the sense of wanting everything for himself but of being concerned first and always with his own self-discovery as an artist. The artist, Cummings is saying, must consider himself (his art) first, or he will not be an artist. Him realizes the fantastic precariousness of the artist's position: he is as far above and different from other people as "a human being who balances three chairs, one on top of another, on a wire, eighty feet in air with no net underneath, and then climbs into the top chair, sits down, and begins to swing" (p. 12). But he realizes above all the necessity of proceeding, of paying no attention to anything except himself, even though he feels that as an artist he is, "except at timeless moments, a would-be artist." [16]

Him cannot, then, be concerned with Me, with the matter of whether their relationship will continue and whether they are suited for each other. To him she represents woman: loving, unthinking, feminine, the perfect complement for himself; and this is all he wants her to be. But although she realizes she is woman through and through, Me cannot accept herself simply as such but feels that she must try to figure out Him and what he is doing: "I dare say," she tells Him, "everything is interesting if you understand it" (p. 49). The paradox here is that Me is the one who *can* "understand," in Cummings' sense of the word, for understanding, as opposed to knowing, is intuitive, and is possible only for those persons who do not try to think through things but who instinctively "understand" by feeling.

At the end of this scene Cummings brings in one of his few props, which is to figure prominently and symbolically in the action: Him's battered old felt hat. In their next scene together (Act I, Scene IV) Him returns to the room, again wearing his hat. Me, obviously worrying about her pregnancy, soon begins sobbing and lies down on the sofa with her back to him. While she is there he goes to the mirror (which is now a tangible one on the left-hand wall); seems to be berating himself for his stupidity in making her unhappy (since he doesn't know about the pregnancy, he can't imagine what she is crying about); pulls an automatic out of his jacket pocket and puts it to his head. He does not, however, mean to commit suicide: he has been talking to his "other self" in the mirror, the self he thinks she loves; it is this man that he would like to kill, but he realizes that to do so would be impossible—that, should he pull the trigger, he would be killing not the man in the mirror but his real self.

Me catches sight of him with the pistol to his head, and, although she is at first terribly frightened, suddenly she relaxes utterly and, womanlike, makes an instantaneous change of mood. When Him asks how things are with her, she says, "It's wonderful with me" (p. 24); and one has the feeling that this is so because she is resigned to the coming of the baby and at the same time is beginning to accept him in the intuitive, unquestioning way that would enable them to be happy. But Him is unable to let things alone; when she starts to joke about the moth-eaten condition of his hat, he reveals that he has all along been thinking about the problem of who he is, the same problem that had concerned him as he inspected his face in the mirror. He says:

[16] *i:Six Nonlectures,* p. 81.

HIM: . . . Here's something queer: I can say "that's not my hat." And it's true.
ME: Is it, now: you mean you've given that dreadful old hat away to somebody? Not to me, I hope?
HIM: How could I give it away when it doesn't belong to me?
ME: You mean it's just a horrid old hat you've rented—by the year, I suppose?
HIM: Not rented. Borrowed.
ME: Well now, that's interesting: the dirty old thing—it belongs to somebody else, you mean?
HIM: It belongs . . . to a friend of ours.
ME: Of ours? That nasty old crooked disagreeable hat?
HIM: It's the Other Man's hat. (pp. 25–26)

He goes to the mirror and shows her the Other Man. ("O. Him." she says, when she sees what it is he is talking about.) He speaks to the Mirror Man: ". . . you yourself know that you're the only fellow she's ever seriously been really in love with . . ." (p. 27). Me is paying no attention; she is looking at herself in the mirror. Him suddenly picks up and puts on his hat, which has now become a symbol of his other self—the part that is not the artist, the part that he thinks Me is in love with. One sees that now he, too, is beginning to worry about love; he is no longer satisfied to think of himself solely as the artist but is beginning to see himself as two people, the artist and the man whom a woman could love. Just as Me has almost reached an equilibrium between herself, the baby, and Him—she is willing, one thinks, to go on or to leave him, whichever seems to be necessary—he begins to tilt the balance by wondering whether "an artist, a man, a failure" *is* all that he needs to know. As the scene ends, Me asks him about his play, and when she wants to know who the hero is he says, "This hero is called 'Mr. O. Him, the Man in the Mirror' " (p. 30).

Interposed between this scene and the beginning of Act III, when the lovers appear again, are the nine scenes of Act II, which Him is showing to Me as the play that Mr. O. Him would write to make money. Since this drama is much too wild for the conventional Mr. O. Him to have composed, it must be seen as satire, almost all the way through, on his respected kind of peephole theatre, as well as on various phases of American life or popular ideas or types of people. Cummings' sketches, although they added the intellectual dimension of satire to the burlesque skit, were by all accounts of the Provincetown performances as uproariously funny as anything the Minsky brothers were offering at that time.

Two scenes of the second act, the first and the last, are not comic. The first scene is the one in which the curtain rises on an empty stage and falls again; Him explains it as meaning "nothing, or rather: death" (p. 35). Each of scenes II through VIII represents a different kind of death: Scene II, for instance, shows three middle-aged drunks whose particular brand of fun—they play tennis and croquet without implements in the wee small hours—is a rather sad commentary on American maturity. Scene III is a long monologue by a soapbox orator trying to sell a cure-all for the disease of modern civilization. Scene IV is a comic broadside delivered against the whole question of "Who Am I?"; here Cummings is not only satirizing Him's preoccupation with his own identity but also making a parody on Eugene O'Neill's *The Great God Brown.* He goes on, in the Frankie and Johnny burlesque of folk drama, to satirize Comstock's attempts to regulate decency; to make fun of Freudian psychology in a scene involving an Englishman who carries his unconscious around in a trunk; to ridicule American Babbitts in a transatlantic liner scene; and to parody Shaw and Sherwood by making a burlesque skit out of Mussolini.

The last scene of the act, which is bitter rather than amusing, shows an insensitive American businessman in the midst of a European city in which everyone is starving. After a long dialogue between the American and a mob of almost-skeletons, the American is symbolically reborn when he throws to them a crust of black bread that he had been refusing to share. After the negativism of the first eight scenes, the act ends affirmatively with an event representing Cummings' conviction that giving is the foremost requirement for aliveness. In this scene the tone changes to one of bitterness, sadness, and finally redemption, as Cummings leads into the feelings and events of the third act; the American's rebirth foreshadows the birth of Me's child, which will occur at the end of the play.

Scene I of Act III starts out with a bit of action: Me and Him are sitting on the sofa; Him starts to caress her, to make love to her; she refuses by jumping up and screaming "No!" One sees at once that the lovers are no longer "as is"; something has happened to Me to make her decide to end the affair. Him doesn't want to accept her decision; he can't understand what has made her change, unless she has found someone else, which she denies. It is apparent that Me still loves him very much, but she tries to convince him that he isn't really in love with her:

> Only think, dear, that you and I have never been really in love. Think that I am not a bit the sort of person you think. Think that you fell in love with someone you invented—someone who wasn't me at all. Now you are trying to feel things; but that doesn't work, because the nicest things happen by themselves. (p. 93)

He says, "You are a very remarkable person—among other reasons, because you can make me afraid." She insists that she is not, doesn't want to be remarkable. She says:

> I know perfectly well it's foolish of you to waste your time with me, when there are people who will understand you. . . . You know what you really are, and really you're always sure of yourself; whereas I'm never sure. . . . You know you will go on, and all your life you've known. (p. 94)

To which Him replies:

> May I tell you a great secret? . . . All my life I've wondered if I am any good. If my head and my heart are made out of something firmer or more living than what I see everywhere covering itself with hats and with linen. (pp. 94–95)

And when Me says, "You mean I'm like everybody else," he responds fiercely:

> I mean that you have something which I supremely envy. That you are something which I supremely would like to discover: knowing that it exists in itself as I do not exist and as I never have existed. How do I know this? Because through you I have come to understand that whatever I may have been or may have done is mediocre. You have made me realize that in the course of living I have created several less or more interesting people—none of whom was myself. (pp. 95–96)

Me refuses, or is unable, to listen to what he is saying. "I know," she says, ". . . that you liked me for something else. . . . Tell me (as if I was dead and you were talking to someone else with your hands on her breasts) what there was, once, about me." And he can only reply, "I hoped that I had—perhaps—told you" (pp. 96–97). She tells him that her dream of him will live for a hundred years, and she dismisses him.

It is impossible to reproduce the sharp feeling of futility, of unnecessary suffering that Cummings conveys in this scene. The conversation is full of tragic illogicalities: her belief that he fell in love with someone he invented when actually the love he has dreamed of is herself: the perception of her "you know you will go on" and yet the blindness of her not being able to see that he too is unsure of himself; her thinking that he means she is like everyone else when he is trying to explain to her that she is unique; her final obtuseness is not knowing, still, what it is about her that appeals to him; and her stubbornness in keeping to the decision she has made.

In this scene the former positions of Him and Me are reversed. Where in the beginning he had been the one who was firm in his position, even though it may have been wrong, now he admits that he has never been sure who was really himself; he releases the uncertainty he has been holding back all his life and, without saying so, cries for her to help him. She, on the other hand, becomes more sure of herself. She has made a tremendously unselfish decision: to give up everything that she wants because she thinks it best for him to go on alone. She will not, now, ever tell him about the baby, for that would be asking him to stay with her, and this she has the strength not to do. Significantly, he does not leave the room until she indicates that he should. When he leaves, he is wearing his hat.

Before Me and Him appear on the stage again Cummings inserts the long grotesque scene at "Le Père Tranquille," the Paris nightclub, in which he depicts Americans abroad at their subhuman worst. Near the end of the scene Him wanders in, a little drunk and carrying a cabbage. Perhaps the nightmarish quality of this scene, in contrast to the rationality of the scenes Me is remembering, is due to the fact that this is an episode in Him's life which she can only imagine and about which her suppositions, even when awake, must have been fantastic. It is ironic that she conceives of the club as "Le Père Tranquille"; is she bitterly picturing Him enjoying himself in Paris while she, awaiting the birth of her baby, is quite the opposite of tranquil? Perhaps, too, the "cabbage" contributed to her unrest; she quite naturally thought that Him would have another woman in Paris.

As Scene V of Act III opens there is a conspicuous absence from the setting: Him's hat. In its place on the table is a vase of flowers. Since the hat has gone, one must assume that the owner of the hat, Mr. O. Him, is also absent; that Him has disposed of his troublesome Other Self once and for all. In the nightclub scene Him had remarked, "I was born day before yesterday" (p. 113), and while one was likely to pass over this remark as part of an obviously drunken conversation, now the absence of Mr. O. Him's hat and the presence of flowers—which in Cummings' work have always signified birth, growing, aliveness—lead one to suspect that the statement was significant. In commenting later on the play, Cummings said that Him is, throughout, "in his birth-agony." [17] While Him and Me's child is going through her actual birth-agony, Him is undergoing a symbolic one; he is being born into himself.

One learns that Him has not gone back to her on his return from Paris but that they had met quite by accident, in the rain, and had walked along together under his umbrella until they reached the door. Now they talk to each other, quite sadly; Me hints that her decision for them to part may be the wrong one: "—suppose I made a mistake; and it was the mistake of my life. And suppose: O suppose—I'm making it!" He tells her that she is ruining not her life, but his:

[17] [*i:Six Nonlectures,* p. 81.]

"You're wrong, quite wrong. It's the mistake of my life." They go on to talk obliquely, hinting, reaching out to each other:

ME: It may take two people to make a really beautiful mistake.
HIM: The nicest things happen by themselves.—Which reminds me: I had a dream only the other day. A very queer dream: may I tell it to you?

(p. 125)

He is implying that his dream is about one of those "nicest things"—one of those "really beautiful mistakes"—that happen by themselves. He relates that in the dream he was standing next to her in the darkness, in a room, and that she led him somewhere else in the room and pointed to something. Through the darkness he could not see but he "seemed to feel—another person:"

> When I could see, this other person's eyes and my eyes were looking at each other. Hers were big and new in the darkness. . . . Then I stooped a little lower and kissed her hair with my lips. . . . Then the darkness seemed to open: I know what I saw then: it was a piece of myself, a child in a crib, lying very quietly with her head in the middle of a biggish pillow, with her hands out of the blankets and crossing very quietly and with a doll in the keeping fingers of each hand. . . . So you and I together went out of this opened darkness where a part of ourselves somehow seemed to be lying—where something which had happened to us lay awake and in the softness held a girl doll and a boy doll.

(pp. 126–127)

After telling her the dream of their baby, Him searches the face of Me, hoping to find some response; one does not know whether he has actually dreamed it and is hoping it could be true, or whether he suspects Me's secret and is trying to tell her in this way that he very much wants their child. At any rate, in Me's face he finds "a different nothing;" he quickly goes to the mirror and throws his dream away. In a mood of complete sadness he says, "Hark. That was my dream which just fell into my soul and broke;" and Me replies, "I guess it took so long to fall because it was made of nothing." (p. 127)

Now that he sees there is no hope of changing her decision, he draws his protective skin of bumptiousness over him: "You have a bright idea," he says. But he is unable to keep it up; he desperately wants love now and he wants to find out why things have gone wrong, why Me rejects him:

HIM: . . . But if I ask you something, now, will you promise to answer truthfully? (*She shakes her head*) Because you can't?—Tell me; why can't you answer me truthfully, now?
ME (*Rising*): Now you want—truth?
HIM: With all my life: yes!

ME (*Advancing toward him slowly*): You wanted beauty once.
HIM (*Brokenly*): I believed that they were the same.
ME: You don't think so any longer?
HIM: I shall never believe that again.
Me (*Pauses, standing before him*): What will you believe?
HIM (*Bitterly*): That beauty has shut me from truth; that beauty has walls—is like this room, in which we are together for the last time, whose walls shut us from everything outside. (p. 130)

She asks him, "If what you are looking for is not here, why don't you go where it is?"—knowing, of course, that what he is looking for *is* there: both beauty and truth (for she sees that the walls do not shut them from the outside), both art and love. He replies brokenly, "In all directions I cannot move. . . . I cannot feel that everything has been a mistake. . . . How should what is desirable shut us entirely from what is?" Him's birth pangs, one sees, are not yet finished; he has grown enough to know that his former conception of art as all, and of love as possibly inimical to art, has been wrong; but he is not yet able to achieve complete self-transcendence by discovering how to make the synthesis of art and love. He knows that he must discover this, and he feels desperately that he must do it now.

Suddenly the scene ends as Me hears drumbeats (used as the symbol of labor pains), the stage begins to darken, and the drumbeats are drowned by swirling voices, out of which juts the raucous tone of a circus barker. His announcement of the freak show leads into the next scene, a depiction of a sideshow with freaks sitting on nine platforms arranged in a semicircle. At the center position the freak is hidden inside a curtained booth. At the climax of the barker's spiel he reaches the booth, which conceals "Princess Anankay"; when he pulls the curtain the princess turns out to be Me, draped in white and "holding in [her] arms a newborn babe at whom [she] looks fondly" (p. 144).[18] When he sees Me with the baby, Him, who is part of the crowd (since he is wearing his hat, one must assume that this is his Other Self, Mr. O. Him), utters a cry of terror.

The stage darkens and the last scene of the play begins with Me and Him occupying the same positions with respect to each other and to

[18] Cummings' freak-show name for Me is significant. In Greek mythology Ananke, or Necessity, is identified as the mother of the Morae, the three Fates, and she was supposed to have presided along with Tyche, goddess of fortune, over one's birth. Probably Cummings means here to indicate that the separation of Him and Me was to some degree the unavoidable working out of their separate destinies, she as a woman and mother, he as an artist and lover. In contrast to the three Weird Sisters, who might be thought of as burlesque fates, Princess Anankay is no doubt intended to inject the note of tragic determinism that is the characteristic of classical Grecian drama.

the room as at the end of their former scene; but the room, having made one revolution for each of the previous four scenes, has now described a complete circle, and the invisible wall between the players and the audience is again the one on which hangs the mirror. Him and Me take up their conversation where it had left off; a moment ago he had told her that the walls of the room "shut us from everything outside." Now Me tells him that the room has only three walls. He is astonished; he points in turn to the three visible walls and she admits that, yes each of these is a wall. Finally he points to the invisible mirror wall and asks her "What do you see there?" To which she replies:

ME: People.
HIM (*Starts*): What sort of people?
ME: Real People. And do you know what they're doing?
HIM (*Stares at her*): What are they doing?
ME (*Walking slowly upstage toward the door*): They're pretending that this room and you and I are real. (*At the door, turning, faces the audience.*)
HIM (*Standing in the middle of the room, whispers*): I wish I could believe this.
ME (*Smiles, shaking her head*): You can't.
HIM (*Staring at the invisible wall*): Why?
ME: Because this is true. (p. 145)

And the curtain falls. She is telling him that beauty has, indeed, shut him from the truth; that although beauty and truth—the room and the world outside—are open to each other, he is too preoccupied with himself, his artist's search for beauty, to be able to see through the mirror. What she doesn't realize is how desperately and genuinely he wants to do this and how she, with her unique aliveness and capacity for love, could be the path to his self-transcendence. Giving, to Cummings, has always been the primary indication of love; and Me, convinced that to Him art will always precede love and that love will, in truth, interfere with his single-mindedness as an artist, sacrifices herself—the possible joys of a life with Him and with their child—to the loneliness of his position as an artist. Tragically, Him had not wanted the sacrifice.

"Attraction, intimacy, estrangement, departure, return"—all are present, and in order, and with results. But the most enthusiastic champion of *Him* would admit that it takes more than even knowing the whole text almost by heart to make oneself sure of the order and the results. The play is saturated with difficulties and with confusions; it does not surrender its meaning on first sight or after a first reading. What makes the play a work of art is that the meaning is worth finding.

If one must read and re-read it in order to comprehend it fully, one is not wasting his time, for he will have been enriched when he understands.

There are many thorny problems in *Him,* some of which would trouble a spectator and not a reader, and vice versa. Even such an important symbol as the hat is used so sparingly and so subtly that a spectator is probably not aware of its importance. Actually the hat is one of the chief keys to understanding the play; with its help, the reader can figure out many puzzling details. But the spectator might not consider the hat at all except in the scene quoted above, when Me and Him discuss it. In the last act, when Him's hat is absent from the room and a vase of flowers is present, would a spectator realize that the "other self" had been disposed of and that Him had been re-born? In the circus scene, when Him, wearing his hat, screams at sight of the baby, would an observer realize instantly that it is Mr. O. Him who screams?

Cummings' wit, too, is too rapid and subtle to come across adequately on the stage. If one is not constantly aware of Him's predilection to explore the possibilities of metaphor and language, much of what he says appears to be meaningless. (It is an upsetting fact that some of what he says *is* meaningless; the reader must use his judgment and decide.) Not only quick wit but nonsense can be hilarious to Cummings, and if it is hard to tell what is nonsense and what is truth in disguise, perhaps that too is a reflection of life. Those of the 1928 spectators of *Him* who remember the play recall the fun of it, but many of them have only a fuzzy recollection of the love story, which, it is obvious to a reader, is the real meat of the work.

Surely when Cummings puts *Him* among the works by which he wants to be remembered, he does not do so for the cleverness of the second act sketches but for his presentation of the problem of the artist; and if the burlesque aspects of *Him* have an impact stronger than the serious theme, that must be considered a fault. It was not that the adverse critics felt that a disproportionate emphasis had resulted from Cummings' device for incorporating precision and movement into his play, but that they objected to the device itself. They were unable to see the propriety of combining burlesque with lyricism, buffoonery with near-tragedy.

Cummings, however, does not feel that life is a dichotomy of comedy and tragedy; for him the funny and the terrible are inextricably mixed, and the work of art that tries not merely to imitate life but to become life must embody this duality. He must have realized, too, that it would be necessary to provide a sizable portion of relief somewhere within the Me-Him story. Talk on the stage, even wonderful talk, cannot be carried on indefinitely; rather than falsify his conception of the love story by bringing in other characters or inventing artificial actions, he presented the affair of the lovers truly and provided a respite for the audience by leavening his seriousness with light-hearted recognition of the follies of modern life. Who can say whether the fault of wrong emphasis lies with Cummings for making his skits too humorous and his love affair too delicate, or with the audience for taking the line of least resistance?

It is unfortunate to think that the dazzling scenes of the second act, the new twist on the three fates, the wit and sheer exuberant nonsense of Him's dialogue become a hindrance to the understanding of the serious theme, or even that to some spectators they might appear to be the primary justification for the play and the love story merely another kind of nonsense. Perhaps it is a fault in the play, from the viewpoint of comprehending it, that Cummings chose to interlard his love story with skyrockets. But Cummings has said, " 'The chairs will all fall by themselves down from the wire;' and who catches or who doesn't catch them is none of his immortal business." [19] Ostensibly speaking about his character Him, Cummings is also referring to himself, to his own conviction that the artist works in the way that is peculiar to him and that he neither considers nor explains to his public. The meaning of *Him,* then, is difficult to see clearly through the blazing light of the exploding fireworks—which may have been set off intentionally in order to distract from the face of the person who is touching the match—but it is eminently worthwhile, after the glitter has been enjoyed, to turn one's eyes back to the life which remains.

Unique as it may seem, *Him* must not be thought of as an isolated example of experimentation in drama; Cummings' technique of viewing the world in terms of Me's peculiar state of mind, his heavy use of symbols, his magnifications and distortions of reality, look both forward and backward to similar dramatic productions. In America during the twenties expressionism was looked upon as the most promising technique for creating a more penetrating and imaginative insight into life than could be arrived at through the increasingly more realistic techniques prominent on the American stage. The little theatres, influenced to a large degree by European experiments in expressionistic drama, were giving American authors the chance to attempt new techniques. Eugene O'Neill's *The Emperor Jones* (1920), *The Hairy Ape* (1922), and *The Great God Brown* (1926), John Dos Passos' *The Garbage Man* (1925), Elmer Rice's *The Adding Machine* (1923), Kaufman and Connelly's *Beggar on Horseback* (1924), were some of the notable examples of American experimentation produced before *Him;* and all these were paralleled by similar European plays by

[19] *i:Six Nonlectures,* p. 82.

Strindberg, Kaiser, Toller, Cocteau, Marinetti, and others that were concurrently being produced on American stages.

Him was the only [full-length] play Cummings wrote; and, though the furor that arose when it was produced was great, it is doubtful that *Him* exerted any strong influence on the experimental dramatists who later continued the attempt to counteract the limitations of the realistic stage—Thornton Wilder in America, for example, or Auden, MacNeice, and Priestley in England. Direct influence is traceable in the work of only one playwright, Tennessee Williams, whose *Camino Real* comes close in technique and in purpose—a conscious revolt against the domination of the theatre by conventional realism—to duplicating the attributes of *Him*. Although *Camino Real* suffered, just as *Him* did, from critical disapprobation and lack of box office success, it is a play that means a great deal to Williams, just as *Him* represents to Cummings one of the works by which he wants to be remembered.

And again Cummings has expressed why this should be so: "With success, as any world or unworld comprehends it, he has essentially nothing to do." [20] Again Cummings is speaking of Him, of himself, of the artist—without quotation marks. The artist does not work for "success," nor is he deterred by failures. The play *Him* represents an artist's initiation into the world of creation; and, conjectural though it may seem, there is good basis for the inference that while Cummings wrote *Him* the possibility of artistic failure did exist in his mind despite the fact that he continually felt the necessity to proceed, to create. When one says, then, that there are failures in *Him,* one is merely expressing what Cummings candidly admits is to be expected of any artist.

The failures in *Him* are attributable to Cummings' sincere attempt to write for the stage in a way that would bring it alive. That he was genuinely writing for the stage and not composing a "book play" is shown by the fact that he sacrificed the peculiarities of style that characterize his poetry and other prose works, which depend so much for their effects upon the appearance of print on the page. The spoken word makes impossible the most unconventional typographical excursions that typify his poetry; and, though the language Cummings employs bears the stamp of his individuality, by and large the play is the most self-effacing major work he has produced.

Cummings has called *Him* a "quarter-of-a-century young play," and indeed it will be as fresh another quarter of a century from now as it is today. Perhaps before long the advertising slogans will have been forgotten, satires on folk dramas and Freudian psychology will lose

[20] *Ibid.*, p. 81.

their point, and experimental staging will become conventional, but the problem of the artist in society will be a vital one as long as there is society; and the convictions that Cummings has expressed about the artist—his fidelity to himself, his necessity to proceed, his unconcern with success or failure—will be as true in the unimaginable then as they have been in the chartable past or the living present; and, assuming the continuance of men and women and the continued possibility of love, Cummings' exploration of the "mysteries" of "love, art, and selftranscendence or growing" will remain a thoughtful probing into three things that are necessary for human greatness.

The Voyages[1] [*EIMI*]

by Paul Rosenfeld

People have pinned the oakleaves of the soldier on writer's coat-lapels, on Heine's, on Péguy's: the oakleaves of the soldier of Liberty. People also have honored poets for having fulfilled the Poet's ancient function, the guardianship of his nation's spiritual life. Rarely have their two actions been combined. They might be so in reference to E. E. Cummings. The reason mainly is *Eimi* (*I Am*), his scrupulously faithful record of his journey to the Soviets in 1931.

The Aristophanic *Eimi* does not have its like among Voyages. The book's typography and style to begin with are its author's invention and new toy. Frequently, at times ingeniously and gracefully, boldly oftentimes, the style distorts the normal syntax; the typography, the normal prose arrangement. These torsions often express extremely staccato feeling; sometimes legato feeling equally extreme. Their purpose in some instances is objective correlatives of sensations of complex motion. In others it is correlatives of motion betraying the stream of inner life in the object under observation:

> she slowly floated about a smallest room,she stepped crisply in and smoothly out of(handling the things, gifts,opening this which skilfully and touching this)sunlight . . . (p. 65)

Eimi besides incorporates an account of the event of the formation, on the road, of its author's most intimate experience of the Great Impellent of Things in a mass of perceptions preponderantly comic, wittily-ironic and sarcastic. Other Voyages also recount the event of the formation on the road of similar experiences of the ultimate impellent; similarly embed accounts of the stages by which they come to life in the mass of the perceptions of the author-voyagers. But none with so inimitable a mixture of satire, with hymnic praise and lyric expression of divine bliss. This, is cosmic comedy.

"The Voyages," by Paul Rosenfeld. From *The Harvard Wake*, 5 (*Cummings Number*—Spring 1946), 31–44 © 1946 by Harvard University. Reprinted by permission of Seymour Lawrence.

[1] An extract from a chapter in a piece of work in progress. [I do not find that this work was ever completed. —Editor's note.]

Eimi's main symbol is a grotesque personal accident, the absurd contradiction of an expectation by an event. It was the shock of travelling to the allegedly most advanced of lands, changing trains at the frontier, and stumbling into "a world of Was":

> inexorably has a magic wand been waved;miraculously did reality disintegrate:where am I? . . .—everything shoddy;everywhere dirt and cracked fingernails—guarded by 1 helplessly handsome implausibly immaculate soldier. Look! A rickety train,centuries BC. Tiny rednosed genial antique wasman,swallowed by outfit of patches,nods almost merrily as I climb cautiously aboard. . . . But tell,O tell me:where are we? Who lives? Who has died? (pp. 8–9)

There was a dining-car on the international train to Moscow:

> Diner:outmiracling of miracle. Deer in snow(a painting). Pink plant (real?) Customer without necktie(real). 3 roubles for 2 boot-air-broat(a half of a ham-and a half of a cheese-sandwich)1 bottle(vile)beer(but I was warned—Horrors Of Making The Mistake Of Expecting To Find In Russia What You Elsewhere Find Without Expecting)& 1 glass tea. Round bit of Austrian sits opposite;we talk finance,in Goethe which am beginning to remember. And where(O,where)may I be?—and the headwaiter(no less, probably more)has a bandaged 1stfinger. The tea,however, is good. The headwaiter sits,sullenly reading a perfectly blank piece of paper. The deer are in the snow,a painting;and everywhere exist motheaten flyspecked unnecessaries of ultraornamentation(if only everything did smell like a stableor something smelled like a stable;but something and everywhere distinctly don't)and nobody seems anything except lonesome;hideously lonesome in hideousness,in rundownness, in outatthe heelness,in neglectedness,in strictly omnipotent whichnessandwhatness. Ah well,the tea is excellent. But everybody's actually elsewhere. . . . Elsewhere being where? Perhaps in Russia—for obviously this whateveritis or defunct-Ritz-on-square-wheels isn't anywhere or anything,isn't Russia, isn't a diningcar,isn't(incredibly enough)Isn't. Never hath been begotten, never shall be conceived,such head-and such waiter;such Deer and such In Snow:such nonlife and such undeath and such grim prolifically cruel most infraSuch (pp. 9–10)

Almost the whole is comic surprise, astonishment, amazement. Accurate in its evocation of the great whiffy, dusty barracks of Moscow, Kiev and Odessa, the Russia of Leninism and its weird, tormented, pathetic, sometimes beautiful inhabitants, with its new style *Eimi* pictures a marvellous but incoherent, dislocated world. Here is Lenin's tomb

> a rigid pyramidal composition of blocks;an impurely mathematical game of edges:not quite cruelly a cubic cerebration—equally glamourless and emphatic,withal childish . . . perhaps the architectural equivalent for "boo!—I scared you that time!"(hard by are buried martyrs) (p. 25)

To characterize this "realm of machine-tortured ideal-ridden ghosts" Cummings softly has likened it to that of the beginning of Dante's Dream-Voyage: indeed he has represented it with a comic re-individuation of *The Divine Comedy.* As in the *Inferno,* the Essence of Evil at first is hidden from our eyes. We merely encounter its victims "writhing in the ridiculous tortures of a perverted Nature." We meet Virgil who comes from Cambridge and happily vanishes as Beatrice, who is a lovely American, arrives. There are Geryons of propaganda and Malebolges of ratoinization [sic].[2] We stumble into an arsenal, not that of mediaeval Venice but of contemporary Odessa. We leave Purgatory by a sea-change across the Black Seas which "makes us seafellow of Glaucus and the other gods." Appears the Paradiso relative to the hell of "cruelly superficial categories of perfection, sickly mediocrities, fanatical compulsions, definitions." It is the ordinary liberties of life: space above Stamboul becomes a vault sown with "the sun and the other stars." In all his splendor the Author of the Show reveals himself. And, lo! his face is as our own.

To find the closest relative to Cummings' book we have indeed to look across the boundary of Voyages toward the comedies of Aristophanes. There we find amalgams of a mirth-provoking, astonishing matter and religious revelation not dissimilar to that in *Eimi;* similar combination of surprises of language and incident and expressions of sympathy for physical nature; exuberant, self-swayed fantasy, ridiculization of the visionary utopias of political theorists, Attic melody, the statements of a prudent far-seeing moralist. Cummings, this is to say, is one of the drolls who have seen. We feel him fundamentally a poetic merrimaker radiating gaiety with work in prose and verse as a blond poll diffuses light; the primitive comedian, with the perpetual ticklishness, pell-mell of negative and affirmative emotions, love of astonishment, self-dramatizing child-likeness, passion for fun. The majority of his lyrics, the very ones in the tone of pathos, make love:

> if i should sleep with a lady called death
> get another man with firmer lips
> to take your new mouth in his teeth
> (hips pumping pleasure into hips). (121: X)

Every feeling of his bursts spontaneously into exaggeration. He plays amusedly with the associations of his fancy; throws off his gaiety and satire, in his mature prose and verse at least, in concise anecdotes and epigrams, gracefully pointed, metallically hard of edge.

It is that, while giving him contact with the incongruities and ab-

[2] [This reads as it does in the original publication. I would guess that the word is either "rationalization" or "ratiocination." —Editor's note.]

surdities of existence—its thorough mixtures of ugliness with beauty, sublimity with ridiculousness, the acute difference between the actual and the desirable, between human pretense and performance—simultaneously his merriment like an ecstacy has made him too the medium of the sublimities. By temperament he is a mystic.

One great dissimilarity exists to be sure between the comedies of the old Ionian pessimist and *Eimi*. The impellent unveiled by the former is a deep-lying Mephistophelian, destructive one: in Heine's phrase a *Weltvernichtungsidee* the source of "human disappointments, sorrows, disgusts." That unveiled by *Eimi* is the ultimate object of the Idealist vision, the Author of Liberty; the origin not only of the fact that we ourselves are inwardly impelled and impelled to express and fulfill our own inherent life-forms, but equally of the fact that we are blessed only in proportion to the degree to which we derive ideal springs of conduct from within our own consciousness; in fine, of the fact that only a society of sovereign individuals can be harmonious.

For the Idealist, the Divinity made the world to be outside Divinity; and the activity in it is not completely God's. Complete determinism, predestination are absent from the world; Law by no means thoroughly rules it. It is impelled from within by the Ideas, its spiritual content, the provisions of this benevolent God; [it] floats of its own force almost like an architecture in space; and Man is able to interfere with its energies. Curiously enough, this ability of his flows from the very fact that to a pronounced degree Man shares in the nature of God. Man's life extends to the beginning of creation; and "within him is the soul of the whole, the wise silence, the universal beauty, to which every part and particle is equally related, the eternal One"; and the individual soul mingles with the universal soul, whose beatitude is accessible to us. Now, one of the attributes of God is freedom. God cannot be compelled; He was not compelled; He acted through internal necessity the result of His essential Being, which was love. And Man shares in God's freedom in enjoying an independence from his very Maker, since he has a dependent root in Nature and yet is independent of her, for the Divine is awake in him. Man thus need not be compelled by anything outside himself, can act by the law of his own being; and faced with an infinite universe and endowed with the power of choice, can mar or make . . . In ignorance of the Ideas and hatred of God—as the theologians would say, in Self-will—he can for example desire to rival God, desire that he himself become the creative basis, the "whole thing" and rule over things. As we might say, he can remain whole in a childhood or even prenatal concept rather than adjust to the natural situation where opposites are accepted as complemental. Or in self-consciousness, consciousness of the Ideas, the inner impellents, Man can accept his limitations, the perhaps very different forces inside various sorts and degrees of men, and struggling to work out his own form, can bring them into some sort of order; adjust other things to himself and himself to other things. Ignorance of the Ideas and denial of God, however, is self-destruction. Self-consciousness on the other hand is junior partnership with God. It is participation in creation.

One is tempted to consider this Idealistic world-picture an archetype in E. E. Cummings' mind; pressing there for the opportunity to release itself and become cosmos; that in some way it ever is in search of the comic objects which permit themselves to be explained in its terms. The appearances are this picture may be his paternal inheritance. Cummings' charming poem about his father, "my father moved through dooms of love," goes far to make Idealism seem to have been the paternal philosophy. It shows the Unitarian divine "scorning the pomp of must and shall;" cries:

then let men kill which cannot share
let blood and flesh be mud and mire,
scheming imagine,passion willed,
freedom a drug that's bought and sold. . . .

—i say though hate were why men breathe—
because my father lived his soul
love is the whole and more than all (373–5: 34)

So too does this equally charming extract from a personal letter of the poet's:

> I wot not how to answer your query about my father. He was a New Hampshire man, 6 foot 2, a crack shot & a famous fly-fisherman & a firstrate sailor (his sloop was named The Actress) & a woodsman who could find his way through forests primeval without a compass & a canoeist who'd stillpaddle you up to a deer without ruffling the surface of a pond & an ornithologist & taxidermist & (when he gave up hunting) an expert photographer (the best I've ever seen) & an actor who portrayed Julius Caesar in Sanders Theatre & a painter (both in oils and watercolours) & a better carpenter than any professional & an architect who designed his own houses before building them & (when he liked) a plumber who just for the fun of it installed all his own waterworks & (while at Harvard) a teacher with small use for professors—by whom (Royce, Lanman, Taussig, etc.) we were literally surrounded (but not defeated)—& later (at Doctor Hale's socalled South Congregational really Unitarian church) a preacher who announced, during the last war, that the Gott Mit Uns boys were in error since the only thing which mattered was for man to be on God's side (& one beautiful Sunday in Spring remarked from the pulpit that he couldn't understand why anyone had

> come to hear him on such a day) & horribly shocked his pewholders by crying "the Kingdom of Heaven is no spiritual roofgarden: it's inside you" & my father had the first telephone in Cambridge & (long before any Model T Ford) he piloted an Orient Buckboard with Friction Drive produced by the Waltham watch company & my father sent me to a certain public school because its principal was a gentle immense coal-black negress & when he became a diplomat (for World Peace) he gave me and my friends a tremendous party up in a tree at Sceaux Robinson & my father was a servant of the people who fought Boston's biggest and crookedest politician fiercely all day & a few evenings later sat down with him cheerfully at the Rotary Club & my father's voice was so magnificent that he was called on to impersonate God speaking from Beacon Hill (he was heard all over the common) & my father gave me Plato's metaphor of the cave with my mother's milk.[3]

Of course Idealism existed in his special cultural milieu. He saw the light as an American, and here all are told early that "we are free." Washington, we are told, "set us free" by driving out the King. What is important: the law forbids schoolmasters physically to coerce their pupils; and it is the child that is reared with gentleness, whose Idea never has been broken, that wishes neither to rule nor to be ruled. Cummings moreover was born on the little fleck of earth about Massachusetts Bay, and the people of "Channing, Emerson and Parker" specially asserted the existence and the possibility of human freedom:

> Our fathers' God, to Thee,
> Author of Liberty,
> To Thee we sing!

Most significantly on one occasion previous to the composition of *Eimi,* Cummings had taken up a challenge delivered to Idealism and sought to read the deeper secret of things in Idealist terms and project Idealism's world-picture through objective perceptions.

This was the event of the composition of his first crisply fresh contribution to literature, *The Enormous Room,* a comic and fanciful Voyage in many respects the child [who is] the father of *Eimi.* Its main symbol too is a grotesque personal accident, the absurd contradiction of an expectation by an event: it was the misadventure of the author when, green from Havard Yard, he went to France in the first years of World War I and landed in a concentration camp. Ultimately this was the adventure of the born poet who, yearning for perfection, awakens to find himself in an incoherent, dislocated world and one of a motley, by no means entirely unhappy crowd of helpless, ragged, suspect, or even partly insane individuals called artists: lost souls all; perhaps "found" souls. As in *Eimi,* everything in *The Enormous Room*

[3] [Cummings reprinted this letter in *i:Six Nonlectures,* pp. 8–9. —Editor's note.]

is surprise, astonishment, amazement. Accurate in its evocation of the concentration-camp of La Ferté Macé—a concentration-camp that was to Hitler's as France is to Germany, as the civilization of 1914 was to that of 1940; building it up in definite outlines, brick on brick, stench on stench in all its squalid color, with its pathetic sometimes beautiful prisoners, the book took us through a marvellous but incoherent, dislocated world. Odd and inordinate accidents continually befell us. We endured abrupt personal transformations and changes of scene, unpredictable vicissitudes of fortune. We encountered personages with peculiar or morbid idiosyncrasies of shape or disposition. Unsuspected edges of flint led 'round corners to equally unsuspected surfaces of silk. A gun was shoved against our ribs: we were transformed from Norton-Harjes ambulance chauffers into criminals and led away to dungeons; small Charlie-Chaplinesque figures staggering under heavy loads. Objects behaved like monkey-men abrupt and ludicrous of movement, and people like whirring mechanisms and terrible wound-up toys.

The prose in *The Enormous Room* teemed with excited over-statements, ingenious exaggerations:

> The smile was ample and black. You saw through it into the back of her neck— (p. 162)

> an incoherent personage enveloped in a buffoonery of amazing rags and patches, with a shabby head on which excited wisps of dirty hair stood upright in excitement— (p. 65)

As in the fairy-tale world, things had personalities and behaved as personalities do.

> Like a sharp, black, mechanical cry in the spongy organism of gloom stood the coarse and sudden sculpture of his torment; the big mouth of night carefully spurted the angular actual language of his martyred body. I had seen him before in the dream of some medieval saint with a thief sagging on either side, surrounded by crisp angels. To-night he was alone; save for myself, and the moon's minute flower pushing between slabs of fractured cloud. (p. 54)

> The shrinking light which my guide held had become suddenly minute; it was beating, senseless and futile, with shrill fists upon a thick enormous moisture of gloom. To the left and right through lean oblongs of stained glass burst dirty burglars of moonlight. (p. 58)

The very main defect of *Eimi* forecast itself, for here as there after a swift inception the movement stagnated a little, milled about, and only toward the end recovered supervisibility and line. But not only the defect of *Eimi*: as we have said the attitude of *Eimi* cast its shadow before it in *The Enormous Room*. The great object of satire in this voyage is of course the wartime *gouvernement Français*, the hysterical jailor of the author and the other suspects in La Ferté Macé; and the wartime *gouvernement Français*, of course, was nothing if not a symbol of the abhorred and fatal self-will, the desire of the part to play the whole of things, to compel obedience, to suppress every opposition. Half the dislocation in the squalid scenes through which we pass is connected with its despotism and oppression. Life's intensity on the other hand is associated with its antithesis, with the object whose celebration and affirmation composed the book's last page:

> My God, what an ugly island. Hope we don't stay here long. All the red-bloods first-class much excited about land. Damned ugly, I think.
>
> Hullo.
>
> The tall, impossibly tall, incomparably tall, city shoulderingly upward into hard sunlight leaned a little through the octaves of its parallel edges, leaningly strode upward into firm, hard, snowy sunlight; the noises of America nearingly throbbed with smokes and hurrying dots which are men and which are women and which are things new and curious and hard and strange and vibrant and immense, lifting with a great ondulous stride firmly into immortal sunlight. . . . (pp. 331–32)

What is herewith lyrically celebrated and embraced not only is freedom in the sense of personal sovereignty. At the base it is the political, philosophical, religious attitude with which the author associates man's capacity for intensity and most perfect fulfillment of his life-form, and his own will to live his own clamorous soul and lift his inner life "firmly into immortal sunlight." To be sure in this book we remain on the level of a semi-conscious reading of the deeper secrets. The attentive, however, will recognize the whole picture betokened by the opaque symbols.

Suddenly, in the years about the composition of *Eimi*, in the financially rotten, ruined United States of the early 1930's, Cummings like every other man of letters was surrounded by Comrades and Fellow-Travellers: persons who, abandoning Idealism, fought it in the Revolution. The massive Swing to the Left had occurred among litterateurs, and the weapon of assault was a Marxism, which denies the independence of the world from God, the existence of the Ideals and the spiritual content of life. Man, claims Marxism, is determined from without. The activity of the world entirely is determined by a mysterious power called History. The ideal merely is "the material world reflected by the human mind and translated into forms of thought." Man entirely is a means to the self-realization of History; events ultimately are independent of him. Saving that he help realize History, he is eternally cast out. History in this era was about to realize the Socialist State, the society of individuals without property and devoid of the profit-motive. . . . The motivation of humanity is economic and functional. The world is a battle between classes, the possessing and the proletarian. Ideas have been produced in the interests of the battling classes; artists all were propagandists, interested purveyors of doctrine, mainly in the pay of the ruling classes. One of these doctrines was the religion of love. Love, declared V. F. Calverton, one of the spokesmen of the Left, was "for the bourgeoisie; hate was the instrument of the proletariat." Unless they helped realize the Socialist State, artists were damned. The realization of this had begun in Russia; and "spring was nowhere else."

Cummings for his part would seem to have met this phenomenon at its source. In *Eimi* he records an occasion when in Moscow he

> tumbled into exactly 180 minutes of "materialist dialectic" which(among other miracles)makes sun while hay shines,opens the key of life with the lock of science,juggles(without dropping)the unworld the unflesh and the undevil,and justifies from soup to nuts the ways of Marx to man.
> (p. 83)

and relays several "feasts from which crumb of reason." Part of Communistic propaganda was the allurement of visitors to Russia with pictures ranging from the plentifulness of vintage wines from the cellars of the aristocrats to pictures of the new bloom of the theatre-arts. The latter, Cummings pretends, allured himself; probably the mirage had been drawn for him by members of the circle of his friend Louis Aragon. There then, in Marxism, the Swing to the Left, Leninist Russia, as we see it, he found challenging material exquisitely susceptible of comic and satiric interpretation in the terms of Idealism and corroborating its world-picture. . . . The years succeeding the composition of *The Enormous Room* meanwhile had seen the author's growth of insight. They were the years in which he wrote the play *Him,* itself a picture of the advent of self-consciousness in a hero sportingly and ingeniously engaged in battling an erotic fate; incidentally, a stylization of what in all probability is the debased survivor of the Aristophanic Comedy, the Burlesque Show - - - notable for the skill [with] which the author manages and organizes opposing comic-burlesque and romantic-sentimental insights. Cummings besides was in the period of life when consciousness of the profounder psyche, of its correspondence with God, and the unity of visible nature and the invisible soul. . . . Cosmic Consciousness in Maurice Roucke's famous phrase . . . overwhelmingly makes its appearance. Bit by bit, then, while ironically he observed "the soul of man under Sovietism" the total interior world-picture worked itself out into clarity in him: the expression, confession, affirmation of Idealism that became *Eimi.* Bit by bit the ultimate impellent of things that is Idealism's center revealed himself, in constructive memories, in lyrical imaginings in words, in feeling streaming in from skies: possibly the insurmountable conclusion, sum, basis of all Ideas, "the Idea of the Good;" probably the benevolent Deity whose provision the Ideas are - - - the source of the free, ultimately indefeasible spark of divinity lodged in the being of each one of us; knowledge of whom almost is salvation. For Cummings calls this impellent He and by the ancient name I AM. Comically seen at first as

> a certain Mr. Cosmic Ray,Mary mother of Joshua ben Lenin ben Joseph ben Franklin ben Stalin ben Roosevelt ben Big Ben ben Big Stick ben Evolent ben Lightningrod— (p. 52)

caught during another conversation on the wing in a flash of constructive memory

> Over and over again,during those hours . . . [I] find myself standing before A Portrait Of The Artist As A Young Man;watching a certain Jesuit father move heaven and earth to persuade a certain Stephen Daedalus that he,Stephen, is fit for the holy task . . . which Stephen(forever, but only after meditation)knows is not true:only knows because of something around(under throughout behind above)him,or which is always the artist;his destiny. (p. 87)

apprehended again as

> the giving walls of this single house—only whose ceiling and whose floors frame the Self's full perfect doom of imperfection:doom untranslatable, doom of which all exhortations constitute unplastic parodies— (pp. 187–88)

confessed in still another argument

> "Actually,the world is a part of me. And—I'll egocentrically tell the world —a very small part" (p. 212)

in Kiev it was embraced with hymnic praise

> The churches are drowning with stars,everywhere stars blossom,frank and gold and keen. Among these starry miracles time stops,lives a silence which thought cannot capture. Now(touched by a reasonance of sexually celestial forms)the little murdered adventure called Humanity becomes a selfless symbol(the doomed assertion of impermanence recoils;falters the loud insignificant intrusion)whereas these stars eternally and all their cathedrals march to some harmony beyond themselves(here the lone star of socialism dies;defeated by all stars) (p. 265)

Still clearer in Constantinople at the ecstatic moment before debarcation at sundown, it was accompanied by feelings of divine bliss

> . . . O, now everything begins
> Everything expands increasing now even the air celebrates(the sky's building within the sky a steep incredi"

ble pleasure out of what far Forms unbelievable;springs a sun,but no mere world:1 atom—of blood of life of all)every-and-thing & opens lifting quietly rising growing-and-upward infinitely opening & and throughout coolness alive always deepening growing beside wonder and height rising among promise and dream lifting upon immeasurable

whereless
silence. . . .
look—
(new Stars!Stars not-of-heaven awfully
begin; here
multiplying suddenly become the
very arising magically
is:looms!a
. . . now . . .

allblossoming finite Firmament of throbbing frenzied Ifs of leaping fiercely Whys. Now insane structure of To Be;finally sprouting terror ecstasy and semblance—now a profound a trivial an architecture of mortality—moves at us like a

Yes)unfaltering
& toward our ghostship comes,inhabited by thousands upon millions of manlights,the World (pp. 376–77)

Finally on the Orient Express to Paris it rapturously became a possession to the rhythm of the carriage-wheels

& "metal steed,very treacherously wherefrom descending the promiscuous urbans plundered rus!through you I greet all itgods. And I tell them of a singular He,indivisible or individual,one Being natural or unafraid, for whom exists no sign no path no distance and no time. Strutcringing inexistence!through you I greet all cruely enslaving deities of perfection. And I tell them of a totally adventuring Is Who breathes,not hope and not despair, but timeless deep unspace—I prophesy to handless them that they shall fall by His hand,even by the hand of Poietes;for guilt may not cancel instinct and logic defeat wish,nor shall tasteless hate obtain against the fragrance of amazement. Unspontaneous sterility!through docile you I greet all deathless,all the not alive,wheelgods of real. And I tell them of a million or a trillion selves,musically which are one always who cannot perish;I prophesy to faultless them a moving within feelfully Himself Artist,Whose will is dream,only Whose language is silence—

(p. 418)

Clearing, the philosophy penetrated the objective perceptions of the trip. They were the pervasion of life, in this dictatorship summoned into being by the cry "You have nothing to lose but your chains!", by the very antithesis of intensity: a universal sluggishness, an ineptitude monumental in proportions, "bandaged firstfingers," a deadly resignation; the prevalence of theorists and rationalizers; the prevalence of desire to interfere with other people, those in especial with spontaneity and liberty of conscience and of act. Everywhere, the expressions of instincts that had felt interfering hands. Significantly the rationalizations and desire to interfere with others showed itself nowhere more strongly than in the behaviour of a certain poor devil of a Comrade who in the name of the Classless Society had to endure his wife's display of her love-affairs at his board. No self-consciousness: not even awareness of "Our Lord Sigmund Freud." Their secret was "a joyless experiment in force and fear" (p. 49). They were effects of a desire of a part—an individual, a class, a nation—to be the creative basis, the "whole thing," to rival God Himself; the Titanic egotism which rationalizes itself by claiming that all things are predestined to fulfill its wishes; the Egotism born of self-unconsciousness. Life's intensity was elsewhere. It existed in a hurly-burly as savage as that of Constantinople, as extravagant as that of the USA. Efficiency and grace, perspicuity and brilliance were elsewhere. They existed in a survivor of the old Russia such as the personage distinguished as "the flower-buyer"; in individualistic rebels such as The Noo Inglundur of Odessa; in the sceptical and ironic American spectators of the "joyless experiment in force and fear." It danced in all that possessed a fierce intolerance of dictation and constraint; a profound unwillingness to act in accordance with any law other than that of the inner being; an equal reluctance to impose force upon Nature or any of her creatures. It danced, as it dances in all whose spirit at a first glance might seem to be indifferent to natural injustices, imperfections, waste; tolerant of disorder and lawlessness, incapable of discipline of any sort; but which really is the spirit at once of independence and strict and conscientious discipline in the formation of personality; of self-reliance and reverence of something within the self not in our power, something we are not but that is ourselves and impenetrable, inflexible, supernormal; the spirit of acceptance along with our own selves of the selves of others and joyous subjection to the Universal Will.

The equilibration of the Swing to the Left, *Eimi* was met with almost total silence, and the fewest of readers know the book. But, to have mocked a slave-religion, comically, lyrically, exuberantly, emotionally above all; to have affirmed impulse and its belief, is to have fought for their salvation in these US., perhaps the world. A fearless deed, *Eimi;* the great poetic deed of its decade, and one of the American books!

E. E. Cummings and His Fathers [*i:Six Nonlectures*]

by Alfred Kazin

The Charles Eliot Norton Professorship at Harvard is awarded each year to a distinguished modern writer, composer, or critic of the fine arts. For the academic year 1952–53, the Norton Professor was E. E. Cummings, Harvard '15, who told his delighted audience that "I haven't the remotest intention of posing as a lecturer," [1] and then proceeded, in his highly personal style, to summarize his life and opinions and to campaign for love, beauty, and individuality by reading from his own works and from no one else more contemporary than Dante, Chaucer, Shakespeare, Donne, Wordsworth, and Swinburne. His talks have now been published, by the Harvard University Press, under the inevitable title of *i:Six Nonlectures.*

Although Cummings considers himself a dangerous crank and the last individualist of our collectivist and totalitarian century, he is probably regarded by most people who read him—and certainly by those who don't—as a funnyman, a great card, a deliberate showman. This is the reputation of many leading poets now, for although they naturally complain of the age, on a platform they tend to become the very incarnation of literature, the only literary performers around who recall such famous actors as Dickens and Mark Twain. But Dickens and Mark Twain pretended to play characters from their own works, to audiences that doted on these books. Today a poet like Cummings simply plays himself, in the role that is always, provokingly and unerringly, that of the "poet"—the last of the clowns, the one fool left with innocence or brass enough to stand up before a crowd, bare his heart, and sass the age. Many a literary audience in this country, composed of people as liberal as anyone else, has roared with laughter when Cummings has denounced trade unions as slavery or has said

"E. E. Cummings and His Fathers," by Alfred Kazin. From *The New Yorker,* 24, no. 46 (January 2, 1954), 57–59.

[1] [*i:Six Nonlectures,* p. 3. —Editor's note.]

things about the New Deal that, if found on the editorial page of a newspaper, would reduce this audience to despair. It is not always the poetry that comes through; it is the poet himself—in the marvellous, the ineradicable difference from other people that gets him to be a poet at all. The result is that his opinions are regarded not even as quaint but as the portable furniture that is part of his public performance. There must be thousands of people in this country who can never look at Cummings' name in lower-case type without seeing in him what their grandfathers saw in Mark Twain or Mr. Dooley.

Cummings has certainly assisted in making this reputation. He has done this by creating a style whose trademark is by now as instantly recognizable as an automobile's—by giving to its very appearance on the page the instant feel of spontaneity, of lyric bitterness against the mob age; by constantly unhorsing all words sacred to our conformism and replacing them with private words; by the living contrasts within a language that is full of abstractions but that is always coming apart at the seams, slangy and mock-important. A lifelong addict of the circus, vaudeville, and burlesque, Cummings loves to puncture words so that he can fling their stale rhetoric like straw all over the floor of his circus tent, to take a pompous stance that collapses under him, to come out with an ad-lib that seems positively to stagger him. But the very point of all this is that it occurs within a vocabulary that is essentially abstract and romantic, and that the performance is by a man who remains always aloof, whose invocation of love, spring, roses, balloons, and the free human heart stems from a permanent mistrust of any audience.

This duality of the traditionalist and the clown, of the self-consciously arrogant individualist and the slapstick artist, makes up Cummings' world, and it is this that gives special interest to the autobiographical sections of a book that otherwise, though as delightful as anything he has ever written, tends to lapse into defensive quotations from his own writings and opinions. For in coming to Harvard he came back to his own—to the town he was born in, to the university whose intellectual inheritance he so particularly represents, to the memory of his father, a Boston minister and onetime Harvard instructor, whose influence is so dominant in his best work. The remarkably exalted memories Cummings gives us of his Cambridge boyhood—his loving, characteristically idyllic picture of the big house in Cambridge; of the trees; of the great English poems his mother copied into a little book and read to him; of William James, who introduced his parents to each other; of Josiah Royce, who introduced him to the beauties of the English sonnet—all this, which is no less a fairy tale, as Cummings tells it, for being true, is the background of his familiar opposition between the idyllic past and the New York world in which he has to live. Cummings is not merely a traditionalist in the mold of so many American poets, a mold that recalls those other American inventors and originals, such as Ford and Edison and Lindbergh, who are forever trying to reclaim the past their own feats have changed; he is the personification of the old transcendentalist passion for abstract ideals. In his knowingness with words, in his passion for Greek and Latin, he takes one back to Emerson and Thoreau, who were perpetually pulling words apart to illustrate their lost spiritual meaning. Underneath the slapstick and the typographical squiggles, Cummings likes to play with words so that he can show the ideals they once referred to—and this always with the same admonitory, didactic intent and much of Thoreau's shrewd emphasis on his own singularity.

It is these old traits that give such delightfulness, and occasionally something of his hoped-for disagreeableness, to Cummings' "egocentricity," which he pretends in these lectures to apologize for yet which is actually, of course, not a subjective or narcissistic quality at all but the very heart of his Protestant and fiercely individualistic tradition. And certainly that tradition has in no recent literature received such tributes as Cummings pays here to his father, who was killed when a railroad train ran into his car. One of Cummings' best poems is called "my father moved through dooms of love" (373–5: 34), in which the dead man's probity, lovingness, and joyfulness are so achingly contrasted with the lives of most men that by the time the poem swells to its triumphant conclusion he has taken on virtually the attributes of Christ. In this book, Cummings quotes an old letter of his, which reported (and it is interesting to note the rush of these details) that his father "was a New Hampshire man. . . ." [2]

In the new American scriptures, fathers don't count. But Cummings' cult of his father is, precisely because it will strike many Americans as wholly unreal, the clue to all that makes Cummings so elusive and uncharacteristic a figure today. For just as the occasional frivolousness of his poetry is irritating because it is *not* gay, because it is snobbish and querulous and self-consciously forlorn in its distance from the great urban mob he dislikes, so the nobility and elevation of his poetry—which has become steadily more solid, more experimental and moving—is unreal to many people because of the positive way in which he flings the *true* tradition in our faces with an air that betrays his confidence that he will not be understood.

Cummings' wit always starts from the same tone in which Thoreau said that "I should not talk so much about myself if there were anybody else whom I knew as well." It is both a conscious insulation of

[2] [The remainder of the quotation is omitted here; it is given in full on pp. 160–61. —Editor's note.]

his "eccentricity" and an exploitation of his role. But Emerson and Thoreau, even in the rosy haze of transcendentalism, were resolute thinkers, provokers of disorder, revolutionaries who were always working on the minds of their contemporaries; Cummings' recourse is not to the present, to the opportunities of the age, but to the past. And that past has now become so ideal, and the mildly bawdy satires he used to write against the Cambridge ladies of yesteryear have yielded to such an ecstasy of provincial self-approval, that we find him in these lectures openly pitying his audience because it did not have the good sense to be born in his father's house, and quoting never from his contemporaries but only from the familiar masterpieces of English poetry his mother read to him. He has always made a point of defying the Philistines, but at Harvard he stood up against our terrible century armed only with his memories and the Golden Treasury.

Cummings' poetry has ripened amazingly of recent years, but it has not grown. And charming and touching as he is in this little autobiography, he remains incurably sentimental. This sentimentality, I hasten to add, is not in his values, in his dislike of collectivism, in his rousing sense of human freedom; it is in his failure to clothe the abstractions of his fathers with the flesh of actuality, with love for the living. The greatness of the New England transcendentalists was their ability to reclaim, from the commonsensical despairs of a dying religion, faith in the visionary powers of the mind. More and more, in Cummings' recent books, one sees how this belief in imagination, this ability to see life from within, has enabled him to develop, out of the provocative mannerisms of his early work, a verse that is like lyric shorthand—extraordinarily elastic, light, fresh, and resonant of feeling. At a time when a good deal of "advanced" poetry has begun to wear under its convention of anxiety, Cummings' verse has seemed particularly felt, astringent, and musical. But it is precisely because Cummings is a poet one always encounters with excitement and delight, precisely because it is his gift to make the world seem more joyful, that one reads a book like this with disappointment at hearing so many familiar jokes told over again, while the poet escapes into a fairyland of his fathers and points with a shudder to all who are not, equally with him, his father's son.

Review of *i:Six Nonlectures*

by Robert Graves

I get a warm feeling when I remember that, in the late Twenties, I was probably the first Englishman to say a good word for E. E. Cummings as the author of *is 5* and other poems; and that I persuaded Jonathan Cape to publish his *Enormous Room,* the most hilarious account of prison-camp life that two world wars have produced. Since then Cummings has written little—his only other long work, *Eimi,* a cross-grained comic diary of a visit to Soviet Russia is twenty years old now—and gone forward little; but neither has he gone backwards nor sold any pass. I bought his *Collected Poems* a year or two ago to see what had been happening since *is 5* and *XLI POEMS* and the play *Him*: and the poems stood up, all stalwart and American, saying: "Sure, read us if you like!"; which I did with a deal of pleasure. But —if *but* be the right copulative—I realised for the first time his close kinship with Nicholas Vachel Lindsay, who though neither so classically educated, so tough-shelled, so precise in language and punctuation; nor capable of such wicked and often pornographic satire; nor (being born into an elder generation of Puritan Progressives) so openly and happily devoted to carnality—nevertheless was as ingenuous, noble-hearted, gentle, courageous and liberty-loving as Cummings. And Lindsay proved equally apt, when least expected, to write an unforgettable line or two, or even six or seven in a row; and also equally capable of deep, brilliant unblushing folksy-homesy sentimentality.

Both in fact are/were ideally representative of what an American poet might once hope to be: a thing which apparently, as Lindsay admitted by his suicide, and as Cummings here indicates by his rage against the "spiritually impotent pseudocommunity . . . grovelling before the materialization of its own deathwish" (p. 103),[1] no American poet can plausibly hope to be again.

Lindsay in his youth tramped around the States peddling *The*

"Review of *i:Six Nonlectures,*" by Robert Graves. From *The New Statesman and Nation,* June 12, 1954, pp. 761–62.

[1] [Page references to *i:Six Nonlectures*; poems referred to as before. —Editor's note.]

Village Magazine, written and illustrated by himself—I remember one pretty stanza:

"Which is superior to which?"
Asked the snob when she came to the City.
"I want to know people to kick,
I want to know people to pity."

—and preaching the Gospel of Beauty. Antisnob Cummings has been preaching the Gospel of *Is*ness, as he calls poetic or artistic integrity, since at least 1922; and recently Harvard University, a beleaguered stronghold of U.S. academic freedom, invited him to lecture on it. This is the poetic *is*ness he then defined:

> Fine and dandy: but, so far as I am concerned, poetry and every other art was and is and forever will be strictly and distinctly a question of individuality. If poetry were anything—like dropping an atom bomb—which anyone did, anyone could become a poet merely by doing the necessary anything; whatever that anything might or might not entail. But (as it happens) poetry is being, not doing. If you wish to follow, even at a distance, the poet's calling (and here, as always, I speak from my own totally biased and entirely personal point of view) you've got to come out of the measurable doing universe into the immeasurable house of being. I am quite aware that, wherever our so-called civilization has slithered, there's every reward and no punishment for unbeing. But if poetry is your goal, you've got to forget all about punishments and all about rewards and all about selfstyled obligations and duties and responsibilities etcetera ad infinitum and remember one thing only: that it's you—nobody else—who determine your destiny and decide your fate. Nobody else can be alive for you; nor can you be alive for anybody else. Toms can be Dicks and Dicks can be Harrys, but none of them can ever be you. There's the artist's responsibility; and the most awful responsibility on earth. If you can take it, take it—and be. If you can't, cheer up and go about other people's business; and do (or undo) till you drop. (p. 24)

In the first two nonlectures, as he prefers to call them, he described his old-hickory-cut New Hampshire father: crack shot, fly-fisherman, cameraman, woodsman, clergyman, sailer, actor, photographer, painter, carpenter, plumber, ornithologist, taxidermist, Harvard lecturer and hero. And his Roxbury mother: poetry-lover, Quaker, charity worker, heroine. And himself as a child, secure in a home which was all that an ideal American poet's home should be: and where he read Scott, Dickens, Jules Verne, Harrison Ainsworth, Malory, Froissart, the Bible, *Robinson Crusoe, The Swiss Family Robinson, Gulliver's Travels, Lorna Doone, Treasure Island* and *The Arabian Nights*—odd! no Twain, Alger, Fenimore Cooper or Melville!—and now thanks a beneficent Providence that he passed through his childhood without

> . . . ever once glimpsing that typical item of an era of at least penultimate confusion—the uncomic nonbook. No paltry supermen, no shadowy space-cadets, no trifling hyperjungle-queens and pantless pantherwomen insulted my virginal imagination. (p. 27)

One of the penalties of this New English education was that he learned at an early age "the one and only thing which mattered about any poem . . . was what the poem said; its socalled meaning" (p. 29). He records:

> —A good poem was a poem which did good, and a bad poem was a poem which didn't: Julia Ward Howe's Battle Hymn of The Republic being a good poem because it helped free the slaves. Armed with this ethical immutability, I composed canticles of comfort on behalf of the griefstricken relatives of persons recently deceased; I implored healthy Christians to assist poor-whites afflicted with The Curse Of The Worm (short for hookworm); and I exhorted right-minded patriots to abstain from dangerous fireworks on the 4th of July. (p. 29)

And being a good son and citizen he has never altogether divested himself of this obsession about goodness, even after celebrating a sort of Doge-wedding with the vicious Seine at Montparnasse; nor indeed of the red H which his mother knitted into his first jersey and which, printed on his heart, sent him to read Classics at Harvard 40 years ago and has now called him back there again to deliver his nonlectures. Towards the close of each of these he read out his favourite poems, and what were they? "The Ode on the Intimations of Immortality," in full, for his mother's sake; a passage from *Prometheus Unbound,* for Liberty's sake; a border ballad in memory of Harvard's Professor Francis James Child, who had baptized him; two pieces from Dante; three from Shakespeare; Burns's "Red Red Rose"; Keats's "Grecian Urn"; Swinburne's "When the Hounds of Spring"; and (in frank tribute to Old Carnality) Donne's "To His Mistress Going to Bed."

By thus loyally keeping his first loves in poetry always before his eyes, and not realizing how unworthy some of these are (judged by his own standards of *Is*ness) to be set beside some of the others, he does his heart more credit than his five sound senses. Nor is he abashed to write, endite and publicly recite so intrinsically corny a sonnet as the one beginning:

> i thank You God for most this amazing
> day:for the leaping greenly spirits of trees
> and a blue true dream of sky;and for everything
> which is natural which is infinite which is yes

(i who have died am alive again today,
and this is the sun's birthday;this is the birth
day of life and of love and wings:and of the gay
great happening illimitably earth) (p. 91; 464: 65)

In 1945 he ran, as he reminds his nonlectured, to the rescue of "this selfstyled world's greatest and most generous literary figure: who had arrived at our nation's capital, attired in half a GI uniform and ready to be hanged as a traitor by the only country which ever made even a pretense of fighting for freedom of speech"—with the plea that this nontraitor had been true to the "illimitable country" of his own personal art. Thereupon he rages against the "supermechanized submorons . . . dedicated to the proposition that massacre is a social virtue because murder is an individual vice" (p. 69). Here I personally cannot follow him; the self-styled world's literary figure had compromised his *is*ness by raving anti-poetic generalities over the Fascist radio, and recommending that all Jews in Italy, as in Germany, should be sent to the gas-chamber. And the G.I.s who made a buck-show of him when they caught him were, I assume, acting *is*ly, on individual impulse; castigating not the artist but the truth-perverting tool of *is*lessness.

Cummings is at his best here when, as a "burlesk addict of long standing," he mimics the voice of the America that he hates yet continues to live among:

John, viii, 7.

So now let us talk about something else. This is a free country because compulsory education. This is a free country because nobody has to eat. This is a free country because not any other country was is or ever will be free. So now you know and knowledge is power.

An interesting fact when you come right down to it is that simple people like complex things. But what amounts to an extraordinary coincidence is mediocre people liking firstrate things. The explanation can't be because complex things are simple. It must be because mediocre people are firstrate.

So now let us pull the wool over each other's toes and go to Hell.

John, viii, 7. (p. 67)

I regret that he did not include in the readings from his own work such jocund verses as "she being Brand/-new" (178–9: XIX), describing Old Carnality in terms of the internal combustion engine; and the well-worn but ever-living mock-heroic stanzas beginning:

come, gaze with me upon this dome
of many coloured glass, and see
his mother's pride, his father's joy,
unto whom duty whispers low

"thou must!" and who replies "I can!"
—yon clean upstanding well dressed boy
that with his peers full oft hath quaffed
the wine of life and found it sweet—

a tear within his stern blue eye,
upon his firm white lips a smile,
one thought alone: to do or die
for God for country and for Yale (195–6: VIII)

. . . Yale, not Harvard! And therefore with the shocking pay-off at the close.

Chronology of Important Dates

1894	Edward Estlin Cummings born, Cambridge, Mass., October 14, first of two children born to Edward Cummings and Rebecca Haswell Clarke.
1911	Enters Harvard.
1912	First published poems in *Harvard Monthly.*
1915	Graduated from Harvard *magna cum laude.* Delivers Commencement Address, "The New Art."
1916	Receives M.A. from Harvard.
1917	Living in New York City.
1917	April. Sails for France.
1917	June. Joins Norton Harjes Ambulance Corps, American Red Cross, in France.
1917	Fall. Published in *Eight Harvard Poets.*
1917	September–December. Imprisoned by French authorities on suspicion of disloyalty.
1918	New Year's Day. Released, returns to New York City.
1918	Summer. Drafted into Army, Camp Devens, Massachusetts, until Armistice. Returns to New York City.
1920	First major appearance as a poet in the *Dial.*
1921–23	First sojourn in Paris, where he meets many avant-garde figures. Lives in Paris intermittently throughout the 1920s; makes many trips abroad thereafter.
1922	Publication of *The Enormous Room,* based on the experiences of 1917.
1923	Returns to New York City, living at 4 Patchin Place in Greenwich Village, which becomes his permanent home—along with Joy Farm, his family's summer place, in Silver Lake, N.H.

1923	Publication of first volume of poetry, *Tulips and Chimneys.*
1924	Marries Elaine Orr; divorced soon after. They have one child, a daughter.
1925	Receives the Dial Award for "distinguished service to American letters." Publication of *&* and *XLI POEMS.*
1925–27	Writing essays for *Vanity Fair* and others.
1926	Publication of *is 5.*
1926	November. Father dies in auto accident.
1927	Marries Anne Barton; this marriage also ends in divorce. Publication of *Him.*
1928	April 18–May 13. Production of *Him* at the Provincetown Playhouse.
1930	Publication of *No Title* and *Anthropos.*
1931	Spring. Trip to Russia.
1931	First major showing of paintings at the Painters and Sculptors Gallery, New York City. Publication of *CIOPW,* a collection of works done in charcoal, ink, oil, pencil, and watercolor. Publication of *VV* (*ViVa*).
1932	Marries Marion Morehouse, well-known model, actress, and photographer.
1933	Guggenheim Fellowship. *Eimi,* based on trip to Russia, published.
1935	Publication of *Tom* and *no thanks.*
1938	Publication of *Collected Poems.*
1940	*50 POEMS* published.
1944	*1 x 1* published. Show at American British Art Center, New York City.
1946	Publication of *Santa Claus.*
1947	January. Mother dies.
1948	*Him* produced once again in New York City.
1949	One man show of paintings, American British Art Center.
1950	Awarded Fellowship of American Academy of Poets for "great achievement." Publication of *XAIPE.*
1951	Guggenheim Fellowship.
1952–53	Charles Eliot Norton Professor at Harvard.

1953	Publication of *i:six Nonlectures.*
1954	*Poems 1923–1954* published.
1955	Awarded special citation by National Book Awards for *Poems 1923–1954*.
1957	Receives Bollingen Prize in Poetry and Boston Arts Festival Award.
1958	Publication of *95 poems* and *E. E. Cummings: A Miscellany.*
1959	One man show at Rochester Memorial Art Gallery, Rochester, N.Y.
1962	September 2. Dies, North Conway, N.H.
1962	*Adventures in Value* (with Marion Morehouse Cummings) published.
1963	Publication of *73 poems.*
1965	*Fairy Tales* published.
1967	Publication of *E. E. Cummings: Three Plays and a Ballet.*
1969	*Selected Letters of E. E. Cummings* published. Marion Morehouse Cummings, the poet's widow, dies.

Notes on the Editor and Contributors

NORMAN FRIEDMAN, editor of this volume, teaches at Queens College of The City University of New York, and has published two books on Cummings, as well as several textbooks (with C. A. McLaughlin) and a number of poems and articles.

S. V. BAUM has edited a collection of essays on Cummings. He teaches at Newark College of Arts and Sciences of Rutgers University.

R. P. BLACKMUR taught at Princeton and was among the most influential of modern American critics. His best-known books are *The Double Agent* (1935), *The Expense of Greatness* (1940), *Language as Gesture* (1952), and *The Lion and the Honeycomb* (1955).

PATRICIA BUCHANAN TAL-MASON CLINE is bringing out a book on Cummings; she teaches at Miami-Dade Junior College in Miami, Fla.

ROBERT GRAVES, one of the most distinguished of contemporary British poets, lives in Majorca, Spain. He is also well known for his fiction and criticism. *Good-Bye to All That* (1929), *I, Claudius* (1934), and *The White Goddess* (1948) are his prominent prose works.

GEORGE HAINES IV taught history at Connecticut College in New London until his death in 1964. His publications include *German Influences upon English Education and Science, 1800–1866* (1957).

ALFRED KAZIN teaches at the State University of New York at Stony Brook, Long Island, New York. Beginning with *On Native Grounds* (1942), his writings and reviews have made him an important influence.

ROBERT E. MAURER wrote his doctoral dissertation on Cummings and has published many articles and reviews on contemporary literature. He teaches at Antioch College.

PAUL ROSENFELD was one of our most versatile freelance critics of the arts until his death in 1946. Among his books are *Port of New York* (1924) and *Men Seen* (1925).

DAVID E. SMITH teaches at Hampshire College in Amherst, Mass., and has published *John Bunyan in America* (1966) and numerous articles on American literature and culture.

ALLEN TATE has long been acknowledged as one of our chief critics and poets. His main books are *Reactionary Essays* (1936), *Reason in Madness* (1941), and *The Forlorn Demon* (1953).

BARBARA WATSON has published *A Shavian Guide to the Intelligent Woman* (1964) and a number of poems in the journals. She teaches at The City College of the City University of New York.

WILLIAM CARLOS WILLIAMS, who died in 1963, was among the poetic giants of the post-World War I generation. A busy practicing physician, he found time to write poems, plays, stories, novels, essays, and autobiography. His largest poetic achievement is *Paterson,* a modernist epic.

Selected Bibliography

BIBLIOGRAPHICAL AIDS

Firmage, George J. *E. E. Cummings: A Bibliography*. Middletown, Conn.: Wesleyan University Press, 1960. A full descriptive bibliography of Cummings' writings, translations of his writings, musical settings for his poems, recorded readings, and reproductions of his drawings, water colors, and oils.

For extensive secondary bibliographies of writings on Cummings, see Baum and Friedman in "About E. E. Cummings," below.

BY E. E. CUMMINGS

All of the poetry will be found in:

Poems 1923–1954. New York: Harcourt Brace Jovanovich, Inc. 1954.

95 poems. New York: Harcourt Brace Jovanovich, Inc. 1958.

73 poems. New York: Harcourt Brace Jovanovich, Inc. 1963. Published posthumously.

The prose works, listed chronologically, are as follows:

E. E. Cummings: A Miscellany, ed. George J. Firmage. New York: Argophile Press, 1958. *E. E. Cummings: A Miscellany Revised,* ed. George J. Firmage. New York: October House, 1965. Contains essays by Cummings dating back to 1915.

The Enormous Room. New York: Random House, Modern Library Edition, 1934. Originally published by Boni and Liveright, 1922; reprinted in paperback by Liveright, 1970.

Him. New York: Liveright, 1927. Reprinted by Firmage (see *Santa Claus* below). Full-length play.

No Title. New York: Covici, Friede, 1930. Reprinted in *A Miscellany Revised*. Surrealistic burlesque satirical sketches plus drawings.

Anthropos: The Future of Art. Mount Vernon, N.Y.: Golden Eagle Press, 1944. Originally published, 1930. Reprinted by Firmage (see below). Short didactic play.

Eimi. New York: Grove Press, Evergreen Paperback, 1958. Originally published, 1933. Journal of trip to Soviet Russia.

Tom. New York: Arrow Editions, 1935. Reprinted by Firmage (see below). Scenario for a ballet based on *Uncle Tom's Cabin*.

Fairy Tales. New York: Harcourt Brace Jovanovich, Inc., 1965. Illustrated by John Eaton. Four tales, probably written in the 1930s, three of which were published in 1946, 1948, and 1950.

Santa Claus (A Morality). New York: Henry Holt, 1946. Medium-length didactic play. *Him, Anthropos, Tom,* and *Santa Claus* have been reprinted by George J. Firmage in *E. E. Cummings: Three Plays and a Ballet.* Cloth and Paperback eds., New York: October House, 1967; London: Peter Owen, 1968.

i:Six Nonlectures. Cambridge, Mass.: Harvard University Press, 1953. Cummings' autobiographical Charles Eliot Norton lectures.

Adventures in Value (with Marion Morehouse). New York: Harcourt Brace Jovanovich, Inc., 1962. Mrs. Cummings' photographs, with Cummings' commentaries.

Selected Letters of E. E. Cummings, F. W. Dupee and George Stade, eds. New York: Harcourt Brace Jovanovich, 1969. Letters spanning the period 1899–1962.

ABOUT E. E. CUMMINGS

Books:

Baum, S. V., ed., *ΕΣΤΙ: e e c: E. E. Cummings and the Critics.* East Lansing, Mich.: Michigan State University Press, 1962. Contains thirty-two essays by various writers, plus secondary bibliography.

Friedman, Norman, *E. E. Cummings: The Art of His Poetry.* Baltimore, Md.: Johns Hopkins Press, 1960. Paperback edition, plus secondary bibliography, 1967. Vision, forms, techniques, and so forth, in the poetry.

——— *E. E. Cummings: The Growth of a Writer.* Carbondale, Ill.: Southern Illinois University Press, 1964. Chronological study of all of Cummings' writings through 1958.

Marks, Barry A., *E. E. Cummings.* New York: Twayne Publishers, United States Authors Series, 1964. Mainly on the poetry:Cummings' aesthetic beliefs and practices, his treatment of the themes of children and sex, and his relation to the United States.

Norman, Charles, *The Magic-Maker: E. E. Cummings.* New York: Macmillan, 1958. *E. E. Cummings: The Magic-Maker,* rev. and abr. ed., New York: Duell, Sloan and Pearce, 1964. Biography.

Wegner, Robert E., *The Poetry and Prose of E. E. Cummings.* New York: Harcourt Brace Jovanovich, Inc., 1965. Mainly on the poetry: subjects and images, freedom and the individual, techniques and forms, and so forth.

Articles, chapters, and reviews published since the appearance of the bibliography in the 1967 paperback edition of E. E. Cummings: The Art of His poetry:

Babcock, Sister Mary David, "Cummings' Typography: An Ideogrammatic Style," *Renascence,* 15 (1963), 115–23.

Bautista, Cirilo F., "The Bright Monolith: A Note on the Poetry of E. E. Cummings," *Saint Louis Quarterly,* 3 (1968), 517–54.

Bentley, Eric, *From the Modern Repertoire: Series Two.* Indiana University Press, 1952, pp. 485–94 (On *Him.*)

Clark, David R., "Cummings' 'anyone' and 'noone'," *Arizona Quarterly,* 25 (1969), 36–43.

Clendenning, John, "Cummings, Comedy, and Criticism," *Colorado Quarterly,* 12 (1963), 44–53.

Cline, Patricia Buchanan Tal-Mason, "The Whole E. E. Cummings," *Twentieth Century Literature,* 14 (July 1968), 90–97.

Cooperman, Stanley, "Between Tears and Laughter: E. E. Cummings," in *World War I and the American Novel.* Baltimore: Johns Hopkins Press, 1967, pp. 169–75. (On *The Enormous Room.*)

Dembo, L. S., *"E. E. Cummings:* The Now Man," in *Conceptions of Reality in Modern American Poetry.* Berkeley and Los Angeles: University of California Press, 1966, pp. 118–28.

Dickey, James, "E. E. Cummings" (1959), in *The Suspect in Poetry.* Madison, Wisc.: The Sixties Press, 1964, pp. 85–91. Review of *95 poems.* Reprinted in Dickey's *Babel to Byzantium: Poets and Poetry Now.* New York: Farrar, Straus and Giroux, 1968, pp. 100–6.

Dougherty, James P., "Language and Reality in E. E. Cummings," *Bucknell Review,* 16 (1968), 112–22.

——— "E. E. Cummings: *The Enormous Room,"* in *Landmarks of American Writing,* ed. Hennig Cohen. New York: Basic Books, 1969, pp. 288–302.

Fairley, Irene I., "Syntax as Style: An Analysis of Three Cummings Poems," in *Studies Presented to Professor Roman Jakobson by His Students,* ed. Charles E. Gribble. Cambridge, Mass.: Slavica Publications, 1968, pp. 105–11.

Friedman, Norman, "E. E. Cummings and His Critics," *Criticism,* 6 (Spring 1964), 114–33.

Gaull, Marilyn, "Language and Identity: A Study of E. E. Cummings' *The Enormous Room," American Quarterly,* 19 (1967), 645–62.

Gidley, Mick, "Picture and Poem: E. E. Cummings in Perspective," *Poetry Review,* 59 (1968), 179–98.

Jacobsen, J., "Legacy of Three Poets," *Commonweal,* 78 (May 10, 1963), 189–92. (On Frost, Cummings, and William Carlos Williams.)

Kennedy, Richard S., "Edward Cummings, the Father of the Poet," *Bulletin of the New York Public Library,* 70 (1966), 437–49.

Lawrence, Floyd B., "Two Novelists of the Great War: Dos Passos and Cummings," *University Review* (Kansas City), 36 (1969), 35–41. (On *Three Soldiers* and *The Enormous Room.*)

Logan, John, "The Organ-Grinder and the Cockatoo: An Introduction to E. E. Cummings," in *Modern American Poetry: Essays in Criticism,* ed. Jerome Mazzaro. New York: David McKay, 1970, pp. 249–71. (Expanded version of Logan's earlier piece in *The Critic,* 1961.)

Macksoud, S. John, "Anyone's How Town: Interpretation as Rhetorical Discipline," *Speech Monographs,* 35 (1968), 70–76.

Patty, Austin, "Cummings' Impressions of Communist Russia," *Rendezvous,* 2 (1967), 15–22. (On *Eimi.*)

Pearce, Roy Harvey, "Cummings," in *The Continuity of American Poetry.* Princeton, N. J.: Princeton University Press, 1961, pp. 359–66.

Phillips, Paul, "A Note on E. E. Cummings," *Mainstream,* 15 (1962), 22–25.

Read, Donald R., "E. E. Cummings: The Lay of the Duckbilled Platitude," *Satire Newsletter,* 3 (1965), 30–33.

Springer, Haskell S., "The Poetics of E. E. Cummings," *South Atlantic Bulletin,* 32 (1967), 8–10.

Stetler, Charles, "E. E. Cummings' *73 poems:* With Life's Eye," *Xavier University Studies,* 7 (1968), 5–16.

Thorne, James Peter, "Stylistics and Generative Grammars," *Journal of Linguistics,* 1 (1965), 49–59. (On "anyone lived.")

Tucker, Robert G., "Cummings the Chivalrous," in *The Twenties,* R. E. Langford and W. E. Taylor, eds. DeLand, Fla.: Everett Edwards Press, 1966, pp. 25–27.

Waggoner, Hyatt H., *"The Transcendental and Extraordinary:* E. E. Cummings," in *American Poets From the Puritans to the Present.* Boston: Houghton Mifflin, 1968, pp. 493–94, 511–25.

Weimer, David R., "Grassblades Assassinated," in *The City as Metaphor.* New York: Random House, 1966, pp. 78–87.

Wesolek, George., "e. e. cummings: A Reconsideration," *Renascence,* 18 (1965), 3–8.

Wickes, George, "E. E. Cummings at War," *Columbia Forum,* 12 (Fall 1969), 31–33. (On the *Enormous Room.*)

——— *"The View from the Windows of Nowhere," "Typographic Verse,"* in *Americans in Paris 1903–1939.* Garden City, New York: Doubleday, Paris Review Editions, 1969, pp. 69–82, 103–18.

Wilson, David B., " 'O To Be in Finland'," *Neuphilologische Mitteilungen* (Helsinki, Finland), 2, LXXI (1970), 270–76.

Worth, Katherine J., "The Poets in the American Theatre," in *American Theatre* (Stratford-upon-Avon Studies 10), J. R. Brown and B. Harris, eds. New York: St. Martin's Press, 1967, pp. 86–107. (On *Him,* pp. 102–7.)